Lou Halsell Rodenberger

THE LOU HALSELL RODENBERGER PRIZE IN HISTORY, CULTURE, AND LITERATURE

ALSO IN THIS SERIES:

Dressing Modern Maternity: The Frankfurt Sisters of Dallas and the Page Boy Label
by Kay Goldman

A Promise Fulfilled: The Kitty Anderson Diary and Civil War Texas, 1861
edited by Nancy Draves

Their Lives, Their Wills: Women in the Borderlands, 1750–1846
by Amy M. Porter

THE LADY MAKES BOOTS

ENID JUSTIN & THE NOCONA BOOT COMPANY

CAROL A. LIPSCOMB

TEXAS TECH UNIVERSITY PRESS

Copyright © 2021 by Texas Tech University Press
All rights reserved. No portion of this book may be reproduced in any form or by any means, including electronic storage and retrieval systems, except by explicit prior written permission of the publisher. Brief passages excerpted for review and critical purposes are excepted.
This book is typeset in EB Garamond. The paper used in this book meets the minimum requirements of ANSI/NISO Z39.48-1992 (R1997). ∞

Designed by Hannah Gaskamp

Library of Congress Cataloging-in-Publication Data

Names: Lipscomb, Carol A., 1946– author. Title: The lady makes boots: Enid Justin and the Nocona boot company / Carol A. Lipscomb. Description: Lubbock, Texas: Texas Tech University Press, [2021] | Series: Lou Halsell Rodenberger prize in history, culture, and literature | Includes bibliographical references and index. | Summary: "Chronicle of the life of Enid Justin, female entrepreneur and creator of an iconic Western business, the Nocona Boot Company—Provided by publisher. Identifiers: LCCN 2021012091 (print) | LCCN 2021012092 (ebook) | ISBN 978-1-68283-095-6 (cloth) | ISBN 978-1-68283-240-0 (paperback) | ISBN 978-1-68283-096-3 (ebook)
Subjects: LCSH: Justin, Enid. | Businesswomen—Texas—Nocona—Biography. | Boots—Texas—Nocona. Classification: LCC HD6072.6.U5 L56 2021 (print) | LCC HD6072.6.U5 (ebook) | DDC 338.7/685310092 [B]—dc23

LC record available at https://lccn.loc.gov/2021012091
LC ebook record available at https://lccn.loc.gov/2021012092

First paperback edition 2024

Texas Tech University Press
Box 41037
Lubbock, Texas 79409-1037 USA
800.832.4042
ttup@ttu.edu
www.ttupress.org

To Richard

CONTENTS

IX	ILLUSTRATIONS
XI	ACKNOWLEDGMENTS
XV	INTRODUCTION
3	CHAPTER 1
25	CHAPTER 2
47	CHAPTER 3
71	CHAPTER 4
91	CHAPTER 5
117	CHAPTER 6
147	CHAPTER 7
179	CHAPTER 8
199	EPILOGUE
205	NOTES
235	BIBLIOGRAPHY
243	INDEX

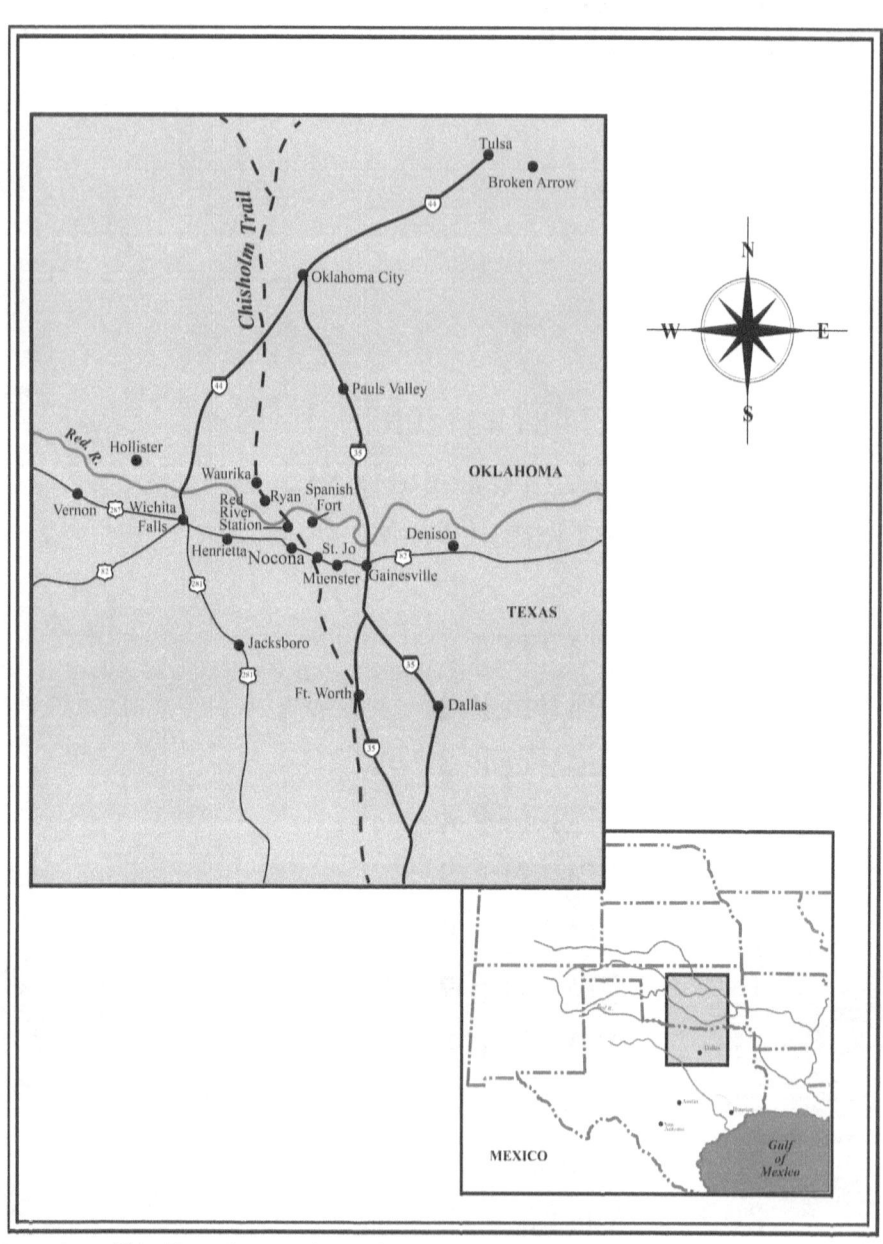

Map created by Alexander Mendoza, PhD

ILLUSTRATIONS

11	Young Joe Justin, c. 1887
13	Young Justin family, c. 1905
14	Justin home in Nocona
15	Justin clubhouse, 1951
16	Interior of the H. J. Justin boot factory, c. 1905, with Daddy Joe, Earl, and John
19	Daddy Joe, employees, and boot-drying racks, Justin Boot Company, c. 1910
21	Justin family on front porch, with Enid and Julius
27	H. J. Justin & Sons new factory, c. 1920
29	"Powder River" boot, 1923 Justin catalog
35	Enid Justin, portrait, c. 1925
41	Nocona Boot Company, early 1940s
42	Nocona Boot Company factory interior, c. 1930
43	Early Nocona boot with moon and star, c. 1930
50	McChesney portrait on 1906 price list
53	McChesney "Gal Leg" spur
56	McChesney-Nocona spurs with silver heart pattern
65	Enid at ribbon-cutting ceremony of Pony Express Race, 1939
66	Amon Carter and Enid Justin at start of Pony Express Race
68	Pony Express riders
69	Pony Express Race winner Shannon Davidson

ILLUSTRATIONS

83	Architect's sketch of new Nocona Boot Factory completed in 1948
85	New factory grand opening
87	Enid observing her employees inside factory
88	Enid in front of boot display, c. 1950
89	Enid, Ken Maynard, and horse Tarzan, Fort Worth Stock Show, 1941
92	Enid with boots on desk
93	Fancy 1950s boots
98	Models with Leon A. Harris Jr. at "Texas on the Riviera"
100	Governor Talmadge tries on Nocona boots as Enid watches
107	Enid in buckboard for Nocona's Chisholm Trail Round-up Rodeo Parade, 1954
125	Enid with revolving shoe tree
127	1960s boots, one with cut diamond shapes, 1969 catalog
133	"Hereford" boot
142	"Let's Rodeo" ad campaign posters
144	Bicentennial boot
149	Enid with nephew Joe Justin at Vernon groundbreaking
151	Spanish boots
157	Enid with Jerry Jeff Walker
161	NBC ad with Earl Campbell
163	Late 1970s exotic skin boots
177	Photo of smiling Enid
181	Wildflower roper
182	Shoe boot
186	Enid and Walt Disney, grand opening of the Disneyland Hotel, 1956
189	Enid's nieces and nephews advertise for the company

ACKNOWLEDGMENTS

Telling Enid Justin's story has been both an honor and a dream project for this historian. The journey was made even more enjoyable by the many people who helped along the way. My family has been constant in their support and encouragement. My husband Richard grew up in Nocona and provided my first connection to Enid Justin. My Wichita Falls family, Rik, Shaye, Carson, and Dani, and my Colorado family, Clark, Meredith, Liz, and Mason, have been staunch supporters throughout this process. Their most-asked question, "Gram, how's your book going?" My son Kelly, a writer and filmmaker, always willingly gave his time to consult on this project and offered invaluable advice on questions of content and story structure as well as continual inspiration. He was also my technical wizard. In addition, I wish to thank Kelley Kosar, who used Photoshop magic to improve many of the aging photographs and catalog illustrations included in this book. And thanks also to our extended family, Juan, Monika, and Juan Carlos Zirion, and Jessica and Chris Frazer, who enthusiastically supported my project.

Dr. Donald E. Chipman, friend, mentor, and historian par excellence, read this manuscript, chapter by chapter (some more than once), and offered insightful suggestions along with his editing expertise, an exercise I am sure must have led him to question if his former graduate student would ever learn the proper use of a hyphen. I am also indebted to Dr. Randolph B. (Mike) Campbell, who was instrumental in my taking on this project and offered help and encouragement along the way. And to the late Robert S. Weddle, whose high standards for researching and writing history I always strive to emulate.

ACKNOWLEDGMENTS

The Tales 'N' Trails Museum in Nocona, Texas, is a wonderful repository for all things Nocona Boot Company. In addition to documents, personal papers, catalogs, and photographs, the collection has many examples of Nocona boots, the patterns used to cut them, and an assemblage of early boot-making tools. A recent addition to the boot company exhibit is a life-size animatronic Miss Enid who tells her story in her own voice—that alone is worth a trip to Nocona. I owe special thanks to Museum Director Nell Ann McBroom, who provided invaluable help in locating specific items in the collection as well as alerts when the museum received new acquisitions. While I was working on the book, Enid's divorce papers were found in an NBC safe that was purchased by Toby Booth when the company went out of business, and Steve Pickens donated an old metal file box that contained documents relating to Enid's salary dispute with the War Production Board in the 1940s. I am very grateful to Nell Ann and the staff and volunteers at the museum and to Noconans who have helped to preserve boot company history.

I also want to thank Tracy Mesler, editor of *The Nocona News* since 1981, whose unfailing coverage of news and events surrounding Nocona Boot Company preserved much of the history of the company. The *News* has been in continual operation since 1905, and it was a valuable resource for information on the early Justin Boot Company as well as its successor, the Nocona Boot Company. I owe a special word of appreciation to Nocona librarian Karen Teague, who kept an aging microfilm reader in working order while I scanned the many years of weekly issues. Good news for future researchers: *The Nocona News* has now been digitized.

I owe a debt of gratitude to Meagan May and the staff at the University of North Texas Special Collections, who were always helpful as I sifted through the many boxes that contain the Enid Justin - Nocona Boot Company Collection. Nancie Thomas, who oversees the Justin Archives in Fort Worth, also deserves special consideration for helping to locate pertinent documents in that collection.

Over the years that I have worked on this project, I have had the pleasure of interviewing members of Enid's family as well as Nocona Boot Company employees—their words brought this story to life. Joe Justin, Luciel Leonard, and Marcia Taylor, all now deceased, provided personal stories and enriching details. I also want to thank John Tillotson and

ACKNOWLEDGMENTS

Steve Pickens, whose interviews provided insight into the final years of NBC. Thanks also to Melanie Chapman Howington, Enid's great-niece and one of the children in the photo on page 189, whose description of her "auntie" revealed a personality quite different from that of the staunch businesswoman.

I would like to thank my friend of many years, Ann Stevenson, for always having time to listen to my stories about Enid and offering unrelenting encouragement and enthusiasm about this project.

A special word of appreciation goes to fellow Texan and boot historian Tyler Beard, whom I have never met but whose beautiful books inspired my telling of Enid's story.

And finally, to Texas Tech University Press and its managing director Joanna Conrad, who "made my day" on June 5, 2017, when she offered to publish my manuscript. And to acquisitions editor Travis Snyder, who guided me through the publication process; to editor Christie Perlmutter, whose eagle eyes let nothing slip by; to John Brock, for marketing expertise; and to Hannah Gaskamp, whose creative design made the book beautiful—you have been a pleasure to work with.

Thanks to all.

INTRODUCTION

It was early fall 1925 when Enid Justin opened her new company to manufacture cowboy boots in the small North Texas town of Nocona. The odds for success were not in her favor. As a woman taking on a man's trade, she would undoubtedly face disparagement and discrimination along with the usual challenges of starting a new business. She had no funds of her own to invest in the venture, and only a small loan obtained from the local banker who was a family friend. Had she not had that relationship, it is doubtful that, as a woman, she could have secured even that small amount of capital to fund her new business. To further compound the difficulties she faced, her family disapproved of her enterprise and forecast failure.

It would be an uphill road for the young bootmaker, but she was confident in her ability to make cowboy boots. After all, she had grown up in a boot-making family and, starting at a young age, she had learned every aspect of the business. A knowledge of boot-making would be her greatest asset, followed closely by a commitment to the idea of creating her own company and a willingness to work hard to realize her dream. Timing was also on her side, as the economy of the mid-1920s was booming. Just a few months before Enid Justin opened her Nocona Boot Company, President Calvin Coolidge had declared, "The chief business of the American people is business," a statement that echoed the optimistic business climate of the time. Although the president probably did not have businesswomen in mind when he made that declaration, there was also optimism on that front.[1]

INTRODUCTION

"The 1920s was a breakthrough decade for women in business and other professions," wrote historian Donald L. Miller in an article on women entrepreneurs in the Jazz Age. Building on the social reforms of the Progressive Era, women gained confidence that they could succeed in the workplace as equals to men. For the most part, women entrepreneurs found their best opportunities in businesses that catered to women—especially beauty products and fashion. As prominent examples, Elizabeth Arden and her main competitor Helena Rubinstein both created successful cosmetics companies, while Hattie Carnegie built a multimillion-dollar couture business. There were also women who succeeded in typically male arenas of enterprise, but those women most often inherited rather than initiated those businesses. Marjorie Merriweather Post inherited her father's Postum Cereals company and expanded it into General Foods Corporation, and Rose Knox took over the family's gelatin business when her husband died and captained it for almost four decades. The Norton sisters, who played a small part in this story, provide a Texas example. They inherited their father's shoe company in Gainesville and ran it successfully for some thirty years. Enid Justin fit neither of those patterns—she was not creating a business for women, nor did she inherit her company. She was starting her own business in a traditionally male industry, but like other enterprising women of her era, she was optimistic about her chances for success.[2]

The cowboy boot business that Enid Justin ventured into had been in existence for just over fifty years. It originated in the 1870s to meet the footwear needs of men herding cattle on horseback over long distances, often spending all day in the saddle. By the time Justin entered the business, boots were no longer the exclusive footwear of working cowboys; they were slowly being appropriated by the culture at large. The unique footwear became a symbol of the "Old West," a romanticized era that had gained great popularity by the 1920s. As cowboy boot expert Jennifer June so aptly noted, boots had gone "from fact to fantasy."[3]

The cowboy boot is an American creation—it evolved to meet specific needs, making it a perfect example of form follows function. It was not a new style of footwear but rather one adapted to particular circumstances, one that grew out of myriad styles of riding boots that came before. Boots have been around for as long as horsemen have needed protective footwear. In the fifth century, Attila, whose very name may have meant "horseman," and his nomadic Huns wore tall-top boots in their invasion of Central Europe. Genghis Khan's mounted warriors, who rode out of the Mongolian steppes in the late twelfth century, were wearing boots with heels painted bright red. And then there were Spain's conquistadors, whose booted tradition may have come from the Moors along with the Arabian stallion. In their sixteenth-century conquest of the Americas, the Spanish invaders wore thigh-high boots with belt-like straps near the top to hold them up. The seventeenth-century cavaliers of England's King Charles I wore wide-legged boots with tops turned down. Another English boot, the Wellington, adapted from earlier Hessian boots, gained popularity in the early nineteenth century. The namesake of the First Duke of Wellington, the boots had lower heels and fitted tops that only reached mid-calf. And Mexican *vaqueros*, who carried on the ranching tradition begun by early Spanish settlers, wore tall-top boots with spurs. Boots had evolved over time to meet the needs of a man on a horse, and variations were many.[4]

The popularity of the Wellington spread to America, and in 1847, Pennsylvanian S. C. Shive patented the pattern for what came to be called the Full Wellington, described as "a two-piece boot that found wide acceptance among soldiers, horsemen, and adventurers of the time." When the Civil War ended and many Americans headed west for new opportunities, they were shod mainly in military-style boots, often patterned after Wellingtons, or coarse work boots called "stogy" boots, usually made of stiff black leather. Those styles, along with the *vaquero* boot from south of the border, were the prototypes for what would become the cowboy boot.[5]

With demand created by the beef-starved Northeast, men began trailing cattle from Texas to railheads in Missouri and Kansas for shipment to points east shortly after the war ended. An estimated three million cattle—some say as many as five million—roamed free in Texas, and the cowboys who rounded up those vast herds and drove them north found themselves in need of specialized footwear. They spent long days in the saddle, often traversing brushy country that threatened all manner of hazards along the trail, like cactus, mesquite thorns, and rattlesnakes, and then there was saddle chafing that left their legs raw. They required boots

INTRODUCTION

with close-fitting high tops to shield their legs, sturdy toes to protect from errant hooves, and high underslung heels to keep the foot from slipping through the stirrup. High heels also gave the cowboy sure footing on the ground and enabled him to dig in when he was roping on foot. "Then, too," wrote Ramon F. Adams in his dictionary of western words, "the high heel is a tradition, a mark of distinction, the sign that the one wearing it is a riding man, and a riding man has always held himself above the man on foot." In Spanish, for example, *caballero* means "gentleman."[6]

The first known bootmaker to cater to the drovers' needs was T. C. McInerney, who set up shop in Abilene, Kansas, in 1868, and others soon followed. In towns that grew up along the cattle trails, from Kansas to Texas, small shops that made and repaired boots became common, but there were some bootmakers who distinguished themselves from the ordinary. In the early 1870s, two independent bootmakers in Coffeyville, Kansas—John Cobine and William Bright—began constructing boots that came to be called Coffeyville Pattern Boots. Usually black leather, the tall-top boots were crowned by a red-leather panel that curved up in the front like the Hessian boot. The Coffeyville boot, with its distinctive red accent, provided a mark of individuality that cowboys favored, an early forecast of decorations to come. Just a few years after the Coffeyville boot gained popularity, two bootmakers who would become legendary in the industry came on the scene, one in Kansas and one in Texas.[7]

The first was Charles Hyer, who started making boots in 1876 in Olathe, Kansas, a town close enough to the railheads and stockyards of Kansas City to attract a cowboy clientele. Hyer was an innovator: he fashioned custom wooden lasts in the shape of customers' feet to facilitate reordering, and he printed mail-order catalogs with self-measuring kits to help grow his business. By 1889, Hyer had five men working in his shop, and by 1898, according to the *Olathe Mirror*, C. H. Hyer & Sons was "probably the biggest cowboy boot manufacturer of its time." When skilled labor was hard to find, Hyer hired unskilled workers and taught each one a specific step in the boot-making process. That assembly-line production proved successful, and in 1910 Hyer's factory produced ten thousand pairs of boots.[8]

Another famous bootmaker, this one in Texas, started his shop just three years after Charles Hyer launched his enterprise. Herman Joseph

INTRODUCTION

Justin, who figures prominently in this story, began making boots in Spanish Fort, a cattle-drive town on the Chisholm Trail, in 1879, and his quality boots quickly found favor with drovers. Justin moved his boot shop twenty miles south to the railroad town of Nocona in 1889, where his business grew from an artisan shop to an actual factory. Justin's sons joined the business in 1908, and by 1915, H. J. Justin & Sons was producing around 6,500 pairs a year.[9]

Justin also designed a successful self-measuring system for mail-order boots. Both Justin and Hyer claimed to be first to invent self-measurement kits, but because exact dates are lacking, it is impossible to determine the winner of that title. In fact, another bootmaker, Henry Erdman in El Paso, Texas, was advertising "rules for self-measurement" as early as 1883. Controversy aside, Justin and Hyer were both exceptional bootmakers, and in the early decades of the twentieth century they became the largest manufacturers of cowboy boots. Cowboy movie star Tim McCoy, who was a working cowboy before he became an actor, recalled outfitting himself for a job as a horse wrangler in Wyoming in 1909: "The all-important boots were, by custom, either Hyer or Justin, available in town for $9.50."[10]

A talented bootmaker who challenged the hegemony of Hyer and Justin came on the scene in 1912. Tony Lama, formerly a cobbler for the US Army at Fort Bliss, opened a boot shop in El Paso, Texas, and his quality boots soon attracted local ranchers and cowboys who became his loyal customers. Lama, also an innovator, developed methods for producing larger quantities of boots while maintaining his signature handcrafting. Tony Lama Company eventually grew to be the largest boot producer in Texas.[11]

Another successful bootmaker, Salvatore "Sam" Lucchese, also began his career as an Army cobbler, but at Fort Sam Houston in San Antonio. Sam and his brother Joseph, later joined by brothers Michael and Antonio, started Lucchese Boot and Shoe Factory in the Alamo City in 1883. Although on a smaller scale, Lucchese's quality boots added to the competition. So also did Blucher Custom Boot Company, begun in 1915 in Cheyenne, Wyoming, and later moved to Olathe, Kansas. Gus Blucher learned the trade from H. J. Justin, where he worked for seven years before going out on his own. Blucher was an expert designer, and his boots were prized by the working cowboy. M. L. Leddy joined the growing list of bootmakers in 1922 when he opened a shop in Brady, Texas, and brought in five of his younger brothers to help make boots for the growing business. Moreover, there were many small, and successful, "one-man" shops that made boots on a custom-order basis, one pair at a time.[12]

Cowboy boot manufacturers, large and small, continued to thrive in the early 1920s, more than three decades after the cattle drives that spurred their design had come to an end. It was a time of prosperity, the postwar years when patriotism fueled a desire for all things American, including the cowboy boot. Saturday afternoons were often spent at the movie theater, where "Westerns" with stars like Tim McCoy, Hoot Gibson, Tom Mix, and the queen of silent Western serials, Ruth Roland, captivated audiences in their exaggerated Western attire. And rodeo became a popular sport, even in places like Boston and New York City. Cowboy boots were no longer the exclusive domain of ranchers and cowboys. They had become fashionable across the country, and the boot business, like the rest of the economy, was booming.[13]

That was the "world" of cowboy boots and their makers in the second decade of the twentieth century. The bootmakers all had one thing in common: they were men. Women, sometimes wives of the bootmakers, occasionally worked in boot shops but never in an ownership capacity—their names were not on the door. Boot-making was a man's profession, always had been, but that changed in 1925 when Enid Justin, daughter of pioneer cowboy bootmaker H. J. Justin, decided to start her own boot company. Author Dale Terry wrote, "To say that Enid is one of a kind is an understatement—you'll never meet another lady like her." This is her story.[14]

[Postscript: Because there are so many Justin family members involved in this story, they will generally be referred to throughout by their given names.]

THE
LADY
MAKES
BOOTS

CHAPTER 1

IT'S NOT WHAT YOU KNOW, IT'S WHAT YOU DO WITH WHAT YOU KNOW.

—ENID JUSTIN[1]

The story of Nocona Boot Company began in spring 1925, when Enid Justin declared that she was going to start her own boot company in her small hometown. The announcement shocked her family, who immediately prophesied failure and begged her to reconsider, but her mind was made up. When she arrived at this decision, Enid was thirty-one years old, married, and enjoying a comfortable life. The fact that her husband, Julius Stelzer, worked in the family's original boot business only made her announcement seem more irrational to the rest of the family.

Enid had pondered this surprising decision for some months; it was a proclamation that had its genesis in another decision recently made by the Justin family. The Justins had been in the boot business in North Texas for more than four decades, but in early 1925, the family decided to move the thriving H. J. Justin & Sons from the small North Texas town of Nocona to the growing city of Fort Worth, some eighty miles south. That decision triggered Enid's unexpected announcement. She believed her father and founder of the company, the late Herman Joseph Justin, wanted his boot factory to stay in Nocona. If her brothers were intent on moving the company, she would start her own boot factory in the town her father had helped to build. Enid had worked by her father's side in the

Justin factory since she was ten years old, and she believed that of all the Justin children she was her father's favorite. She felt a compelling obligation to honor her father's memory by keeping a boot factory in Nocona. If daunted by the fact that boot-making was a man's profession, she never let it be known, but her plan would truly test her mettle.[2]

Business was good in 1925 when the Justins initiated their move to Fort Worth. As it was in the rest of the nation, the economy in Texas was thriving. The state's prosperity was tied primarily to the growing oil industry and the production of cotton and cattle, but manufacturing was also expanding. Although Texas remained more rural than urban, urbanization was a growing trend, and Fort Worth was the state's fourth-largest city. With its burgeoning economy, it is not surprising that the Justin family saw opportunity in that growing city.[3]

When the decision was made to move to Fort Worth, the Justin Boot Company already had a storied history. Herman Joseph Justin, Enid's "Daddy Joe," came to Texas in 1877 from his native state of Indiana. He was the son of Prussian immigrants Nicholas and Katherine Hubertz Justin, who had lived in England and New York before settling in Lafayette in the 1850s. Joe was born in 1859, the second of seven children.[4]

Census records as well as the Lafayette, Indiana, directory list Nick Justin's occupation as tailor, but family history suggests he was a cigar maker. Whatever his father's trade, Joe Justin had no interest in following in his father's footsteps. As a teenager, he became interested in working with leather, and he hoped someday to earn his living as a bootmaker. He began learning the cobbler's craft in Lafayette, and when he turned eighteen, the handsome brown-haired young man announced to his family that he intended to pursue his dreams in Texas. His decision to leave home had much to do with the family's financial condition: there were simply more mouths than his father could feed.[5]

The decision to leave his home and family must have been difficult. Joe had never been west of Indiana, he knew no one in Texas, and he had no job prospects there. The spirit embodied in the popular phrase "Go west, young man, and grow up with the country" may have enveloped young Joe. He obviously believed there were opportunities in the frontier state, and he was confident that he could make a life for himself there.

CHAPTER I

Justin was not alone in venturing to Texas. With the end of the Civil War, the number of immigrants heading west greatly increased. Western states and territories were growing in population, and Texas was no exception. Between 1870 and 1890, the state's population almost tripled. By 1880, the last of Texas's Indians had been defeated and the buffalo herds slaughtered, opening vast prairies to cattle and cowboys. A huge demand for beef in northern states at war's end led to Texas cattle being driven north along established trails to various railheads in Missouri and Kansas, where they could be transported by rail to the northeast. At the same time, rail lines in Texas were rapidly expanding, crisscrossing the eastern half of the state. The railroad brought young Joe Justin to Texas in 1877, and a storied cattle trail would later provide the first customers for his boots.[6]

Joe got off the train in Denison, Texas, then the end of the line for the Missouri, Kansas & Texas Railway, and he continued his journey west some forty miles, probably by wagon, to Gainesville, the county seat of Cooke County. The growing town benefited from Texas's expanding cattle industry as it became a supply point for cowboys driving herds north to Missouri and later to Kansas. Just seven miles south of the Red River and Indian Territory, the town was ideally situated between the early Shawnee Trail and its successor to the west, the Chisholm Trail. Young Justin found a job as a cobbler in the Norton Shoe Shop, owned by two sisters who had inherited the business from their father.[7]

Joe spent two years in Gainesville perfecting his trade, and during that time he witnessed the possibilities for growth and prosperity in a cattle-trail town. When he arrived, Gainesville was still very much a frontier community. Dirt streets surrounded the courthouse square, and wooden-plank walks fronted stores to help patrons avoid the mud. But the town was changing, and just a year after his arrival construction began on a new stone courthouse, considered very fine for its time and financed by cattle money. Horse-drawn wagons crowded the streets as customers conducted business with dry goods and hardware merchants, banks, hotels, and bars like George Holsapple's Saloon and Boarding House that catered to thirsty cowboys just off the trail.[8]

By the late 1870s, the city was striving to overcome its bawdy cow town image. Although Gainesville citizens drew the line at voting for prohibition in 1877, they did pass an ordinance that same year that prohibited nude bathing in Elm Creek between the hours of 5 a.m. and 8 p.m. Cattle money made Gainesville the financial capital of north-central Texas, as local banks held millions of dollars deposited by wealthy cattlemen. The cattle business provided much of the tax revenue that improved local schools and built better roads. As Justin worked at the shoe shop, he witnessed the growing prosperity of the town and surely heard the news of the trail from newly arrived drovers as he repaired their trail-worn boots. Perhaps he heard of the new cattle trail community of Spanish Fort and learned that the town had no cobbler. Whatever the impetus, the aspiring bootmaker decided to leave Gainesville in 1879 and head west to Montague County.[9]

His chance came when three freight wagons rolled into town. They were headed to Spanish Fort, some forty-five miles northwest of Gainesville, with a cargo of liquor for the Cowboy Saloon. Joe approached one of the teamsters, J. I. Sewell, and asked what the fare would be to ride along. The driver answered with another question: How much money do you have? When Justin replied that he had six dollars, the wagon master set his fare at $5.75. The young cobbler tossed his meager possessions into Sewell's wagon and climbed aboard. In an interesting coincidence, a few years after Joe left Gainesville, another young artisan whose craft was also directly related to the cattle industry set up shop in that Cooke County town. He was John Robert McChesney, and he made bridle bits and spurs. The two craftsmen would later cross paths and develop a business relationship as well as a friendship that would last for years.[10]

Justin arrived in Spanish Fort and found a small but bustling town. When the community began just a few years earlier, Montague County was still considered a frontier county. It was carved from Cooke County and formally organized in 1858, taking its name from Daniel Montague, a surveyor and veteran of the Mexican War. Bands of Comanches and Wichitas raided the area into the 1870s, when an organized effort successfully drove the Indians from the county. In 1878, only a year before Joe arrived in Spanish Fort, Texas governor Richard B. Hubbard announced that Montague County was no longer a frontier county.[11]

Despite the governor's pronouncement, Spanish Fort in 1879 was still very much a frontier settlement. The town was situated on a big bend of the Red River, such that the river was both north and east of the settlement. The heavily wooded area surrounding the town, a part of the Western Cross Timbers, provided a stark contrast to the prairies just to the west. The community was originally named Burlington, but when citizens applied for a post office in 1876, postal authorities denied their request because Texas already had a town with that name. Two local men suggested the name Spanish Fort because of nearby ruins of a stockaded fort. The new name was accepted, and the Spanish Fort post office opened in 1877. Ironically, the ruins were not Spanish but Indian.[12]

The town of Spanish Fort occupied the same location that a century earlier had been a major settlement of Taovaya Indians, a Wichita group. Two permanent villages on opposite banks of the Red River were established in the early 1700s and continuously inhabited until the 1830s when the tribe, decimated by smallpox and pressured by Anglo encroachment, abandoned the site. The Taovaya villages were the target of a major attack by Spanish forces in 1759 in retaliation for an earlier Indian attack on a Spanish mission on the San Saba River in present-day Menard County. After a daylong battle, the Spanish expedition of some six hundred men was forced to retreat. They were no match for the fortified villages defended by an estimated two thousand warriors armed with French muskets. As a result of that battle, later settlers often found Spanish artifacts and assumed the ruins were Spanish—thus the misnomer.[13]

Spanish Fort was a last stop for drovers before crossing the river into Indian Territory. Cowboys would bed down their herds at Red River Station, a primary crossing on the Chisholm Trail, then ride some eleven miles east to Spanish Fort for supplies and recreation.[14]

Red River Station predated Spanish Fort by more than a decade. The small settlement located at a well-known river crossing got its name when a Confederate Frontier Regiment was stationed there during the Civil War to guard the border between Texas and Indian Territory. The crossing was a main artery of travel into and out of the territory; after the war, as cattle drives became a lucrative enterprise, Red River Station became the crossing of choice on the Chisholm Trail. The community had an outfitters store, a saloon, a ferry, and even a post office for a few years, but the movement of so many cattle through the area became a drawback. The dust, the smell, and the noise as thousands of cattle waited to ford the river led to the establishment of other communities more distant from the chaos, and Spanish Fort met that need.[15]

Joe was twenty years old when he arrived in Spanish Fort. He had a few personal belongings, his cobbler's tools, enough leather to make one pair of boots, and twenty-five cents in shinplasters, a form of paper currency widely circulated in frontier economies. Thanks to a young barber, Frank P. See, also newly arrived in Spanish Fort, Joe found a place to ply his trade in a small 2' x 4' lean-to attached to Frank's barbershop. While he waited for potential customers, Justin swept the floors of the one-chair shop and did other odd jobs for Mr. See. One day he observed a cowboy waiting for a shave whose boots were badly in need of repair, and he offered to mend the tattered footwear. The cowboy, probably thinking he had nothing to lose, agreed to let Joe have a go at it. Pleased with the job, the drover told his friends, and word quickly spread, by way of the local saloons, that there was an experienced cobbler working at the barbershop. More cowboys whose boots needed patching sought him out, and his repair business grew. But repairing boots was not what he really wanted to do; he wanted to make them.[16]

Justin was making enough money to "get by" but not enough to buy the leather and other supplies he needed to begin boot-making. As his frustration grew, he considered giving up and going back to Indiana. In desperation, he told his friend See about his dilemma and asked if the barber had any money that he could borrow. Years later, in recounting the story to a reporter, See remembered:

> One evening after supper, Joe came in and said, "Frank, I am going to have to leave. I can't get by at this unless I can get hold of some money. Have you any money?"
>
> I said, "Mighty little, Joe."
>
> "Well," he said, "if I can get enough to buy a little stock, just two or three hides, I'll make the world sit up and take notice that H. J. Justin can make the best boots in the world. How much have you got?"
>
> I said that I had just an even $35, not a cent more, but I told him he could have it and counted it out to him and said, "Now, Joe, go do your best."
>
> In a week, he was hammering out a pair of boots for me and soon I was wearing the first pair of boots made by H. J. Justin. They cost me $9. Sandy Horton got the second pair and Meel Morris got the third pair.[17]

CHAPTER I

See also told the story of a cowboy named Joe who worked for rancher Meel Morris and, after seeing his boss's boots, asked Justin to make him a pair. Joe was a big man, and See remarked, "The cowboy's foot was as long as my arm and as big as a ham." He asked Justin, "How are you going to work on his boots in this little place?" Joe's answer: "We'll work when it's not raining so we can go outside to turn them around."[18]

It was not long before young Justin needed a larger place, so he rented a one-story frame building located just off the town square. According to See, the new place measured about eight feet by eight feet. There was space for a workbench, storage for hides and other supplies, and even room to hire a helper. His first employee was an elderly man named Bill Grace. Joe hung a painted wooden sign in the shape of a boot from the corner of the building and painted "H. J. Justin, Boot Maker" over the front door. With a popular saloon only a few doors away, the drovers soon found their way to the bootmaker's door.[19]

Justin's boots were comfortable and durable, and his reputation began to grow. Word spread along the trail that good boots could be bought in Spanish Fort, and cowboys driving their herds north would stop at Joe's shop to order boots, then pick them up several weeks later on their way back south. The boots were not fancy; that would come later. They were made of heavy oil-tanned leather and had high heels to keep the cowboy's feet from slipping through the stirrups and high tops to protect his legs from hazards of the trail like thorny brush and snakes. They were tight fitting for sure footing on rough ground. The average price for a pair of Justin boots was $8.50, a cost roughly equal to a week's wages for a cowboy. In his one-room shop, Justin produced an average of two pairs of boots a week.[20]

In addition to the new boot shop and the barbershop, Spanish Fort had all the usual cow town establishments. There were four hotels and several saloons, the most popular "watering hole" being J. W. Schrock's Cowboy Saloon. An early history of the town noted, "It was the custom of the cowboys when they reached the Red River to bed down their cattle and come to Spanish Fort to quench their thirst and display their marksmanship." A favorite target was a large painting of a bull that adorned the front of the Cowboy Saloon. Schrock was finally forced to board up that painting to stop the target practice. Spanish Fort was a rough town, as court dockets and "boot hill" attest, but the town also had respectable citizens just trying to make a living for themselves and their families.[21]

The community had a number of businesses that provided goods and services for local ranchers and farmers as well as for cattlemen and drovers who were just passing through. McNatt's General Store was a popular stop for supplies. There were several churches, a newspaper, a school, and even a Masonic lodge. In 1885, the population reached 300, and by 1887, the town boasted 500 residents. Surprisingly, the town had five physicians, who were kept busy treating the numerous injuries and ailments that arose on the trail.[22]

One of those doctors, S. A. Allen, came to Spanish Fort from Lipan in Hood County in 1876 with his wife Elijah Jane and his daughter Annie. Annie grew up in the raucous cattle town and often accompanied her father as he made his rounds to treat patients. Annie was a pretty young lady, and when she and Joe met at one of the town's weekly square dances, the young bootmaker was immediately smitten. He and Annie married on January 12, 1887.[23]

When the couple married, Joe had been working in Spanish Fort for eight years, during which time he had established a reputable boot shop; but he worked long hours to meet the demands of his growing business. When his elderly helper quit due to bad health, Annie took his place. She worked alongside Joe measuring cowboys' feet by day and cutting patterns at night in the tiny shop lit by kerosene lamps. The couple could not keep up with the work, and Justin wrote to his younger brother William in Lafayette asking him to come to Spanish Fort, "a new and exciting country," to work in the business. Willie soon arrived and was a welcome addition to the small shop. As Justin's reputation for producing quality boots grew, so did his business, and in 1889, he saw a new opportunity in a town twenty miles to the south.[24]

Justin recognized that times had changed. The cattle drives that had fueled the economy of Spanish Fort and provided Justin a steady stream of customers were ending. There were a variety of reasons for the demise of the trail drive. With the invention of barbed wire in 1874, the cost of fencing large tracts of land was no longer prohibitive, and cattlemen began to enclose their pasturelands, ultimately bringing an end to the open range. In addition, quarantines imposed by northern states to stop the spread of

CHAPTER I

Joe Justin was approximately twenty-eight years old (c. 1887) and resided in Spanish Fort when this photo was taken. The young bootmaker would move to Nocona in 1889. (Courtesy of the Enid Justin - Nocona Boot Company Collection, University of North Texas Special Collections.)

Texas fever often resulted in whole herds being turned back at the Kansas border. Texas cattle had developed immunity to the disease, spread by ticks, but the fever was almost always fatal to other livestock that came into contact with Texas herds. To compound those problems, a severe drought in the mid-1880s dried up sources of food and water along the trails. But the end of the great cattle drives was clinched by the expansion of railroads. Shipping cattle by rail proved to be more efficient and less costly, and by the late 1880s the trailing of cattle over long distances had almost ended.[25]

While the expanding railroads brought an end to the cattle drives that built Justin's business, at the same time they offered the bootmaker new opportunities. Joe recognized the possibilities of reaching new markets by rail, and when the approaching rail line bypassed Spanish Fort in favor of a route further south, he made the decision to move his shop to the railroad town of Nocona. The town had begun in 1887 as a tent city to house workers laying track for the new Gainesville, Henrietta, and Western line from Denison to Henrietta.[26]

The GH&W's decision to use the more southern route did not happen by chance. Topography favored that route, as a more northern path through Spanish Fort would require costly bridges. But the decision was finalized in 1887 when ranchers D. C. Jordan and William Broadus, who established a ranch in northern Montague County in the early 1870s when it was still open range, offered to donate railroad right-of-way as well as one square mile of land for a townsite. The land was surveyed by Major B. S. Wathen, and the town's name was suggested by Wathen's friend John L. Davis, a Texas Ranger who had served under Sul Ross at the 1860 Battle of Pease River. Davis told Wathen the story of that fight between Rangers and Comanches that resulted in the death of legendary war chief Peta Nocona and the "rescue" of his wife Cynthia Ann Parker. After hearing Davis's account, Wathen agreed that Nocona would be a fine name for the new town.[27]

Nocona enjoyed rapid growth as citizens from surrounding communities like Spanish Fort, Illinois Bend, and Eagle Point moved to the new town to take advantage of the railroad. By the time Justin moved to Nocona in 1889, there was a bank, dry goods store, hardware store, lumber yard, livery stable and wagon yard, blacksmith shop, restaurant, hotel,

CHAPTER I

The Justin family, c. 1905. Front Row: Daddy Joe, Avis, Anis, and Annie. Back Row: John, Fern, Enid, and Earl. (Courtesy of the Enid Justin - Nocona Boot Company Collection, University of North Texas Special Collections.)

and new railroad depot. Justin opened shop in a small rock building with a wooden front on the east side of Clay Street, but he soon moved to a larger building across the street. The location, less than a block from the depot, facilitated shipping as Justin Boot became the first manufacturing enterprise in Nocona.[28]

The Justins had started their family in Spanish Fort. Their first son, John Sullivan—named after the famed boxer of that era—was born in 1888, just a year before the couple moved to Nocona. John was followed by William Earl in 1890, Fern in 1892, Enid in 1894, another brother Samuel Avis in 1896, and sister Anis in 1898. A fourth daughter, Doris Myrl, was born in 1909. For a short time, the family lived in two tiny rooms at the back of the shop while a modest frame house was being built behind the boot shop. As the family grew, the house underwent numerous expansions, including the addition of a second story and a large wraparound porch. A "family clubhouse" built behind the house served as a playhouse for the children as well as a space for social events and parties.[29]

13

The Justin home was the scene of many fond memories for Enid. The home burned in the late 1920s. (Courtesy of the Enid Justin - Nocona Boot Company Collection, University of North Texas Special Collections.)

Soon after moving to Nocona, Annie and Joe devised a self-measuring system that allowed customers to order boots by mail. The impetus for the technique came from a letter from Montana rancher O. C. Cato, a Justin customer who also became a longtime friend. From his ranch headquarters north of Miles City, Cato wrote that there were many folks in his area who would like to have Justin boots but could not get to Texas to be measured. If Justin could figure out a way to fit boots without having to personally measure a man's foot, Cato felt certain the young bootmaker would have many new customers in Montana.[30]

Justin could not have had a more influential supporter. O. C. Cato, originally from Texas, managed the Montana division of the XIT Ranch, a three-million-acre ranch created in 1882 when the state of Texas sold land in the Panhandle to fund construction of a new capitol building. In 1889, in an effort to improve the quality of the XIT herd, ranch management leased two million acres in Montana between the Yellowstone and Missouri Rivers to serve as feeding grounds for its cattle before shipping them to market in Chicago. Some 12,500 cattle were driven annually to

CHAPTER I

The Clubhouse, located behind the Justin home, was a play space for the Justin children and later the first home of Justin Leather Goods Company. The structure remained long after the home burned, as this photo was taken in 1951. (Courtesy of the Enid Justin - Nocona Boot Company Collection, University of North Texas Special Collections.)

those northern pastures. Cato oversaw that enormous enterprise, and in 1908 when the Texas ranch no longer needed the northern pastures, he bought the XIT's Montana holdings. The rancher and banker also served as sheriff of Custer County and was elected to both the Montana House of Representatives and the state senate. Cato's suggestion proved to be a boon to the Justins' business.[31]

Upon customer request, the couple mailed a packet containing a catalog with price list, order blanks, a small cloth tape measure, and a foot chart with directions for measuring the ball, instep, heel, ankle, and calf. The order blank listed options for the customer to choose toe shape, heel height, sole thickness, and the type and color of leather for the boot top and vamp. The packet was complete with a self-addressed return envelope. The system proved to be popular, and mail orders soon arrived, requiring Justin to hire additional help to meet this new demand. Although Joe is usually given credit for devising the system, family members say it

Interior of the Justin Boot Factory with Daddy Joe and son Earl in the right foreground and eldest son John, already an apprentice bootmaker, in the left foreground. (Courtesy of the Enid Justin - Nocona Boot Company Collection, University of North Texas Special Collections.)

was Annie who was largely responsible for the design of the revolutionary method. Enid later noted that her mother, an accomplished seamstress, was a "whiz with a tape measure and it was she who really figured it out so that it was effective."[32]

The self-measuring kit was a huge success, but Justin refused to patent the system, saying, "If it will help me, let it help others." Before long, bootmakers around the country were using similar self-measuring systems. Another innovation, the use of decorative stitching, is often credited to the young bootmaker. The stitching was applied in rows around the top of the boot to strengthen the leather and keep the boot top from folding down as it became worn. In time, those stitches took on a decorative flair. Justin became known for the quality he stitched into every boot; craftsmanship was his top priority.[33]

By 1898, Justin Boot had five employees, and annual revenue approached $4,000. As the Justin children grew up, they all worked in

CHAPTER I

the boot shop after school and on Saturdays. John, the oldest, went to work in the shop when he was twelve, earning twenty-five cents a day. His brothers Earl and Sam also joined the workforce while still in grammar school. Enid was ten when she started working at the shop. Her first job was to assemble mail-order packets and help with other small jobs around the factory. By age twelve she was stitching boot tops on a foot-pedaled Singer sewing machine and doing the "pasting up," the term for putting the boot backs and fronts together. Enid later recalled, "Daddy Joe was a stern boss.... He demanded quality in everything we did, our living, our work, and our play." She added that he "gave us girls the same opportunity to work as the boys." For Enid, that encouragement and experience would later prove invaluable.[34]

When Enid was thirteen, her life took an unexpected turn. A party was held at the Justin home to celebrate her brother John's twenty-first birthday. Enid later told the story of what happened the next day:

> I had finished the seventh grade and was ready to start in the eighth grade on my brother John's birthday. We had a big party at our house to honor John. There were about twenty couples, his friends, there. We always danced in our home. We had a long, wide hallway that was perfect for dancing. So, after dinner, we retreated to the hall and we danced. The next morning when I went to school, Mr. Paddy [Enid's teacher] asked if I had danced the night before. I said, "Yes, I had a good time." I thought he sounded like he was happy, by the way he asked. I found out different when he said, "Well, I have had instructions from the school board to suspend you for three weeks. You aren't expelled, but you are suspended." It absolutely floored me and I got mad pretty quick. I got my books and I started walking out ... and I told him, "Anybody that thinks there's a party going on in my own home and I'm going upstairs to go to bed has something else to think about!" That wasn't very smart, but I said it anyway ... and I never bothered to go back to school."[35]

Enid had always been a good student and she enjoyed school, but she was also strong-willed. She believed she had been wrongly suspended, and she was determined not to return to the school that had treated her so unjustly. Years later she wondered, "I don't know why Mother and Daddy

Joe didn't make me go back to school," but she speculated it was because they needed her help at the factory. While Enid's brothers and sisters and friends went to school, she went to work full time at her father's boot shop. She obviously spent considerable time with Daddy Joe, and their special bond began to grow. She eventually moved from the factory floor to her father's office and worked closely with him until his retirement in 1916. For a thirteen-year-old, Enid demonstrated an extraordinary work ethic, and with Daddy Joe's encouragement she threw herself into learning the boot business. Her choice not to return to school revealed much about her character. That unique Texas descriptive "maverick" could apply to Enid because, even at that young age, she was not afraid to choose a different path. Perhaps that was a forecast of events to come.[36]

Enid's help was needed as the company grew and made adjustments to meet the challenges brought on by that growth. In 1908, Justin began selling through retail outlets for the first time. No longer would boots be strictly made-to-order for individual customers. This change required Justin to go on the road to search out new merchants who would stock his boots. Because he needed help to run the business while away, he named Enid's two older brothers, John, age twenty, and Earl, age eighteen, full partners and changed the name of the company to H. J. Justin & Sons. When the partnership was formed, Enid was fourteen years old and working beside her brothers to meet the demands of the growing company. That year production exceeded one thousand pairs and annual revenue reached $12,000, with Justin boots being sold in twenty-two states.[37]

The year the partnership was formed, Justin made the decision to mechanize the plant. Up to that point his boots were made by hand except for the stitching around the boot tops that was done with Singer sewing machines. In September 1908, *The Nocona News* reported that H. J. Justin & Sons bought twenty-five pieces of machinery "of the latest make" from the Norton estate at Gainesville. The Norton Shoe Company had given Justin his first job in Texas thirty years earlier; with its closing, it gave him the opportunity to mechanize his factory. Electric lights powered by a gasoline engine were also installed to better illuminate the newly mechanized operation. Justin told the *News* that the machinery was necessary because he had "for the past ten years been unable to take care of his trade,

CHAPTER I

Daddy Joe and his bootmakers pose behind boot drying racks on the sidewalk in front of H. J. Justin Boot Company, c. 1910. (Courtesy of the Enid Justin - Nocona Boot Company Collection, University of North Texas Special Collections.)

as he finds at the end of the week that he has just as many orders as he did at the beginning of the week." The new machinery necessitated increasing the workforce to fifteen men, and the resultant production of standardized, machine-made, assembly-line boots would allow the company to meet current demand and even grow. In addition to the machine-made boot, Justin would continue to produce a more expensive handmade custom line, although in limited numbers.[38]

In addition to machinery, Justin acquired an employee from the Norton Shoe Company. G. C. "Gus" Blucher, who had served as foreman of the Gainesville factory, joined H. J. Justin & Sons as its new foreman, a position he would hold for five years. Blucher would go on to make his own mark on the boot industry. In 1913, he left Justin to start his own custom boot company in Cheyenne, Wyoming. A few years later, he moved his business to Olathe, Kansas, because it was more centrally located and had better railroad access. Blucher became a well-respected custom bootmaker, although on a much smaller scale than H. J. Justin.[39]

Justin had a penchant for advertising and attracting publicity. He ran his first ad in 1903 in the Fort Worth–based *Livestock Reporter*, and

19

through the years his advertising program continued to be aimed primarily at cattlemen and cowboys. Local newspaper ads often featured catchy phrases like "Our competitors are our best advertisers." Advertising brought increased sales, and the mechanized factory was able to meet that demand. In 1909, *The Nocona News* emphasized the importance of the company to the local economy when it announced, "Justin & Sons Boot Factory brings more money to Nocona than any other institution in the town."[40]

The Justins were a close family. Even though Joe Justin worked long hours, he still found time for his family, and he made sure the children had activities to keep them busy. The backyard was filled with playground equipment and, of course, there was the "clubhouse," complete with Victrola and billiard table. Enid recalled, "It was fun being in our home, not only for us but for other people as well. We always had people visiting us and they were always welcome."[41]

Enid grew up to be an imposing young woman. She was tall, almost six feet, and thin, with light brown hair and blue eyes. Enid admitted that as a young woman she never had much interest in boys, but that all changed when she met a charming young telegraph operator named Julius L. Stelzer. In summer 1915, the couple married at Sacred Heart Catholic Church in Muenster, Texas, where Julius lived and worked; they were both twenty-one. At the wedding, Julius's mother remarked about the young couple that she had "never seen two taller or skinnier people." Shortly after their marriage, Daddy Joe offered Julius a position at H. J. Justin & Sons. Julius quit his job in Muenster, and the couple moved to Nocona where Julius went to work for Enid's father and he, too, learned the boot-making trade. Enid later wrote, "I think the reason Daddy Joe hired Julius and taught him the boot trade was because he wanted me back in Nocona. Daddy Joe and I were really close."[42]

By 1915, the boot company had grown to twenty-five employees who were turning out twenty-five pairs of boots a day. John Justin later said of that period, "We sold thousands of pairs of good seventeen-inch calfskin boots at $8.50 a pair." In lauding the company's success, *The Nocona News* noted, "There are today on the ranges of the West thousands of cowboys who would give you the big 'horse-laugh' if the suggestion was made that they wear anything else but Justin boots."

CHAPTER I

The Justin family of the front porch of their Nocona home. Enid leans against the porch pillar on the right with Julius behind her. (Courtesy of the Enid Justin - Nocona Boot Company Collection, University of North Texas Special Collections.)

All was going extremely well at the boot company, but its founder was not faring so well. Joe Justin was stricken with a mysterious illness, sometimes described as "creeping paralysis." His travels took a new direction as he sought medical treatment from specialists across the country.[43] The Justin family kept the factory going during Daddy Joe's illness. Brothers John, Earl, and Sam and sister Anis, along with Enid and her husband Julius, worked side by side managing the factory. Then in December 1916, Enid and Julius had their first child, a daughter, named Anna Jo after both her maternal grandparents, and Enid left her job at the factory to care for the baby. The young couple was devoted to Anna Jo, and Enid remarked, "Everything we did centered on her."[44]

In summer 1917, another Justin left the employ of the boot company. Shortly after the United States entered World War I, Sam joined the Army. He was assigned to the First Division, American Expeditionary Forces, and served in France for the duration of the war. Sam's departure was not the war's only impact on the boot company. Wartime inflation raised prices across the nation, and boot sales slumped. The cost of living actually doubled during the war years, and to compound the problems of a wartime economy, Texas suffered one of the worst droughts in its history in 1917, drastically reducing the production of wheat, cotton, and cattle.[45]

The Justin factory faced shortages of leather and other materials, but because of Daddy Joe's foresight, Justin Boot fared better than some of the competition. When the conflict broke out in Europe, he purchased a large shipment of French wax calf, a quality leather, before it disappeared from the market. As a result, the 1917 Justin catalog boasted, "We are using French Calf. Ask your bootmaker if he is." That same catalog noted apologetically that although Justin boot prices had risen only about two dollars a pair over the previous ten years, the price of wartime materials had necessitated a slight price increase.[46]

The Justin sons made changes in an effort to boost wartime sales and avoid factory layoffs. They increased advertising and began selling boots directly off the factory racks. Those measures increased revenue sufficiently to keep the factory producing on an acceptable level until war's end. Annual sales for 1918 totaled just over $100,000, a slight increase over the previous year. With a son overseas, Daddy Joe was especially eager to support the troops. He received a commendation from Franklin D. Roosevelt, then Assistant Secretary of the Navy, for his contribution to "Eyes for the Navy," a program that provided binoculars, telescopes, spyglasses, and navigation instruments "to protect our warships, transports and supply vessels against the submarine activities of the enemy." Throughout the war, other Noconans did their part to contribute to the war effort. The Justin "clubhouse" was used by the town's women to make bandages for wounded soldiers.[47]

The boot company survived the war years unscathed, but the Justin family experienced personal tragedy in 1918. An outbreak of whooping cough struck the area, and although a vaccine for the disease had been developed in 1906, it would not be used for widespread immunization until 1925. The epidemic was exacerbated by an extreme cold spell. *The Nocona News* reported "zero weather, snow, and a real old time blizzard. . . . The whole week has been about as cold as we ever see in this country." The outbreak itself was not mentioned in the newspaper, but a column titled "Mortuary" began appearing on the front page to list deaths during the previous week, most of them children. That column remained on the front page for several weeks.[48]

Anna Jo was one of the many children who contracted whooping cough, but her illness turned into pneumonia. Enid and Julius lived in a four-room house that Enid purchased with $600 in Liberty Bonds that Daddy Joe had given her. Described as a "box house," the frame structure had single walls and no insulation, so Enid's mother insisted the couple move with the baby to the warmer Justin family home. Despite the best care that the doctor, her family, and a special nurse called in from Wichita Falls could provide, Anna Jo died on January 27. She was only thirteen months old. Enid and Julius were devastated. The doctor told Julius that Enid needed a change of scenery, so the couple moved to Hollister, Oklahoma, where Julius got a job as a railroad depot agent. They had been there two weeks when word arrived that Daddy Joe's condition was worsening. Enid wanted to be with her father, so the couple packed their belongings and moved back to Nocona.[49]

Daddy Joe had suffered a stroke some months earlier that left him partially paralyzed and confined to a wheelchair. Doctors were unable to help him as his condition continued to deteriorate. He died on July 14, 1918; he was only fifty-nine. The Justin family mourned the loss of their patriarch, and the community mourned the loss of an outstanding citizen whose entrepreneurship had been instrumental in Nocona's growth. For Enid, still mourning the loss of her daughter only six months earlier, Daddy Joe's death was an especially cruel blow. In speaking about his death, Enid recalled, "I guess I just never expected Daddy Joe to die . . . when you are the one who is the favorite you just think you've lost everything." After her father died, Enid did not return to work at H. J. Justin & Sons. She would stay away from the boot business until she starting her own factory seven years later.[50]

CHAPTER 2

I CUT MY TEETH ON A PIECE OF LEATHER. I JUST KNEW HOW IT WAS DONE.

—ENID JUSTIN[1]

The years following the deaths of Enid's daughter and father were a difficult time for her, and understandably so. In her memoir, Enid devoted only one sentence to that time: "When Daddy Joe died, my brothers took over the operation of the plant and for the next seven years they stayed in Nocona." It seems it was a time in her life too painful to dwell on.[2]

Enid did not go back to work at the boot factory even though it had been a large part of her life since she was ten years old. Perhaps it was just not the same without Daddy Joe. Perhaps she stayed at home in hopes of having more children. When recalling Anna Jo's death, Enid said, "I wanted a family. I wanted more children after that but fate was unkind to me." Enid's husband Julius, now superintendent of the Justin factory, continued to work alongside Enid's brothers, and the entire family remained close as the boot company continued to thrive.[3]

Daddy Joe had incorporated H. J. Justin & Sons on January 1, 1917. In his will, he stipulated that his five hundred shares of stock in the corporation, each valued at one hundred dollars, be divided among his wife and children. His three sons had been given seventy-five shares each when they became partners in the corporation prior to Joe's death, and they received no additional bequests in his will. Justin's wife Annie and their four daughters each received thirty-seven-and-one-half shares. All of Justin's remaining property was bequeathed to his wife. It is interesting that a father who always treated his sons and daughters equally and who "gave the girls the same opportunity to work as the boys" left the girls half as much as he did the boys. To be fair to Justin, his sons bore the primary responsibility of running the company, and he made sure that his wife and daughters, as shareholders, had a say in business decisions. Except for a few shares sold to outside interests, stock in the corporation was owned exclusively by the Justin family.[4]

A year after Daddy Joe's death, the Justins began a new venture. Because of a leather shortage during the war, the boot company had saved its scraps, and the resulting pile of tanned leather was too valuable to incinerate. As a result, the Justin Leather Goods Company was founded. The new business was the idea of Earl Justin and his brother-in-law G. W. Humphreys. (Earl's wife Florence was Humphreys's sister). They were joined by Reevely A. Moore, head bookkeeper at Justin Boot. Their plan was to use scraps to make purses, wallets, key cases, and other small leather items.[5]

The partners set up shop in the Justin clubhouse, with Earl as president, Moore as vice president, and Humphreys as secretary-treasurer and general manager. According to John Justin Jr., "They hired two or three employees and got an old German-made press with some large dies, and they began cutting pieces, hand-tooling them and making purses." The small handbags, called Purse Pouch Wallets, were made of brown leather hand-tooled with Art Nouveau designs and finished with decorative metal clasps. John Jr. added, "Somebody saw one in New York, and everybody had to have one! They just made those things at a fantastic rate."[6]

The new company quickly outgrew the clubhouse, and in 1920 it was moved to the building vacated when the boot factory moved to a new location at 100 Clay Street. The idea of using scraps was abandoned after the initial production, and the company began ordering its own quality leather. Justin Leather Goods Company became Nocona's second successful leather manufacturer. The company was bought by H. J. Justin & Sons in 1955 and continued to produce handbags and a variety of small leather items sold nationwide until the 1980s. Nocona was on its way to

CHAPTER 2

H. J. Justin & Sons new factory at 100 Clay Street, c. 1920. When Justin Boot moved to Fort Worth, Justin Leather Goods moved into the vacated Justin factory. (Courtesy of the Enid Justin - Nocona Boot Company Collection, University of North Texas Special Collections.)

becoming a center for leather manufacture, owing its beginnings to H. J. Justin, bootmaker.[7]

Justin Boot's new location at 100 Clay Street was a result of Daddy Joe's planning. Before his death, he purchased land on the east side of the town's main street near the rail station as the intended site for a new factory. His sons went forward with his plan and built the modern plant their father envisioned. The new factory, built at a cost of $20,000, was constructed of steel and reinforced concrete with large casement windows. The modern building, flooded with daylight, must have been a welcome change for factory workers. When H. J. Justin & Sons moved to that new location in 1920, the factory had thirty-six employees who produced about nine thousand pairs of boots that year. During the early twenties, standard boots ranged in price from sixteen to twenty-two dollars, but fancy special-order boots sold for as much as sixty-eight dollars.[8]

Much like their father, the Justin brothers proved to be masterful promoters of their brand, and they intended to grow the company they had inherited. With the goal of reaching a larger market, the brothers decided to print an elaborate mail-order catalog. That first catalog, dated 1923, offered thirty-two styles of boots in a variety of designs and leathers. The catalog not only showcased Justin boots but also promoted the Justin brand. Its cover featured a watercolor sketch of an American Indian wrapped in a colorful blanket, sitting on a bluff, pensively observing a herd of buffalo on the plain below. The cover simply read "Justin Boots." The frontispiece dedicated the catalog "To the late H. J. Justin, creator of Justin's Celebrated Cowboy Boots and to that iron-nerved cavalier of the range—The American Cowboy." The fifty-page publication included a history of the company and a variety of testimonials from wearers of Justin boots including western artist Charles M. Russell and famed Texas Ranger Tom R. Hickman. Another photo featured the T. J. Ledbetter family from Mineral Wells, Texas—a father and his nine sons, all wearing Justin boots.[9]

The boots pictured in the catalog were actual photographs cut out and superimposed on a simple background with muted line drawings of western scenes. The boot photos were used so that the customer could be assured "the boot itself will look exactly like the picture." The catalog included detailed ordering instructions as well as a self-measuring order blank with the note, "Take all measurements very carefully and we guarantee you a perfect fit." The price list was attached to the last page of the catalog. A variety of leathers was offered, but the most popular "exotics" were kangaroo, Moroccan kid, and French wax calf, with alligator available at a slightly higher price. The Justin publication also touted its famous "Troutbrook" leather, specially tanned to resist water and barnyard acid.[10]

In addition to producing a catalog, H. J. Justin & Sons broke with a long-held tradition by hiring salesmen to help build its dealer network. For years, the company had proudly advertised that it did not need traveling salesmen, boasting: "Our goods are our representatives. They speak for themselves." Justin Boot had relied on a mix of advertising and direct mail to build its customer base. However, in the early 1920s, the Justin brothers realized the time had come to put salesmen on the road to better serve existing dealers and recruit new ones. Soon, Justin salesmen were traveling the country (there were nine in 1920), and combined with the glossy new catalog, the aggressive sales tactics had the desired effect: in

CHAPTER 2

From the 1923 Justin Catalog, this style, "popular for Rodeos and Roundups," has a kangaroo vamp and white elk top with burned-on design. (Courtesy of the Nocona Boot Company Collection, Tales 'N' Trails Museum, Nocona, Texas.)

1924, sales exceeded $200,000. Sales volume had roughly doubled in only six years. Over the years, when asked if they intended to move their company to a larger city, the Justins had always replied that they intended to stay in Nocona where they could train local workers and not worry about labor issues.[11]

In the first five years of the 1920s, the company grew at a rate of 12 percent a year. With such remarkable growth, the Justins' commitment to remaining in Nocona weakened. They began to consider the advantages of moving their factory to a larger city that would give them access to better banking facilities, a larger labor force, and expanded rail service since Nocona offered only east–west rail lines. The company had been courted by a number of cities in the past, including Dallas, Waco, and Abilene, but either the timing was not right or the incentives were lacking—none seemed to offer the perfect fit. That changed in early 1925 when Fort Worth officials presented H. J. Justin & Sons with a generous relocation package.[12]

Fort Worth offered that "perfect fit" the Justins were seeking, both economically and culturally—the city was steeped in the history of the Old West. It began as one of ten forts established along the Texas frontier to protect settlers from Indians after the Mexican-American War. The line of forts eventually moved farther west, but the settlement that had grown up around Fort Worth remained. In the ten years after the Civil War, Texas's developing cattle industry was a boon to the town's economy. Directly in the path of the Chisholm Trail, the town became a major stop for cattle drives as well as a supply center and headquarters for northern cattle buyers. As the railroad took over livestock transport, cattle shipping became a major industry for the town. At the turn of the twentieth century, livestock-related businesses continued to dominate the economy as Fort Worth added meatpacking to its cattle-related industries. The town came to be called "Cowtown," and citizens proudly adopted the moniker.[13]

By the 1920s, the city that would become home to Justin Boots had a population nearing 125,000, and a building boom was changing the city's skyline. Once again Fort Worth proved to be in an advantageous location as oil was discovered in counties to the north and west. Being the nearest major city, Fort Worth became a center of the booming petroleum industry. By 1925, the city boasted 416 factories, and city leaders actively sought to increase that number.[14]

The Manufacturers and Wholesalers Association of Fort Worth, led by B. B. Buckeridge, courted H. J. Justin & Sons with an incentive package that included a pledge to purchase $50,000 in preferred Justin stock (that generous offer in 1925 would be the equivalent of almost $700,000 in 2018). The association also offered a factory building rent-free for one year and to reimburse the boot company for the cost (not to exceed $5,000) of moving machinery, equipment, and inventory to the new location some eighty miles south of Nocona. An additional incentive was the promise to provide "a great amount of publicity" in local newspapers. Obviously, the offer was hard to resist, but the final decision had to be determined by a vote of stockholders.[15]

The meeting that would decide the home of H. J. Justin & Sons was held in Nocona on April 23, 1925. The entire Justin family, including Enid, who had not been an active participant in the boot company since 1918, attended the gathering. A motion to move the factory and offices to Fort Worth was voted on and passed unanimously. Surprising in light of what happened later, Enid voted her fifty-six shares in favor of the move. The decision was made—Justin Boot was moving to Fort Worth.[16]

On April 24, the front page of the *Fort Worth Star-Telegram* heralded the news with the headline "Justin Boot Factory Comes to Fort Worth." The article detailed the planned move, noting that the local business committee would send a "caravan of automobile trucks to Nocona and move the entire factory here overland." Some seventy employees and their families would also make the move; the *Telegram* estimated a total of six hundred people. The Fort Worth factory was scheduled to begin operation the first of September. Oddly, Justin's announced move did not make the front page of *The Nocona News*. Citizens of Nocona did not learn the devastating news until they turned to page three of the May 1 edition, where the editor had merely reprinted the above-mentioned *Star-Telegram* article. No local article or editorial ever addressed the issue in *The Nocona News*. This peculiar omission almost defies explanation. Perhaps it was meant as a snub to the company that was abandoning the town where it had grown up. Or it may have been a form of defiance, a way of saying "we don't need you and will make it without you." Perhaps it had more to do with the recently discovered North Field, gushing both oil and gas, that had dominated the front page for weeks. Whatever the reason, it is hard to believe that the *News* did not lament the loss of the town's largest employer as well as a sizable portion of its population.[17]

Ultimately, the boot company's planned relocation was the catalyst that drew Enid back into the boot business, a business she had always loved. After years of staying at home, Enid suddenly knew what she wanted to do with her life. She would start her own boot company in Nocona and honor her father's memory in the process. In her memoir, she makes no mention of initially voting for the move to Fort Worth; she tells only of her objection to moving the factory and her strong belief that Daddy Joe wanted the company to stay in Nocona. There is no way of knowing with certainty if she had a change of heart in the months between the vote and the final move or if her favorable vote was part of a strategy that would appease the family and buy time to plan her new venture. Evidence seems to point toward the latter. Enid surely knew that discussions were going on between Justin Boot and Fort Worth promoters before the final vote was taken, and it is possible that during that time she devised a plan to start her own factory in Nocona if her brothers moved south. Undoubtedly, had Justin Boot stayed in Nocona, there would have been no Nocona Boot Company.[18]

In recalling events surrounding the move, John Justin Jr. related, "When the time came for her [Enid] to move to Fort Worth, along with my father and uncles, she told them she needed more time, that she wasn't quite ready to leave. She kept on delaying until she finally said she was going to remain in Nocona and open her own boot factory. It turned out that she had been stockpiling boot-making machinery in a warehouse in Gainesville all that time."[19]

If Enid was indeed "stockpiling" machinery, she omitted that fact from later accounts of creating Nocona Boot Company. Her memoir states that she always opposed the move, and when the decision was made to move the factory to Fort Worth, Enid recounted, "I just bowed my neck and told them I wasn't going. I told them I was going to stay in Nocona and start my own boot business." Her brothers tried to discourage the venture. John told her, "You're going to lose every damned cent you've got in six months." Enid replied that their mother had taught her "how to wash and iron and sew and cook and scrub, and if I go broke, I'll just do something else." Surprisingly, Earl warned, "Don't you know it won't be much longer when there won't be any cowboy boots worn at all?" In fact, the Justins had begun producing shoes as well as boots because they feared the future demand for cowboy boots would decline. To that contention, Enid replied, "Why Earl, we'll always eat meat and the cowboys will always have to ride the range." Enid had made her decision, and no argument would dissuade her.[20]

Enid countered her brothers' objections with her own argument for keeping a boot company in Nocona:

I knew that Daddy Joe would have never left Nocona, he would have never moved the factory away. It was just his nature to give employment to the townspeople, and the people of Nocona were his townspeople. I just knew I had to stay in Nocona and follow in Daddy Joe's footsteps. I had to keep alive the business he started here. I knew how boots should be made, I knew where to buy the materials . . . and I knew a lot more. Daddy Joe had taught me well. And he had trained Julius well in the art of making fine quality boots.[21]

As evidence to back her argument, Enid remembered when her father had been courted by Greenville, Texas. The town fathers asked Joe to consider moving his factory there, but after visiting Greenville, he returned home and told the family, "We're going to stay right here." Justin turned down another proposition in May 1911 when Dallas representatives offered him a large bonus to move his factory to their city. Abilene and Waco were also failed suitors. Enid believed that her father was committed to Nocona and never would have moved his factory to another town.[22]

In an interview years later, Enid recalled telling her husband that she was not going to follow her brothers to Fort Worth. She told Julius, "I am not going." He said, "What are you going to do?" Enid replied, "We will start our own shop." It appears that Julius was surprised by the idea, but he obviously agreed to support her decision. The couple was joined by a handful of Justin Boot employees—including E. D. "Gene" Keller, who had been foreman of the Justin fitting department—who chose to stay in Nocona and become part of the new venture.[23]

Enid tried to raise the capital to fund the new factory by selling her Justin stock, but she couldn't find buyers. She concluded that the people in and around Nocona wanted no part of the company that had moved away. After that failed attempt, Enid's only option was to borrow money, and there she met with success. She obtained a personal loan for $5,000 from the local Farmers and Merchants Bank whose president, C. S. McCall, was a family friend. She noted, "My name was the only one on the loan even though I was married. I guess that was a bit unusual for those days . . ."[24]

A woman starting her own business in "those days," the 1920s, was indeed rare, but women's views of their roles in society had begun to change. Prior to World War I, there was a common belief that a woman could not pursue both family and career successfully. That notion began to crumble when, to meet labor shortages, women were employed in a variety of wartime jobs that ranged from public service to heavy industry. Even though the majority of those jobs halted at war's end, women had seen the opportunity to expand their role in society. In the booming postwar economy, women were increasingly eager to have successful careers as well as families and to seek personal fulfillment. Enid Justin seemed to embody that spirit, even though the women's movement was not a part of her agenda.[25]

The Western ethos may also have contributed to Enid's tenacity. She had grown up in the West of cowboys, cattle drives, and even renegade Indians who on occasion ignored the Red River boundary between Indian Territory and Texas. The frontier was a part of the recent past, and that frontier mentality certainly influenced the young lady who wanted to be a bootmaker. By its very nature, the West encouraged women to be independent and hardworking. Western women had a common remembrance: "When I saw something that needed doing, I did it." Enid personified that philosophy. She once told an interviewer, "Although everyone told me that boot-making was no job for a woman, I wanted to give it a try by myself."[26]

Enid had a "can do" personality that gave others confidence in her ability. Her husband obviously believed in her and thought they could succeed with the new factory, as did the other Justin Boot employees who stayed in Nocona to work with Enid. Her banker evidently also trusted in her ability. As Enid later remarked, "The bank president had been a good friend of my father's, and I guess he figured I could make a go of it." Looking back, Enid admitted the new business had very little going for it. "All I had was the five thousand dollars of borrowed money, a few faithful employees and me." But she also had the support of the town. On July 24, *The Nocona News* headlined "New Boot Shop for Nocona," and this announcement made the front page. The article noted that the Nocona Boot Company "will soon be ready to demonstrate to the world that good boots is [*sic*] still being made in the best town." Understandably, the brothers' move to Fort Worth caused resentment among Nocona residents, and they were eager to support Enid's new endeavor.[27]

CHAPTER 2

Enid Justin, c. 1925. (Courtesy of the Enid Justin - Nocona Boot Company Collection, University of North Texas Special Collections.)

On July 1, 1925, H. J. Justin & Sons left Nocona in a caravan of trucks and vans headed to Fort Worth, and on September 1 Enid's Nocona Boot Company began operations. The new company had been organized in only a few months. Enid rented Daddy Joe's former location, known as the Atkins Building, on the west side of Clay Street for fifteen dollars a month. The building had been home to both the Justin Boot factory and Justin Leather Goods Company. When Justin Boot moved south, the Leather Goods Company moved to the vacated Justin factory at 100 Clay, leaving the Atkins building available for Nocona Boot. The factory space measured 25 x 40 feet.[28]

Enid leased machinery from the United Shoe Machinery Company headquartered in Boston, Massachusetts. Each machine was equipped with an indicator that counted stitches, and the cost of the lease was determined by the number of stitches made on each machine. United Shoe sent representatives to install the machinery, and Enid later reminisced, "I frankly think the United Shoe Machinery Company admired us and wanted to be helpful." United installers even helped Enid's employees build a long table for the Singer sewing machine heads. The Singers, called flat beds, were used to stitch designs on boot tops while the larger United Shoe machines were used to stitch boot tops to soles.[29]

The new boot company was structured as a partnership among Enid, Julius, and Gene Keller. Enid knew there were some individuals who would not do business with a company run by a woman, so Julius was named president. Enid explained that "ranchers and cowhands sort of shied away from women businesspeople at that time." She was aware of the bias against women in business, and she hoped to sidestep that prejudice by letting Julius head the company. Enid later recalled, "Julius was listed as president because that's the way I wanted it, but I actually ran the business." Enid was willing to sacrifice personal recognition for the good of her fledgling company; her venture was not about ego but rather a personal mission to keep a boot company in Nocona and honor her father's memory.[30]

In the weeks leading up to the opening of the new company, *The Nocona News* ran several articles reporting progress on the installation of the new factory. Each of those articles mentioned only Julius and Gene Keller as principals in the company. An article dated July 24 announced that the new company "will be in operation within a short time. . . . Messers. Julius Stelzer and Gene Keller, who have each had years of valuable experience in the making of good boots, are making the venture and we predict success for them." Although many people in town knew that Enid initiated the company, the newspaper did not mention her as an owner until 1934 when a factory expansion was announced. Even then Enid received recognition only as Julius's wife, but that circumstance would eventually change.[31]

CHAPTER 2

As president, Julius oversaw the operation of the company, Keller served as foreman, and Enid did the bookkeeping, ordering, and collecting on accounts. On occasion her job description included "shipping clerk, stenographer, and everything else, just anything they needed me for." The men drew a salary of fifteen dollars a week, while Enid accepted only three dollars. She recalled, "We got by on as little as we could. That's the way I wanted it. . . . I wanted to get the money paid back and get out of debt as soon as possible."[32]

The new factory was divided into departments, each performing a specific task such as cutting, fitting, stitching, and lasting (the process of shaping the leather on a last, a wooden form shaped like a foot). The production line was similar to that of the Justin factory but on a smaller scale. There were only one or two people in each department in that first year, and they required ten days to two weeks to complete a pair of boots. Those early boots were made of cowhide and sold for around eighteen dollars. To bring in additional revenue, the factory also did boot and shoe repair. Money was scarce, and Enid recalled, "One time I walked all the way across town to try to collect a quarter someone owed for repairs . . . we needed the money."[33]

In addition to working all day at the factory, Enid took on a variety of "outside jobs" to bring in extra money. She later recalled, "I wanted the business to be a success so badly that I did other things to make ends meet." She turned her home into a rooming house, cooked meals for her boarders, and sewed and ironed for people. She also cooked meals for other boarders around town. She remembered, "I cooked meals at noon and at night. . . . I had a good boarder business so I guess I was a pretty good cook." Enid also sold washing machines and would go into her customers' homes to teach them how to use the new appliances. She was proud of the fact that she sold the first electric washer in Nocona. And if that weren't enough, she also made extra money selling coal, the primary fuel used in the town at that time. She took customer orders for the coal, and when it arrived by rail, she weighed it on a big scale next to the track, delivered it, and collected the money for it.[34]

To say that Enid was a hard worker is an understatement, but she was not alone—everyone involved in the new company worked hard to make it successful. Despite all their best efforts, however, the financial statement dated December 31, 1925, showed the company had lost $702.58. Enid recalled, "That audit scared me to death. I didn't like being in the hole and I was working so hard. I was determined to succeed, and at this point I developed a trait that has stood me in good stead all my life—just plain, mule-headed persistence." Nocona Boot Company had been operating for only four months when the audit was conducted, and it was not all bad. There were signs that the company was beginning to grow. Merchandise on hand, including "finished stock" and "goods in process of manufacture," was valued at more than $2,000 and, according to *The Nocona News*, "orders are coming in almost faster than they can be filled."[35]

Oddly enough, Nocona Boot Company's early growth can be attributed to the burgeoning oil industry in northern Montague County, between Nocona and the Red River. Exploration began in 1901, but wildcatters had little success until 1916 when a test well showed definite promise. Finally, in July 1923, a drilling site on land owned by J. W. Maddox yielded both oil and natural gas, and a year later the first commercial well in Montague County was connected to a pipeline. Successful drilling continued and production steadily increased in the latter half of the 1920s, averaging close to two million barrels a year and making a significant contribution to the local economy. In 1925, the year that Nocona Boot opened its doors, the area was booming as land leased for $1,000 an acre, and the *News* reported "something near twenty outfits" drilling in the area. The "North Field," as the production area was commonly called, became home to a large number of oil field workers who needed good boots.[36]

Enid's company began producing sixteen-inch lace-up boots designed specifically for the roughnecks. The boot proved to be profitable in more ways than one, as Enid later recalled:

> The cowboys just weren't ready to deal with a woman when it came to their boots . . . but we had this oil field open up north of town and the oil field workers had no problem dealing with a woman bootmaker . . . and as the cowboys watched the oil workers buy from me, the walls came tumbling down and the cowboys decided to give me a try. They found out quick that I had skilled craftsmen building the boots and the problem with the cowboys eventually vanished.[37]

Although the lace-up boot solved one problem, it created another. The tongue of the oil field boot was distinctive—it had been designed by Enid's brother John when the Justin factory was still located in Nocona. The tongue was wider than the standard boot tongue and crafted of soft leather that would spread out and lay comfortably flat behind the laces. It was not long before Enid received a letter from a Fort Worth attorney advising her that Justin Boot Company owned the rights to that tongue, and she could not use it. Never one to give up without a fight, Enid wrote the United States Patent Office requesting a copy of the Justin patent. The copy confirmed what Enid suspected: that she had every right to use the Justin tongue. Her name was on the patent along with those of John and Earl; in fact, all the Justin children were named as patent holders. Enid continued to use the tongue without further protest from her brothers. That incident was the first indication of the rivalry, sometimes bitter, that would exist between the two companies.[38]

A combination of local business and mail-order sales gave Nocona Boot Company its start, but in order to grow, the company needed additional capital. In January 1926, the decision was made to restructure the original partnership as a corporation. The new corporation had five directors, three of them officers. Julius was president, Jess Thompson was vice president, Gene Keller was secretary-treasurer, and Enid and R. R. Alexander were directors. The charter, granted by the state of Texas, authorized the issuance of capital stock totaling $10,000. The stock was sold to investors at one hundred dollars a share, with Enid keeping a controlling interest. The stock sold quickly, as the townspeople wanted to support the new company and hoped to partake in its success. As Enid noted, "Fortunately, our good friends in our little town were glad we stayed at home, kept the payroll"; she added that those investors "really did take a chance, like we did." That infusion of capital from the sale of stock allowed the company to grow, and in August 1927 an amendment was filed to the charter, increasing the capital stock to $20,000.[39]

Growth was also predicated on increased sales volume, and Enid knew the company could no longer rely solely on local sales and mail orders—she wanted to get her boots into retail stores. There was no money to hire an outside salesman, and the men were needed to run the factory, so Enid decided to take on that job herself. In discussing that decision, she noted,

"I knew our boots were good, so all I had to do was get out and let everyone else know about them," and that was just what she did. The lady bootmaker added traveling saleswoman to her already lengthy list of jobs.[40]

Enid felt it was important to "personally call on the stores," and she never seemed to have a second thought about taking on another job traditionally held by men. Accompanied by her younger sister Myrl, Enid loaded samples in her Ford Model T and set out to sell some boots. Roads then were not paved, and Enid described them as little more than cattle trails—"traveling was either dusty or it was muddy."[41]

The sisters' first stop was Jacksboro, a small town some fifty miles southwest of Nocona. They pulled up in front of the Shabay Brothers Store, but Enid could not get her large sample trunk out of the Model T's "turtleback." As she struggled with it, a man hollered, "Enid, what in the hell are you trying to do?" She hollered back, "I'm trying to get this darn case out of the car." The man turned out to be a friend from nearby Saint Jo, and he helped her get the case out of the turtle and into the store. Enid recalled, "I was sure glad to see him . . . and I made my first big sale right there in Jacksboro." She added, "I got fairly good at getting the case out of the car after that."[42]

Enid and Myrl continued on to Mineral Wells, Comanche, Brownwood, and as far southwest as Coleman before they finally returned home. That first trip was successful, and Enid continued to sell on the road, with her goal being to obtain so many orders on each trip that the factory would be challenged to fill them. She and Myrl made many trips together, venturing as far south as Waco and Gatesville. Travel was often difficult, and despite efforts to find decent accommodations, they "did manage to get into a few questionable hotels." They had their share of car trouble, too, and on one occasion Enid was pleased to learn that Myrl knew how to change a tire.[43]

In recalling her role as saleswoman, Enid said, "I never had much trouble on the road in any respect. I found that a woman out selling boots was pretty much like a man out selling boots. The store owners were interested in quality and price. I had both to offer in my boots." Enid stopped selling on the road when the factory could no longer meet the demand that her increased sales were creating. "The men called me in and told me to stay out of the Model T and off the road, that I was selling

Nocona Boot Company in the early 1940s. (Courtesy of the Enid Justin - Nocona Boot Company Collection, University of North Texas Special Collections.)

more boots than they could make." Largely due to Enid's salesmanship, net profits grew from $1,180 in 1926 to $14,998 in 1929. She continued to make occasional trips "more for promotion than for direct sales," because she enjoyed the travel, describing each trip as "an adventure, a challenge and an experience."[44]

By 1930, just five years after its modest beginning, Nocona Boot Company hummed with success. As sales spread beyond Texas, salesmen were hired to fill the job Enid began in her Model T. The factory, with around sixty-five employees, was turning out seventy-five pairs a day. The small building on Clay Street bustled with activity as workers accomplished their tasks amid the ever-present smell of leather and the droning of machinery. Enid was asked if the noise from the machinery bothered her, and she replied, "Only when the noise stops." Production included some eight styles of cowboy boots, sixteen-inch lace-up oil field boots, and lace-up cowboy shoes, a shoe made on a boot last. In tribute to her father, Enid always kept one of Daddy Joe's styles in production. It was a plain boot with just one row of stitching—the same stitching she had learned to do as a young girl.[45]

Enid attributed the company's early success to the quality of her boots. A cowboy boot has fifty-four parts, and "if you don't start out with

The first addition to the original Nocona Boot Company, c. 1930. (Courtesy of the Enid Justin - Nocona Boot Company Collection, University of North Texas Special Collections.)

quality materials, you don't have a chance of ending up with a quality product." The hides came primarily from tanneries in the northeast, particularly Pennsylvania and New Jersey, because Enid believed they produced the best leather. In those early years, leather was hand cut, and many of the steps in boot production were done by hand. But as time went on and technology advanced, the company acquired machinery that performed many tasks formerly done by hand.[46]

In addition to producing a high-quality product, Enid credited her success to producing what customers wanted. According to Enid, cowboys had specific needs that dictated the style of their boots. They wanted high heels to keep their boots from slipping through the stirrups and to "dig in" when roping on foot. The high heel was also traditional, as Enid noted, "the mark of a real riding man." Pointed toes were favored because they slipped into stirrups with ease and could be used for spurring horses, and cowboys preferred thin soles for flexibility and solid leather heels for durability. To protect their legs, they wanted eighteen-inch boot tops

CHAPTER 2

"A snappy dress boot," c. 1930, from Nocona Boot Company features a black calf vamp and tan kid top with inlaid design. (Courtesy of the Nocona Boot Company Collection, Tales 'N' Trails Museum, Nocona, Texas.)

made of lightweight leather. Stitching around the boot top, originated by Enid's father, stiffened the leather and prevented the top from rolling down, while stitching across the toe helped maintain shape and kept the toe from wrinkling with wear.[47]

Over time, boot tops became more decorative. "Cowboys liked good-looking boots as well as good-wearing boots," Enid noted, "so the tops became important features." The decorative stitching was done with silk or linen thread coated with hot beeswax. Boots might have as many as eight rows of stitching, sometimes in different colors. Some of the early stitch patterns were Enid's designs; one was inspired by a sofa's brocade fabric, another originated, oddly enough, at a funeral. Enid was sitting in church and noticed a pattern in the wrinkled skin on the neck of an elderly man sitting in front of her. She remembered, "I did have a problem getting the design though. I would be sketching away and then the preacher would pray. The old man would bow his head and the wrinkles would disappear. Well, that preacher prayed a lot that day and I thought I never would get the sketch finished." That pattern, named "The Neck," remained popular for many years, but Enid never divulged the neck's owner.[48]

Under the leadership of Enid and Julius, Nocona Boot overcame the early obstacles to its success and, as Enid recalled, "We were on our way . . . and I was sitting on top of the world!" While the factory continued to thrive, two events changed Enid's personal life. The first was the loss of the Justin family home to fire, and the second was the loss of her husband.[49]

When Enid's mother moved to Fort Worth to join her sons, she rented the family home to a woman who turned it into a boardinghouse for oil field workers. One of those boarders apparently smoked in bed. He escaped the flames by jumping from the balcony, but the house burned to the ground. Enid wrote that the loss of the family home "nearly broke my heart." She added, "I never had once regretted staying in Nocona . . . but there were some lonely times with my family gone." The loss of the house seemed to rekindle the sadness she felt when most of the family moved to Fort Worth. Now both her family and her family home were gone, and Enid was struck by that finality. In her memoir, she described the house burning as the close of a chapter in her life.[50]

While the loss of the Justin family home was upsetting for Enid, her divorce was devastating. In 1934, after almost twenty years of marriage, Julius left Enid. She was blindsided by his actions, later recalling that she was "the last one in town to find out" that Julius was "running around" with a woman employed at the boot factory. Enid wanted proof of the affair, so one Friday night she and a girlfriend followed Julius and the "other woman" as they drove north and crossed the Red River to Ryan, Oklahoma. The couple was having dinner at Grady Epson's Café when Enid came in with the sheriff. As she later told the story, "It was against the law then to cross a state line with a woman for immoral purposes if you were a married person . . . and they'd get you if they caught you."[51]

CHAPTER 2

The sheriff took the offending couple to jail in the nearby town of Waurika. Enid and her friend followed, and when they arrived, jail officials escorted Enid to the woman's cell. She did not want to see Julius, but she did want to confront the woman. Surprisingly, the jailors gave Enid permission to assault her husband's girlfriend. Enid recalled, "They told me how to take a broom and stick her with the handle between the bars. They said I could punch her good if I could reach her. They said I could do anything I wanted to but they couldn't give me permission to kill her." Enid chose not to physically attack the woman, but she did fire her on the spot.[52]

Julius resigned his position as president of the company, and in the divorce settlement he asked for only three thousand dollars, leaving everything else, including the company, stock, and personal property, with Enid. His generosity seemed to indicate that he truly cared for Enid over the years they were married and felt guilt for his infidelity. Years later, Enid recalled, "He wasn't all bad. He was just weak and got off on the wrong foot, and he didn't feel my equal." Enid was indeed a strong woman, and that may have been threatening for Julius. But she could also be naive and vulnerable, especially when it came to her personal life, and the divorce was shattering for her. She remembered, "I couldn't walk down the street for a long time after the divorce. I was humiliated. I never stopped working but I was so ashamed to get out in public. Finally, one day I said I am going to that bank by myself. I haven't done anything wrong. I am going to walk up that street to the bank." And she did.[53]

Julius moved to nearby Henrietta, in Clay County, and partnered with local bootmaker Carl Olsen to form Olsen-Stelzer Boot and Saddlery. Ironically, Olsen, like Julius, had learned the trade from Enid's father. He had worked for H. J. Justin as a young shoemaker newly arrived from Norway. With Olsen's boot-making talent and Julius's production experience, the company prospered. Olsen-Stelzer became a successful boot manufacturer, although on a smaller scale than that of Nocona Boot Company.[54]

Over the span of fifteen years, Enid Justin's life had changed dramatically. She lost her daughter and her father, her family moved to Fort Worth taking the family business with them, and she went through a difficult divorce. But she had her Nocona Boot Company, and that would become her family. Enid often said, "My boots have been my children and my workers have been my family." Shortly after Julius's departure, Enid became president of Nocona Boot Company, and she held that position for the next forty-six years.[55]

CHAPTER 3

I LIKE MY BUSINESS NOT ONLY FOR WHAT IT DOES FOR ME,
BUT MOSTLY FOR WHAT IT DOES FOR OTHERS.

—ENID JUSTIN[1]

From its uncertain beginning, Enid Justin led Nocona Boot Company with dedication and constancy. She was always fiscally conservative. "The success of the factory didn't go to my head," she explained, "nor did it change the way I lived. I only drew three dollars a week in those early years. Everything else went right back into the business." Enid invested that capital wisely, and in 1926, she purchased the old rock building she had been leasing from her brothers. Enid made a deal with the Fort Worth Justins to trade fifty shares of her Justin stock for the building and three adjacent vacant lots. When her United Shoe Company lease expired, Enid purchased the machinery. As time went on, one of her greatest concerns became controlling company growth. She always feared she would lose control of the company if it grew too fast.[2]

Enid was a hard worker, but from the boot company's founding she exhibited additional traits that contributed to her success. She was well aware that she was entering a man's world, but her resolve and "can do" attitude reduced that fact to a minor obstacle. When asked by an interviewer if she felt that as a woman she had to fight a little bit harder, she replied, "That really didn't occur to me. I was used to working all my life. It [founding Nocona Boot Company] was a challenge, and I didn't want to give up on it." In addition to that determination, she had an intuitive sense of timing, of knowing when the market was right for change, and a knack for being innovative. And, like her father, she had a flair for advertising and promotion. These traits would surface time and time again during her career as a lady bootmaker.[3]

Enid's early success resulted from not only a lot of hard work but also a bit of good luck in that she began her business at a time of unprecedented prosperity in the United States. In the 1920s, the nation's economy was growing with ever-increasing speed. Fueled by postwar optimism, manufacturing expanded, building construction boomed, and retail sales reached record highs. Much like the rest of the nation, Texas experienced that prosperity, but in a slightly different way. Rather than manufacturing, much of the state's economic growth during the 1920s was based on expansion of the oil industry. Major new fields were discovered and developed, and by 1928 Texas led all other states in oil production. Enid witnessed the growth of that industry firsthand and profited from it as North Field roughnecks became some of her first customers and actually helped establish her business. Enid had the good fortune of starting her company during that "prosperity decade" when the economic climate was favorable for business growth. When that climate changed at the end of the Twenties, Enid's young company was strong enough to weather the downturn, and the 1930s would bring a whirlwind of accomplishments as well as challenges.[4]

In 1929, when Nocona Boot Company had been operating for less than five years, Enid was presented with an unexpected opportunity. The family of J. R. McChesney contacted her to see if she would be interested in buying his manufacturing company. McChesney, a well-known bridle bit and spur maker, had died the previous year, and his family was unable to carry on his Pauls Valley, Oklahoma, business. The Justins and McChesneys had been friends for over twenty years, and the patriarchs of both families had much in common.[5]

McChesney, like Joe Justin, was an innovator in his field. He developed a one-piece hand-forged spur that was widely copied by other spur makers. His products, like Justin's boots, were created for the Western lifestyle, and as early as 1909, Justin catalogs offered McChesney spurs and bits along with boots. Considering the longstanding relationship between the

CHAPTER 3

two families and their shared customer base, it is not surprising that the McChesneys approached Enid as a prospective buyer.[6]

McChesney's story is as compelling at that of H. J. Justin. The future artisan was born in South Bend, Indiana, in 1866, the son of Scottish immigrant Thomas Carwin McChesney and Rosetta Madison, a native of New York. At the age of seventeen he became a student at the University of Notre Dame, then offering college academics, preparatory and grade schools, and "manual labor school." Perhaps young McChesney learned blacksmithing there.[7]

In 1884, when John Robert, called J. R., was eighteen, he moved with his family by wagon train to Rogers, Arkansas, where the McChesneys homesteaded farmland. Shortly after the family's arrival there, J. R. met and married Tabitha Thomas. Young McChesney and his brother-in-law, Henry S. Hurst, began making crossties for a nearby railroad construction crew. Each could hand hew eight ties a day, and at twenty-five cents apiece, the men earned a respectable daily wage of two dollars. When the supply of timber on their homestead was depleted, J. R. and Henry began cutting trees on federal land without permission. When authorities came after them, the two men fled to avoid arrest.[8]

They traveled west as far as Broken Arrow, Indian Territory, a small settlement about fifteen miles southeast of the young railroad town of Tulsa. They decided to make Broken Arrow their home, and their wives soon joined them there. McChesney made a living trading horses and repairing all sorts of equipment from guns to plows. When he learned of a bankrupt blacksmith shop in Tulsa that could be bought for five dollars, he traveled there to buy it. Blacksmiths were in great demand in 1887, and Tulsa's town fathers offered McChesney a deed to five city blocks if he would keep the shop in their town. He refused the offer and found a man with a wagon and ox team who would haul the dismantled equipment to Broken Arrow for fifty cents.[9]

McChesney had natural metal-working abilities, and his business prospered in the wild cow town of Broken Arrow. He set wagon wheels, repaired guns, and made branding irons and horseshoes. A local cattleman asked the blacksmith if he would make him a pair of spurs, but McChesney was busy with other interests and put him off. On his next visit to town the cowman emphasized his need for spurs by shooting holes

J. R. McChesney on the cover of his 1906 price list. (Courtesy of Lee C. Jacobs, *J. R. McChesney: A Lifetime, A Legacy*.)

in the shop's ceiling. McChesney relented, and the result was his first pair of one-piece spurs, each made from the tooth of an old harrow. The cattleman paid five dollars for the spurs and another five dollars for a matching one-piece bit.[10]

A few days later a crowd of cowboys gathered in front of McChesney's shop and began shooting their guns and hollering for the blacksmith. When McChesney went out to see what the commotion was about, the cowboys told him they wanted to order some spurs, but their friend had said McChesney would not make them unless they shot their guns and raised a ruckus. The disturbance proved unnecessary, as the blacksmith had learned that spur making could be profitable. He invited the cowboys to tie up their horses and come inside where he took their orders, requiring cash with each transaction. McChesney then made another trip to Tulsa, and this time he purchased three hundred pounds of harrow teeth that he freighted back to Broken Arrow.[11]

McChesney's spur business was born in Indian Territory, but in 1890 the young artisan decided to move his blacksmith shop to the lively trade center of Gainesville, Texas, the same town that had attracted young H. J. Justin thirteen years earlier. In the years since Justin left Gainesville for Spanish Fort, the town had grown from a small frontier settlement to a modern community with a population of ten thousand. The town's economy revolved around cattle shipping and wholesale liquor distribution. The community enjoyed telegraph and telephone service, electric lighting, and gas heating. Cement sidewalks, illuminated by incandescent streetlamps, bordered its gravel streets—quite a change from the boardwalks and dirt of Justin's time there.[12]

McChesney set up shop on Rice Avenue, hired several local blacksmiths, and specialized in general blacksmith work. A few years later, he moved his shop to the corner of Taylor and Olive Streets, on the north side of Gainesville, where he gave up general blacksmithing and concentrated on manufacturing bits and spurs. In 1906, J. R. McChesney issued his first catalog showcasing his creative designs. In the catalog, a photograph of McChesney revealed a handsome dark-haired young man sporting a flamboyant mustache and wearing a three-piece suit, attire that was not typical of him, since contemporaries described his usual dress as bib overalls. McChesney's parents, who had joined him in Gainesville, went on the road to sell his products, and the young artisan's bits and spurs were soon advertised by a number of retailers including W. L. Woods Saddlery in Gainesville, Padgitt Bros. Saddle Company in Dallas, and H. J. Justin & Sons in Nocona. Orders poured in, and before long McChesney was shipping spurs throughout the United States.[13]

McChesney became acquainted with H. J. Justin as their products shared the same market, and the two men developed a business relationship as well as a friendship. Enid remembered visiting the McChesney home as a child, and she noted, "My father cataloged Mr. McChesney's bits and spurs in his little boot catalog while the McChesney Company was still in Gainesville."[14]

Because of McChesney's success in Gainesville, his one-piece spur design became known as the "Texas spur." All spurs had the same basic components—band, shank, rowel, buttons, and leather straps—but they differed in how those pieces were constructed. Before McChesney's innovative one-piece design, most cowboys wore California or Mexican spurs. Both had two-piece construction with the band and shank made separately and riveted together. McChesney touted his design as "one solid piece of metal. No joints or welds to come loose."[15]

McChesney's spurs were originally hand-forged, but over time he added assembly line production techniques that included dies or molds to shape spurs from molten metal. The cast spur was then ground and polished to create a finished product. The company became known for producing lightweight spurs that were described as "almost delicate." McChesney wrote, "They are heavy enough to be substantial, still weigh less per pair than any other make of spurs. I can only attain this by putting more metal where the strains come and making them lighter where there is no strain. In fact, I try to be nothing but a bit and spur maker. I think about nothing else, dream of nothing else and do nothing else."[16]

McChesney is also credited with originating the "goose-neck" spur with a shank gently curved like the neck of a goose and the even more popular "gal-leg" spur with a shank shaped like a woman's leg. The spurs were often embellished with nickel silver, copper, and brass, and all were elaborately engraved. McChesney's son Robert noted, "My father was well known for his gal-leg spurs with copper socks, silver garters, and silver slippers." According to McChesney, each design was "a real piece of

CHAPTER 3

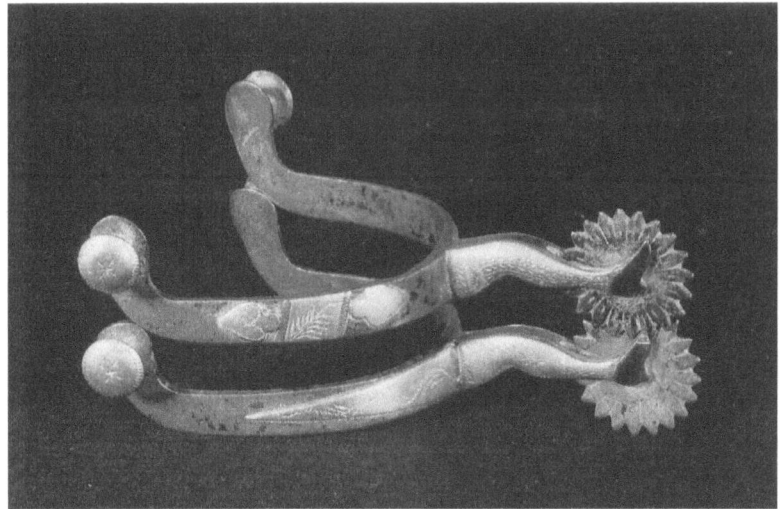

McChesney No. 8 "Gal Leg" spur. (Courtesy of Lee C. Jacobs, *J. R. McChesney: A Lifetime, A Legacy*.)

art." Nature was a favorite subject for the spur maker, and he engraved both bits and spurs with stylized flowers and leaves, snakes, and a variety of birds. Hearts and geometric shapes were common design elements as well. McChesney also created custom designs for special orders, some adorned with sterling silver, gold, gemstones, or Mexican silver coins. The spur maker refused to make a spur that would hurt a horse. The points of his rowels were sharp enough to get the animal's attention but not so sharp that they would penetrate the horse's hide.[17]

In 1910, after almost twenty years in Gainesville, McChesney began looking for a new location for his factory. His decision may have resulted from an economic downturn that began in 1903 when voters approved a countywide local option that restricted alcohol sales, and the town's lucrative liquor business began moving elsewhere. Between 1903 and 1910, more than forty wholesale liquor dealers and saloons closed their doors, and the 1910 census revealed that the county had lost almost a thousand residents. The general decline of commerce in the once-thriving town surely influenced McChesney's decision to move his factory, but a run-in with city officials over his placement of a sewer pipe may have hardened his resolve to relocate.[18]

McChesney boarded a train heading west to search for a new location. His quest ended at Pauls Valley in the new state of Oklahoma. The town, established in the 1840s, was one of the oldest European-American settlements in what was then Indian Territory and home of the Chickasaw Nation. Founded by North Carolina native Smith Paul, who married a Chickasaw woman, the settlement was located in a lush valley where Rush Creek joined the Washita River. Paul described the location as "a section where the bottom land was rich and blue stem grass grew so high that a man on horseback was almost hidden in its foliage." The town acquired a post office in 1871, and in 1887 the Santa Fe Railway reached Pauls Valley, bringing additional growth and prosperity. The town became the county seat of Garvin County, with its courthouse completed in 1895. The progressive community boasted brick buildings and brick streets, and when McChesney arrived in 1910, the population was almost 2,700.[19]

McChesney made Pauls Valley his home after the town's chamber of commerce offered inducements, including $1,500 to help with relocation expenses. He bought a city block across from the railroad depot for $4,500 and built a large two-story brick-and-concrete factory. Some of the spur-maker's Gainesville employees moved with him to Oklahoma, and the Pauls Valley facility eventually employed as many as fifty people who produced 120 spur patterns and sixty-four bit patterns. McChesney became the largest spur manufacturer west of the Mississippi River and the second largest in the United States. His products were shipped all over the nation and to a number of foreign countries, and during World War I he contracted to make spurs for the United States Army. Humorist Will Rogers, author J. Frank Dobie, and cowboy movie stars Tom Mix and Hoot Gibson were among McChesney's famous customers.[20]

Around 1917, McChesney's business began to drop off as his competition began producing less expensive spurs and overall demand for spurs decreased. McChesney's fine spurs continued to have buyers, but his market share had definitely diminished, as a pair of hand-finished McChesney spurs sold for twice as much as a machine-made copy. The spur maker downsized his operation, and in the 1920s he employed only about eight men. In January 1928, J. R. McChesney died of a heart attack at the age of sixty-two. In reporting his death, the *Pauls Valley Democrat* lamented, "Another character of boot and saddle days of the plains has 'gone west.'"[21]

After their father's unexpected death, three of McChesney's children attempted to carry on the family business. Their effort was short-lived, and in late 1929 the family decided to sell the company. "Mrs. McChesney contacted me about buying the business," Enid recalled. "Of course we didn't know much about bits and spurs, but we went up there . . . and talked to them and made a deal . . . we bought the McChesney name, equipment, and stock. They had five families that were real craftsmen in that business then . . . and they came with it." The purchase was finalized in September 1930.[22]

When writing about the longtime relationship of the two families, Enid commented, "It is ironical that after so many years, I bought the McChesney plant." Whether out of family sentimentality or the well-known and respected tradition of McChesney Bits and Spurs, or a combination of both, Enid decided the enterprise was worth saving. It was a company with a reputation for producing quality products, much like Enid's. And the McChesney spurs and bits were a colorful addition to her boot business as well as an opportunity to expand her cowboy market.[23]

The purchase of J. R. McChesney Bits & Spurs, obviously a business risk, demonstrated the level of confidence Enid had, as early as 1930, in the continued success of Nocona Boot Company and in her own ability to salvage the Oklahoma company after family members had failed. Enid was obviously committed to this new segment of her business because just a few months after purchasing McChesney's company, she entered into a contract with R. J. Kerruish of Littleton, Colorado, to be the exclusive manufacturer of his hand-forged bridle bit, a unique design that was patent pending.[24]

Enid named W. D. "Slim" Barnett foreman of her bit and spur department. The former Pauls Valley employee had been with McChesney for fourteen years and was an expert engraver. Barnett, along with the four other Pauls Valley craftsmen, began producing McChesney-Nocona bits and spurs. "One of the most fascinating things was to go back and watch Slim Barnett," office employee Luciel Leonard recalled. "He would engrave the designs on the spurs and bits and things by hand."[25]

The new department was located in the back of the boot factory and set up for assembly-line production of hand-forged bits and spurs. The odors of hot metal and smoke along with the clank of hammer on steel now intermingled with the smell of leather and the drone of machinery

McChesney-Nocona No. 70 spurs with silver heart pattern and McChesney mark on the inside. (Courtesy of Lee C. Jacobs, *J. R. McChesney: A Lifetime, A Legacy*.)

in the small factory. "That hot metal smell would just waft up through the hallway almost out the front door," Leonard remembered. "When you would go back, you could hear the pounding of the anvils and watch them shape the pieces. They would put them in these big furnaces and bring them out—they would just be glowing. Then they would hammer them."[26]

The manufacturing process began with forge work that wrought the metal, followed by grinding and shaping to smooth and refine the rough spur or bit. The product was then polished to create the finished surface necessary for the final steps of mounting and engraving. Mounting involved attaching decorative metal, usually nickel silver, brass, or copper, to the polished item. The mountings were cut from flat metal, shaped to conform to the curve of the spur or bit, and attached with silver solder. For example, the silver stockings, copper slippers, and garters of a gal-leg spur were created with mountings. Rowels, cut in a variety of patterns, were attached to the spur shank with metal pins. The final step was engraving the item with a variety of decorative designs.[27]

The preferred metal for the bits and spurs came from salvaged automobile axles. Enid recalled, "I canvassed many junk yards to buy Model T Ford axles with which to make the bits and spurs—there was no better steel than that at the time, and I had a sense of great pride to find them for our use." The axles could be bought for ten to twenty cents, and each would produce several bits and spurs.[28]

From the beginning of production in Nocona, the bits and spurs were stamped MCCHESNEY, with the mark usually applied to the band of the spur. This was a decided change from earlier production, as McChesney generally did not mark his work. He felt his art needed no signature, that his bits and spurs were identifiable by their superb design and workmanship. That concept had worked for him for many years, but when production began in Nocona, the decision was made to stamp the products with a manufacturer's mark. In addition to identifying the maker, the mark may have been applied for the practical reason of distinguishing McChesney-Nocona bits and spurs from earlier Pauls Valley production.[29]

In 1937, Nocona's bit and spur department began nickel-plating its products. The process, which required several years to perfect, seems to have been exclusive to McChesney-Nocona bits and spurs. The company advertised, "New nickel-plating equipment has been installed—so that all McChesney Bits and Spurs are now rust proof." The innovative process appears to have been popular, as some customers brought in their old spurs to be plated.[30]

Nocona Boot's acquisition of McChesney Bits and Spurs proved to be a successful addition to the business, and the well-known brand lived on, thanks to Enid's commitment to save the company. She proudly announced, "For nearly half a century the name of McChesney has been the hallmark of Bits and Spurs—the sign of precision, balance and high quality. Never have McChesney Bits and Spurs been surpassed in workmanship, metal, strength, and dependability. The standards established by Mr. McChesney have been maintained by Nocona Boot Company." Enid's company continued to produce McChesney bits and spurs until the late 1940s.[31]

The prosperity of the 1920s had been a major factor in Nocona Boot Company's early growth and had given the company an opportunity to establish a firm foundation. When the stock market crashed in October 1929, plunging the country into depression, Nocona Boot Company was financially sound and able to withstand the economic catastrophe that gripped the country. The company continued successful production through the depression years because, as Enid noted, "cowboys and oil field workers had to have boots." While the nation as a whole was experiencing a devastating number of business failures—over 26,000 in 1930 alone—the Nocona Boot Company survived and even experienced modest growth. That year the factory had some sixty-five employees producing on average seventy-five pairs of boots a day. The company never laid off a single employee, no small achievement at a time when the national unemployment rate soared to almost twenty-five percent. Sales in 1930 totaled $61,000, and by 1932 that number had grown to just over $66,000. "We were very fortunate that we didn't feel it," Enid noted, "and I was very grateful and I would remark every day how fortunate we were since so many people much smarter and much larger than we were having a hard time." The biggest problem the company faced during those difficult times was a shortage of leather. Enid attributed her profitability during the depression years to her conservative business practices: "We weren't hit too hard because we weren't trying to be too big too fast."[32]

Despite Enid's worry that her company would become "too big too fast," Nocona Boot Company's growth during the depression years was significant enough to require plant expansion. In 1934, Enid added a brick-and-steel addition that doubled the size of her original factory. In less than ten years, Nocona Boot Company had achieved a level of success that necessitated expanding its facilities despite the nationwide depression. *The Nocona News* reported that the company's increasing sales volume required more floor space and additional equipment, adding that several new machines were being purchased. The 4,500-square-feet addition, at a cost of $5,700, addressed those growing pains. The *News* congratulated the firm on continued success and opined, "The people of Nocona are proud of the Nocona Boot Company." Having lost their original boot company to Fort Worth, it is not surprising that Noconans rooted for Enid's success.[33]

Enid's knack for advertising and promotion became evident during those early years. In summer 1932, *The Nocona News* reported that a "pair of beautiful hand-made ladies riding boots" was presented by Nocona Boot Company to the young lady judged most beautiful at the Texas Cowboy Reunion, an annual event that had been drawing crowds to

Stamford, Texas, since its founding two years earlier. Second prize was a pair of "famous McChesney silver-mounted spurs." That first prize, awarded in 1932, is especially remarkable because rival Justin Boot Company's first lady's boot, called the "Western Gypsy," did not roll off the production line until early 1935. The lady bootmaker had beaten her brothers to the market with ladies' boots.[34]

By the mid-1930s, company sales were nationwide. "Nocona Boots were getting really popular everywhere," Enid noted. "I mean all over the United States." And as the company's reputation grew, so did opportunities for publicity. A representative from Paramount Pictures came to Nocona to ask Enid if she would like to be in the movies. The movie in question was a series of short subject films titled "Unusual Occupations" that premiered in 1937. Produced by Jerry Fairbanks, who went on to become a noted Hollywood producer-director, the series showcased people who had unique and unusual careers. The films were narrated by Ken Carpenter, a longtime broadcast announcer, and produced in the new medium of Magnacolor. The episodes spotlighted people who chose "the path less taken," like Conchita Cintrón, the world's first female bullfighter; a young illustrator whose fanciful creations led to a career as Dr. Seuss; and Enid Justin, a young woman who became a successful bootmaker. In recalling her experience as a movie star, Enid echoed the words of many first-time performers—"It was hot under those lights"—but she noted that the film "did a lot" to promote Nocona Boots.[35]

Another event spurred the company's growth in a more indirect way. The Texas Centennial Celebration of 1936 promoted all things western—cowboys, ten-gallon hats, six shooters, and, of course, high-heeled boots. Celebrities visiting the centennial exposition in Dallas were photographed wearing cowboy garb, and the fad for western wear took off. Enid's company naturally benefitted from this statewide rebranding of Texas's public image as western rather than southern. According to Enid, "The Centennial in Dallas in '36 . . . advocated going western, and that gave a pretty good boost to the boot industry right there."[36]

Another 1930s phenomenon, the growing popularity of the dude ranch, contributed to the clamor for western wear. The origins of dude ranching stretched back to the late nineteenth century, but in the 1920s as railroads expanded across the west, dude ranches became popular destinations. That trend continued into the 1930s as ranchers who experienced hard times during the Great Depression took on paying guests, often from the East Coast or Midwest, to supplement their incomes. The dude ranch offered "city slickers" the opportunity to experience life on a ranch, and the "dudes" had to be dressed for the adventure. That outfit was not complete without a good pair of boots. Much like the Texas Centennial, dude ranching helped to broaden the base of western wear customers.[37]

By 1937, Nocona Boot was producing thirty different styles of footwear that included plain and fancy cowboy boots, lace boots, and cowboy shoes. The cowboy shoe, created by Enid's father, was a boot without the high top that was popular for summer wear. The company's success was a source of pride for the people of Nocona, and in the summer of 1937 *The Nocona News* called the boot factory "one of the city's greatest assets," reporting that the "local firm has carried the name of Nocona to the remotest corners of the Southwest and Far West." But success did not come without problems.[38]

In another of Enid's creative promotions, Nocona Boots were marketed as "The Better Boot," possibly suggesting the product was superior in quality to its Fort Worth competitor. That claim, along with Enid's liberal use of the Justin name, did not go unnoticed by her brothers. In later years, when Enid was asked about the rivalry between the two companies, she explained, "I was in competition with my brothers, my own flesh and blood, but it wasn't my idea for them to move out of Nocona and go to Fort Worth. I didn't feel bad about it at all.... I never have felt bad about it to this day." Over the years, the rivalry would continue to cause problems that consumed the time and resources of both companies.[39]

In April 1938, an article in the *Wichita Daily Times* triggered a clash between the two companies and demonstrated how their rivalry could lead to overreaction on both sides. The headline "West Texans Eye Big Display of Cowboy Boots" was followed by a photo of an elaborate boot display in the window of a Wichita Falls department store. The display was clearly labeled "Nocona Boots," but in the article, the reporter, who obviously did not know the history of the two companies, wrote, "One of the most attractive window displays during the West Texas Chamber of Commerce convention will be the exhibition of Justin Boots in the window of the Hub Clothier." Compounding his error, the reporter added, "Miss Enid Justin, president of the Nocona Boot Company, manufacturers of the famous boots, supervised the arrangement of the display." The confused reporter started a dispute that created a letter-writing barrage involving the newspaper, its attorneys, and both boot companies.[40]

In just two sentences, the reporter managed to offend the owners of both Nocona Boot Company and H. J. Justin & Sons. Enid was angered because Justin was given credit for her boots, and the Justin brothers were angered because Enid was given credit for manufacturing Justin Boots. Enid's brother Earl wrote the *Times* about the mix-up, and the newspaper's attorney replied, "The published statement was based upon facts given the *Times*' reporter by Miss Enid Justin, who came to the Times' office. . . . We regret that the article has given offense to you, as the statements were made in good faith upon information that the *Times* regarded as entirely reliable." Earl then wrote Enid, citing the newspaper's response, and she replied, "This matter was just as embarrassing and provoking to me as it might have been to you." She protested that she was not the source of that false information and added, "It made me pretty darn mad."[41]

Contentious letters continued among all parties as they discussed how to right this wrong. The *Times* offered to print a correction, but Earl considered that inadequate because the article had been read by citizens from all over West Texas who were attending the Chamber of Commerce Convention. Earl proposed that "the *Wichita Times* publish a correction in at least two issues of their paper and cause this statement to be published in at least four West Texas papers—at Lubbock, Amarillo, Abilene and San Angelo."[42]

An attorney for the *Times* replied that the newspaper was willing to print a correction in two issues, but they had no "power" to print the correction in the other four area newspapers—that could only be done by paid advertisement. In an attempt to put this whole issue in perspective, the attorney added, "The readers of those papers, in my judgment, would not know what it was talking about." In a further attempt at conciliation, he offered to give Justin the same publicity by printing a photo of a Justin boot display. He concluded, "Now, I don't see what more we can do. I don't believe that there has been any harm done to you or your company, and there was no intention upon the part of the *Times* to injure you or anyone else." Some three weeks after the offending article, Earl was still not satisfied with the *Times'* corrective proposals. He instructed the newspaper's attorney "to leave the matter in abeyance" because printing the correction "would release you of any responsibility."[43]

By this time, the matter had gone beyond a newspaper correction, as Earl gave Enid a list of suggested actions to help "separate the two concerns" so this mix-up would not happen again. He proposed that Nocona Boot letterheads, invoices, and catalogs display the phrases "Established in 1925" and "We are no part of any other boot manufacturing concern." In return, his correspondence would say "Established in 1879" and "We have no branch factory." Earl closed his letter by saying, "It appears to me that the above is fair, however, if you have any other plan that you think will correct the situation, we will be glad to have it."[44]

Enid, of course, would have no part of Earl's plan and sent him a forceful reply. Expressing a sensible view of the incident, she wrote, "It is okay with us for the Wichita paper to make their correction as that is all that can be done when a mistake is made." With regard to Earl's suggestions for changes to Nocona Boot's letterhead, Enid responded, "We have our cuts for our letter-heads, etc., and do not intend to go to any further expense in making any changes." In a somewhat threatening tone she added, "As far as companies being organized in 1925, and in 1879, I also wish to advise you that it is quite evident that you are misrepresenting things when you say H. J. Justin & SONS being organized in 1879 – that is not true, since Johnnie is only 50 years old. These things can be dug into if I find it necessary. I have thought of that for a number of years, but didn't worry about it, but – misrepresentation is misrepresentation after all." Enid concluded by saying, "May I suggest that you just jerk your white collar off and go back into the factory and see that boots are made good like I know you know how to make them . . . AND, QUIT MAKING A MOUNTAIN OUT OF A MOLE HILL." The incident revealed raw feelings on both sides, and it would not be the last conflict among Justin siblings.[45]

A more serious problem, Enid's first encounter with labor unrest, arose in spring 1937. Enid cared about her employees and treated them well, but she expected loyalty in return. When the incident occurred, the company employees were working six days a week with time-and-a-half pay for Saturdays. A number of employees wanted shorter hours with more pay, and they signed a petition asking for a forty-hour workweek at the same pay they received for forty-eight hours. Obviously concerned that their demands would not be well received by the boss, and not wanting any one person to appear to be the instigator, the employees signed their names in a circle. They mailed the "circle letter" to Enid rather than present it in person.[46]

They were right in suspecting that Enid would not be pleased with their proposal—she saw it as a "demand" that she considered "unfair." She added, "To say I was not happy with the note would be understated. I was mad ... and I was hurt. I always tried to treat my employees fair and square." She described her reaction, "I didn't know but one way to handle the matter and that was to get them together and tell them how I felt. So I called them all to my office and said, 'If you're not happy here, I guess we'll just have to do something else.' They got the idea pretty fast. . . . That put a stop to the demands of the circle note."[47]

Enid failed to mention that the "something else" she did was firing the twenty-five employees who signed the letter. She told the story of the "circle letter" in her autobiography written forty-eight years after the event. In recounting the story, she did not mention the firing. Whether that omission was intentional or a result of the passage of time is impossible to know, but a newspaper clipping in her scrapbook, with the byline Nocona, Texas, May 7, 1937, reported the story in detail under the headline "Boot Factory Is Picketed By 25 'Fired' Men." According to the article, the employees were discharged for asking for shorter hours at increased wages. They decided to picket the factory and "launch a fight that is intended to go to the national labor board created under the Wagner Act."[48]

The now jobless men sent telegrams to President Franklin D. Roosevelt, who happened to be fishing at Port Aransas, Texas, and to John L. Lewis, president of the Congress of Industrial Organizations, claiming they had been "denied the right of collective bargaining" and were "unfairly and unjustly discharged." They signed the telegrams, "Twenty-five jobless bootmakers." The men had chosen an inopportune time to make their demands. The economy was still in the throes of the Depression and jobs were scarce. According to the article, "Immediately there were 150 applications for the open places, and Miss Enid Justin, president of the manufacturing concern, announced that new men would be employed and trained in the work in place of the 25 discharged." She said their pay ranged from eighteen to fifty dollars a week. In defense of her action, Enid added that she "could not let the employees run the plant."[49]

The disgruntled bootmakers were not the only ones to contact government officials. Enid wrote the Wage and Hour Division of the US Department of Labor requesting support for her action, and she also relayed the problem to her congressman, Ed Gossett, who held the 13th District seat. He replied, "I hope the Wage and Hour Administration gave you a satisfactory reply to your request. . . . A bill will come before Congress shortly suggesting numerous amendments to the Fair Labor Standards Act. We will try and take care of you at that time." Enid must have assumed she would face no recriminations from the federal government for the terminations, and her decision stood. The problem was solved, even though twenty-five workers had not received the hearing they probably deserved. But Enid had established her authority, and the company would be free of labor problems for the next twenty years.[50]

In 1939, Enid planned an ambitious promotion—an event that would garner nationwide attention. She sponsored a "Pony Express Race" from Nocona to the Golden Gate Exposition in San Francisco, a distance of almost two thousand miles. The idea for the race came from Nocona Chamber of Commerce manager L. A. Parton, who had organized a race from Lampasas, Texas, to the Centennial Celebration in Dallas in 1936. That race, deemed a "huge success," gave Parton the idea of recreating the race on a much grander scale to publicize Nocona and its developing leather industry. Enid liked the idea: what better publicity than cowboys racing their horses across the Southwest to advertise Nocona Boots? It was a perfect fit for her company image, and after consulting an attorney about possible liability, she agreed to sponsor the race. She would be aided by a group of local businessmen who would help with organizing the grand event.[51]

Rules for the race were relatively simple. A contestant must have two horses and a driver with a truck and trailer to transport the horse that was being rested. The horses would be ridden in twenty-five-mile relays, and judges would be stationed at twenty-five-mile intervals along the route to

CHAPTER 3

Enid cutting the ribbon to begin the Pony Express Race from Nocona to San Francisco, March 1, 1939. She is standing on Clay Street in front of her factory (not shown). (Courtesy of the Enid Justin - Nocona Boot Company Collection, University of North Texas Special Collections.)

verify contestants' progress. Each rider had to finish the race with the same horses that started the race. The winner would receive a cash prize of $750 while second place would receive $250, and Enid promised each contestant who finished the race "the best pair of cowboy boots money can buy."[52]

Each rider was required to carry a maximum five pounds of mail in a replica Pony Express pouch. That mail was picked up and dropped off at various stops along the way, often at stores that sold Nocona Boots—good advertising for Enid's dealers and her boots. Special souvenir stamps issued for the race pictured a cowboy on a horse along with the caption, "Nocona, Texas, the leather goods manufacturing center of the Southwest via Pony Express to Golden Gate Exposition, San Francisco, California." The regulation three-cent stamps sold for fifty cents, and organizers speculated that when "nine million stamp collectors in the U.S. learn of the novel race, the demand for the stamps is expected to be enormous." To

Amon Carter, with Enid alongside, addresses the crowd before the start of the race while spectators watch from the roofs of downtown buildings. (Courtesy of the Enid Justin - Nocona Boot Company Collection, University of North Texas Special Collections.)

help defray the personal costs of the race, each rider would receive 25 percent of the souvenir stamp money for the mail he carried. Contestants were required to pay a twenty-five-dollar entry fee and sign a contract agreeing to abide by race rules.[53]

Forty-two individuals from twenty-six states filed applications to ride in what was possibly the world's longest horse race, but when race day arrived only seventeen riders lined up at the starting line. Fifteen cowboys from Texas, one from Oklahoma, and one Nocona cowgirl hoped to be the first to enter the gates of the San Francisco Exposition. On the morning of March 1, an enthusiastic crowd gathered in downtown Nocona for the start of the race. Enid introduced dignitary Amon Carter, owner of the *Fort Worth Star-Telegram* and a native of Montague County, who made a short speech on the history of the Pony Express. As the jittery horses and their anxious riders waited, Enid cut the starting-line ribbon, and Carter fired an ivory-handled forty-five caliber pistol to start the race. An estimated five thousand people watched the send-off, some from building rooftops, as the contestants thundered down Clay Street.[54]

On the first day out, as riders reached Wichita Falls, town officials welcomed them and presented fifteen dollars to the first to enter the city limits. That prize went to Shorty Hudson from Knox City, who had the early lead. The riders made camp near Olney for a few hours' sleep before climbing into the saddle for the second day. That day ended the competition for Nocona's cowgirl, sixteen-year-old Vennie Greenwood, who was disqualified by judges for riding in her stock truck for a portion of the race.[55]

As the riders continued west, they were greeted with a variety of celebrations in towns along the way. Those festivities must have been a welcome distraction for the saddle-weary cowboys who encountered countless difficulties along the route. Weather was often a challenge as heat, cold, rain, and dust storms added misery to the already tough ride. A sick horse forced Jack Clifton from McClain to leave the race; Crowell's Bob Moyer lost a day near Odessa when his stock truck broke down; and illness caused Taylor Tuck to fall unconscious from his horse and be sent home to St. Jo. And on March 6, Enid threatened to remove one of the riders from the race. She sent a telegram to race judges in Van Horn, Texas, instructing them to "disqualify" L. E. Speers from Crowell, Texas, if he didn't remove the Olsen-Stelzer Boot Company sign from his trailer.[56]

T. J. Sykes from Duval, Oklahoma, who was riding two big plow horses, held the lead for several days, but as the riders approached El Paso, Shannon Davidson from Matador, Texas, took the lead with Nocona's own Chris Uselton in second place. Near Deming, New Mexico, Sykes was forced to drop out when one of his horses became ill. That left Davidson and Uselton battling for the lead with the remaining riders some sixty miles behind. On day sixteen, Davidson, still holding the lead, reached Phoenix, the halfway mark of the race. By maintaining a grueling schedule and barely stopping to eat (his breakfast was pineapple juice and raw eggs) Davidson was the first to reach Santa Barbara, California. Uselton was still a close second, but his plans to overtake the leader on the last leg of the race were dashed when he and his horse were hit by a car. Uselton

THE LADY MAKES BOOTS

And they're off! Pony Express Riders gallop down Clay Street as the race begins. (Courtesy of the Enid Justin - Nocona Boot Company Collection, University of North Texas Special Collections.)

was not seriously injured, but his horse suffered a broken leg. The hometown boy was out of the race.[57]

When Shannon Davidson crossed the finish line, his nearest competitor was nearly one hundred miles behind. The twenty-two-year-old cowboy from Matador, riding ponies Ranger and Rocket, had finished the race in twenty-four days. "What a thrill that was," Enid remembered, "seeing that young cowboy ride in through those gates. A large crowd was there to welcome the winner and all sorts of newspaper people were there shooting pictures." Enid presented Davidson with the weighty prize of 750 newly minted silver dollars. Davidson remarked that he "had figured on coming to California some time, but never thought I would ride a horse here." In addition to his prize money, Davidson came away with a movie contract and landed a few bit parts in Hollywood westerns before returning home to Matador.[58]

Enid's Pony Express Race was not without controversy. As the race's remaining five riders straggled into the Exposition grounds over the

CHAPTER 3

Pony Express Race winner Shannon Davidson. (Courtesy of the Enid Justin - Nocona Boot Company Collection, University of North Texas Special Collections.)

next four days, no one greeted them. The cowboys were exhausted, disappointed, and, according to one newspaper article with the caption "To the Losers Go Nothing," were "stranded financially." Enid, who had returned home, blamed Oakland officials for failing to welcome the lagging contestants. It seems the planning in that respect had fallen short.[59]

Another difficulty arose when the Society for the Prevention of Cruelty to Animals accused Davidson of mistreating his horses. The state humane officer inspected the horses, found them in good health, and cleared the cowboy of any wrongdoing. Enid faced a similar complaint when confronted by a woman from the local Humane Society who accused the contestants of abusing their horses. Enid replied indignantly, "Lady, you don't know what you are talking about. They think more of their horses than they do of their wives." The animal cruelty accusations melted away.[60]

The race was both a resounding success and an unforgettable experience for Enid. She loved to tell the story of presenting the prize money to Davidson and giving him a kiss on the cheek. That kiss embarrassed the young cowboy and made him turn beet red. Much to his consternation, he had to endure the kiss a second time after some photographers complained of missing the shot. The entire event had been great fun, but it was time to get back to work. At a luncheon given in her honor, Enid was approached by an official from the New York World's Fair who asked if she would consider staging a similar race to that exposition. She declined, saying, "No, this is enough of it." The race had accomplished its goal of bringing nationwide publicity to Nocona and Nocona Boots. Enid filled a scrapbook with newspaper clippings from all over the nation that were sent to her by fans who had enjoyed following the race. Years later Enid reminisced, "I guess the Pony Express Race was about the craziest thing I ever got involved in, but believe me, if I had the chance I believe I'd do it all over again."[61]

As the decade came to an end, Nocona Boot Company was prospering—sales volume had continued to increase each year, and thanks to Enid's knack for promotion, her brand was known nationwide. When a reporter asked her if in those early years she had any idea what her company would amount to, she replied, "No, I just worked. I knew we were making money every year. I didn't let it dwell on my mind. I just kept on working."[62]

The coming years would present new challenges for the hard-working entrepreneur as she dealt with wartime regulations, personal disappointment, and construction of a modern factory along with the everyday demands of running a boot company.

CHAPTER 4

LIFE IS NOT ALWAYS KIND. BUT IF YOU JUST KEEP
PLUGGING, YOU'LL FIND IT SURE IS INTERESTING.

—ENID JUSTIN[1]

One Sunday morning in fall 1939, Enid met Harry Whitman as the two walked along Nocona's main street. A few days later, Whitman came to her office and asked if she employed J. R. Welch. According to Enid's new acquaintance, Welch owed money on an automobile, and he was there to collect the debt. Whitman had been hired by a legal firm in Wichita Falls to liquidate a small Nocona auto agency. Enid did not know "the Welch fellow," so the possibility exists that Whitman invented Welch for an excuse to see Enid again. In recalling that encounter, Enid remarked, "Harry seemed like a nice fellow, so when he later asked me out, I went with him."[2]

Enid enjoyed Whitman's company. He was friendly and outgoing, had a good sense of humor, and was a good dancer. She described him as "nice looking, not as handsome as Julius by far, but he was nice looking." Enid remembered one particular evening in Wichita Falls when the couple attended a Christmas dance at the Country Club where Enid was a member. She confessed, "Harry was a wonderful dancer but sometimes I would start leading instead of following and Harry would ask, 'Who's leading this, you or me?'" That same evening Enid received her first warning about Whitman. "One of the oilmen I danced with that night tried to warn me not to marry Harry." Her brother John also cautioned, "Enid, I like Harry just fine, but you be damned careful. You know, you've accumulated something." For a businesswoman who could be described as "tough as a boot," Enid was surprisingly naive and vulnerable when it came to her personal life.[3]

Enid and Whitman were married in John's home in Fort Worth on November 9, 1940. When it became evident that her new husband was no longer gainfully employed, Enid offered him a job at the boot factory. She recalled, "Harry didn't do much at the factory. . . . He just walked around and talked and made friends with the employees," adding that it appeared she had hired a "morale supervisor." Whitman did not contribute monetarily to the marriage, and although he asked her to put a portion of her income in his name, Enid refused and cautiously kept control of her bank account. Despite their financial issues, Enid believed they had "a happy home." She described her husband as "very nice, very courteous," and well-liked by her friends. She did admit, "My strong will might have made Harry feel a little inferior. He sort of played second fiddle to me, I guess. Harry left me on his birthday, October 17."[4]

The marriage had lasted five years when Whitman came to Enid's dressing room and announced, "I'm leaving. I came here broke but I'm not leaving that way." He told Enid to get her "chips out on the table" and call her lawyer. Enid was stunned "I didn't say a word. It had all come so sudden and without cause or warning." Harry apparently believed he would leave the marriage a wealthy man. "He was wanting half of everything I had and didn't deserve it," Enid explained. "He didn't help me make any of it." In the divorce settlement, the judge awarded Harry $1,500. Enid did not marry again.[5]

Harry Whitman, with his five years of boot-making "expertise," moved to Wichita Falls, where he partnered with three local businessmen in a boot manufacturing company called Whitbern Boots. Enid's first husband had started a boot company in Henrietta, and now her second husband was doing the same in Wichita Falls. Enid's brother John, president of Justin Boots and a colorful character in his own right, told her, "I wish to hell you'd quit getting married! You're just creating competition!"[6]

Enid later told the story of going on a shopping trip with her sister to Wichita Falls where they saw Whitbern Boots in a store window. They

CHAPTER 4

went in, and Enid told the salesman she wanted to try on some boots. He brought out a pair of Whitbern Boots and told her, "These boots are made in Wichita Falls by part of the Justin family." The Justin name was obviously a valuable asset for anyone attempting to manufacture boots. When the two women exited the store they had a good laugh. Enid did not buy the boots.[7]

When the Whitbern Boot Company failed a few years later, Enid had the opportunity to buy their equipment in a liquidation sale. An inspection of the Whitbern factory revealed that Whitman was using much the same equipment and supplies used by Nocona Boot Company. Enid concluded that "he'd planned his boot company for a long time and got all the information he could. Maybe that's what he was walking around and talking about in my factory." Whitman's company was even using the same lasts from St. Louis Last Company and had a sizable stockpile on hand. Enid was coping with a shortage of lasts at the time so purchasing the Whitbern supplies and equipment "for a song" was a boon for the Nocona company and possibly a small measure of revenge for Enid.[8]

Despite her personal disappointment, Enid's business continued to flourish. In the early 1940s, the economy of Montague County, along with neighboring Clay and Wise Counties, was booming as oil production steadily increased. Wildcatters continued to make new "strikes," and numerous oil companies competed for a part of the "play." A correspondent for the *Fort Worth Star-Telegram* reported, "Prices for leases in Montague County probably have been the highest of any paid in the present Fort Worth basin play." The reason was the discovery of the Rogers pool one mile west of Nocona and the subsequent sizable production from two deep wells in that formation. Oil was changing lives around Nocona, and *The Nocona News* headlined, "Montague County Citizens Use Oil Money To Pay Off Mortgages." The newspaper offered the example of C. C. Haynes, a local farmer, who celebrated his seventy-sixth birthday by paying off the mortgage on his farm with his lease money.[9]

The thriving oil economy benefited local businesses as well as individuals, and Nocona Boot Company was no exception. Even though boot sales were now nationwide, the local economy still figured prominently in the company's bottom line. As business grew, the factory struggled to keep up with demand. The installation of new machinery in 1940 boosted production from 80 to 100 pairs a day. The new machines, including state-of-the-art automated sole stitchers, sped up production by mechanizing work that had formerly been done by hand. The new machinery increased production, but it also added to already crowded conditions.[10]

Factory space had become inadequate once again, and in summer 1941, construction began on yet another addition to the building. *The Nocona News* reported that the addition was necessary because of "the ever increasing volume of the company's business." The *News* added that the expansion would "for a time at least, make ample room for the installation of more machinery and relieve a somewhat crowded condition in other parts of the plant, thus increasing efficiency and expediting the filling of orders."[11]

The new brick structure was the fourth addition to the building where Nocona Boot started in 1925. The first expansion doubled the building's size by adding 25 x 40 feet to the back of the existing structure. An upstairs stitching room was the second addition. Then, in 1934, a 50 x 90-foot addition that faced south on Front Street was added to the original building, creating an L shape. The 1941 addition, another 50 x 90-foot structure, was added on the west side on the previous addition, turning the L shape into a rectangle. With the completion of that addition, the factory had consumed all the available land at its downtown site.[12]

Nocona Boot Company had come through the Great Depression and was experiencing record growth only to be challenged by another national crisis. As the United States entered World War II in December 1941, war readiness required maximizing defense production, and the footwear industry was a part of that crucial effort. Enid's company was subject to regulations imposed by the War Production Board (WPB), a federal agency created by President Franklin Roosevelt's executive order in January 1942. The agency's main purpose was overseeing the conversion of civilian industry to war production. The WPB allocated scarce resources, rationed certain commodities, established priorities in the distribution of goods and services, and prohibited nonessential production. Like most patriotic citizens, Enid willingly complied with WPB regulations, with one exception.[13]

The new regulations required civilian shoe manufacturers to send in their sole leather so that it could be used for military footwear, but because boot soles are cut narrower than regular shoes, Nocona Boot was allowed to keep soles that were already cut. Enid noted that her company was fortunate to have a large quantity of soles cut when that order was issued. Other WPB requirements, directed toward conserving resources, dictated how civilian footwear could be fashioned. Boots could be produced in only two colors, brown or black. In Enid's opinion, "they were trying to take the eye appeal away from everything so people would buy bonds instead of purchasing other things." In an effort to offer customers more choices, Nocona Boot offered two shades of brown—"turf tan," a lighter brown, and "town brown," not as deep as chocolate—in addition to the basic black.[14]

Regulations allowed only one row of stitching around the boot top to anchor the soft lining to the outer leather. Fancy stitching and inlays were prohibited, but when government authorities tried to eliminate the stitching across the toe of the boot, Enid felt compelled to protest. She called that regulation "ridiculous," as the toe stitching was "one of the fundamental features of the cowboy boot." The stitching on the toe of a boot, called the "wrinkle stitch," strengthened the toe and kept it from stretching out of shape. Enid explained, "A cowboy stands in the stirrups as much as he sits when he is riding hard and that puts a lot of pressure on his boots." The toe stitching is essential to the durability of the boot. Enid added, "Those people who made the rules had never been on a horse or even met a cowboy, but they thought they were real experts." She requested a hearing with the leather division of the War Production Board in Washington, DC, to plead her case for the importance of toe stitching. Her brothers at Justin Boot had made a similar request and been turned down.[15]

But Enid persisted: "The man in charge told me how busy he was and I told him I was busy too, trying to stay busy and make money so I could pay taxes. . . . [I] demanded a hearing." The official finally agreed to meet with her at the regional office in St. Louis, Missouri. She invited several other bootmakers, including the owners of Blucher Boots in Olathe, Kansas, Dehner Boot Company in Omaha, Nebraska, and her brothers from Justin in Fort Worth, to join her in the meeting. Enid and her fellow bootmakers were able to convince the WPB representative that toe stitching was functional rather than decorative, and the restriction was removed.[16]

THE LADY MAKES BOOTS

In addition to complying with wartime regulations, boot company production was hampered by shortages of raw materials. Most critical was the shortage of leather. Enid recalled, "The war kept us looking for leather but we couldn't get enough no matter how hard we tried. We just couldn't buy enough leather to keep the workers busy." She knew her employees wanted and needed to work, and it was not their fault when production stopped because they had run out of leather. Enid refused to lay off her employees and instead purchased a baby grand piano that she placed on the factory's main floor. She paid her workers their full salaries and encouraged them to play the piano and sing when there was no work to be done.[17]

Leather was not the only commodity in short supply. The company suffered shortages of hardwood lasts—plastic lasts were available but, according to Enid, they were a poor substitute for hardwood. Another scarce material was cork, which was used as a cushion between the inner and outer soles. Sheepskin, used for lining boots, was also in short supply, but Enid found a small tannery in Massachusetts that was able to meet her needs. She told the owner, "If he had some overflow he could spare, my brothers in Fort Worth could sure use it. I always helped my brothers when I could." Despite the contentious competition that existed between Enid and her brothers, it appears that familial ties somehow remained strong.[18]

In recalling the war years, Enid noted, "There were a lot of things we were short . . . but we had to take it like everyone else did and do the best we could." Nocona Boot's workforce also changed because of the war. "During 1942," Enid noted, "we lost quite a few employees to the Armed Forces and to the Defense Plants. Some of these employees held jobs that required quite a bit of skill, and as a result, some of our older bootmakers were forced to take on additional work." The experienced workers also helped train new employees, many of them women. The war permanently changed the face of the boot company's workforce, as women continued to hold those factory jobs in the postwar years.[19]

Another wartime agency, the National War Labor Board, presented Enid with a dilemma that lasted for the war's duration. From Nocona Boot Company's inception, Enid had purposely kept her salary low, putting profit back into the business to ensure that the company was financially sound. Enid's salary had been $5,200 a year since the mid-thirties, and in 1943 her board of directors voted to increase her salary to $12,000. The increase was justified by the fact that Enid had worked for many years on less than a fair salary, and "the earnings of the concern have been out of proportion to the salary paid to its president." Enid deserved the raise, but there was a problem with the timing. Salary increases had to be approved by the War Labor Board.[20]

The National War Labor Board was created in January 1942 by another of Roosevelt's executive orders. The purpose of the agency was to forestall labor-management conflicts that might hamper wartime production. In October, the president expanded the board's control to include the stabilization of wages. Control of wage and salary increases was aimed at slowing wartime inflation and the resultant rising cost of living. Any adjustments in wages had to be approved by the WLB that operated under the umbrella of the Internal Revenue Service. On October 6, 1943, Enid submitted the required application to the regional Salary Stabilization Unit in Dallas requesting approval of the salary increase. In late November, she was notified that the board granted an increase of 10 percent, raising her yearly salary by only $520.[21]

When Enid's attorney filed a protest with the Stabilization Board, he was advised that to advance his client's case, Nocona Boot Company must justify the higher salary by providing a list of executive salaries of "like concerns." Enid's attorney complained, "It is extremely difficult to get salary data from competing firms." Some of Enid's inquiries were not answered, but she succeeded in collecting the needed information from three comparable companies, one of those being H. J. Justin & Sons. When she wrote to her brother Earl apologetically asking the amount of his salary, she made no attempt to hide her frustration with the government process:

> I hesitate to ask you for this information, Earl, but it seems this is going to be the only way I will have any chance at all for an adjustment on my own salary here, and my directors are so anxious for me to have it, feeling that through my 19 years of service I have given that I just deserve it, and really I punished myself for several years by not having a larger salary, of course, that is neither here nor there, and it's my own fault, and now (darn the luck) you have to ask some dictator when we know

the business justifies my increase ... but such is life with the New Deal Administration, and that too is neither here nor there.²²

Once again demonstrating the odd dichotomy of business versus family that existed between Enid and her brothers, she closed the letter by saying, "Wish you could have been here the night of the Fourth. We had the best crowd we have ever had for our Sing-Song at the house. Moved the piano out on the south porch, and really had a good one."²³

When the salary information had been gathered, Enid's attorney filed a Petition for Review with the WLB. He began his argument by stating, "The making of cowboy boots is a highly specialized business. There are not many large concerns in the United States who specialize in the making of cowboy boots." He went on to list three competitors—Kirkendall Boot Company in Omaha, Nebraska, C. H. Hyer & Sons in Olathe, Kansas, and H. J. Justin & Sons—and he attached letters testifying that each of their executives' salaries either were comparable to or exceeded the $12,000 Enid was requesting. With regard to her brothers' company, the Petition stated, "The principal officers of H. J. Justin & Sons are four.... Each of them make $8,500 per year, thus that concern pays its executives $34,000 per year for the same work that is done by Miss Justin alone."²⁴

In August 1944, Enid's salary increase had still not been resolved, and she appealed to her congressman, Ed Gossett, for help. His reply surely raised her frustration to a new level. Gossett wrote, "I have just talked on the telephone with the Deputy Commissioner of Internal Revenue in charge of Salary Stabilization, about your salary raise. He tells me the old decision is so out of date they would prefer that you file another application with their Dallas office, and then immediately appeal the case to Washington if the decision on the new application is not favorable." Such is the nature of bureaucracy. Determined as ever, Enid submitted a new application complete with another lengthy written argument supporting her case, but the paper trail ends there. Perhaps Enid received her raise in late 1944, but the possibility exists that the raise had to wait until war's end. The NWLB was discontinued by the Truman administration in December 1945.²⁵

During the war, Nocona Boot employed between sixty and sixty-five people. Factory wages were based on a number of variables including experience, performance, and the skill level required for a specific job. Inexperienced workers started at forty cents an hour with the possibility of a five-cent raise after sixty days and another five cents after six months. Once a worker reached fifty cents an hour, additional increases were based on job performance. Some were paid on a piecework basis after they attained the necessary skills. "When they feel like they can benefit themselves on piece work we let them have it, and they do real well," Enid explained. "The person that does his work and does it well and does more of it, definitely deserves more than the person who just kills time, who doesn't care." She added, "Each person keeps his own books on his piece work. Every day he knows how many pieces and what is paid for that. Of course, they have to be checked and double checked because they could make mistakes, honest mistakes." Supervisors in each department checked the quality of the work.[26]

Nocona Boot had no trouble selling all the boots it could produce during the war years. The company continued to grow despite material shortages, government regulations, and manpower challenges. Longtime employee Luciel Leonard remembered, "We worked six days a week, just the same, all through the war." In 1942, sales exceeded $403,000, and the following year they topped $441,000. In December 1942, the company voluntarily lowered boot prices on a number of its most popular styles. For example, the company's best-selling boot, #299, was lowered from $24.20 to $22.70. In discussing these price reductions, Enid remarked, "We doubt seriously if many products have been reduced in price since Pearl Harbor. If so we would not be burdened with an increase (admitted by government statistics) of 23% in the cost of living."[27]

Nocona Boot Company remained a civilian producer, but Enid made sure that her company contributed to the war effort on the home front. With her encouragement, employees agreed to 100 percent participation in the purchase of war bonds. A small amount was withheld from their checks each week, and when an individual accumulated enough for a bond, Enid would purchase the war bond and present it to them. When Nocona held a scrap metal drive, Enid closed her factory for the day so that all her employees could participate. One employee remembered, "We all went on a search out in the countryside to locate scrap metal." Enid's company also hosted bond rallies when celebrities came to town to entertain for the purpose of encouraging war bond sales. And to aid the numerous military aircraft flying over Nocona, Enid had the town's name painted on her factory's roof in letters twenty-three feet tall. An arrow pointed toward the airstrip north of town in case a pilot needed to land.[28]

Boots were not regulation military footwear, but there were soldiers, even pilots, who made Nocona boots a part of their uniform. "Many of the boys in the service had grown up in cowboy boots and couldn't adjust to military footwear," Enid said. "Many of these boys got permission from their commanding officers to wear cowboy boots and we shipped them all over the world so our fighting men could walk in comfort." Another incident that is telling about Enid's character centered on her determination to make a pair of boots for a "shell shocked" veteran. The soldier's wife asked Enid to duplicate a pair of worn-out boots that her husband was obsessing about. They were fancy boots, prohibited by wartime regulations, so Enid wrote Washington, DC, for permission to make the boots. Much to her surprise, the request was approved, and the factory duplicated the boots. In telling the story of the veteran's boots, Enid noted, "I was going to make those boots whether I got permission or not. . . . That's the way I am when I think I'm right."[29]

Keeping her business afloat for the duration of the war was just one more challenge that Enid met head-on. "It wasn't always easy," she recalled, "but I knew I had to keep Nocona Boots going. . . . I had a responsibility not only to myself, but to my employees and to my town." When the war ended and wartime restrictions were lifted, Nocona Boot Company ramped up production. Dale Terry, editor of Enid's memoir, wrote, "Following World War II, Miss Enid found her business not only in good shape but growing beyond her wildest dreams."[30]

The economy was good and getting better as the country entered what would come to be called the postwar economic boom. In Texas, manufacturing establishments expanded like never before. Technological innovation helped fuel industrial growth, and advances in transportation, including new highway systems, aided distribution of goods. Texas's oil and gas industry continued to grow as the nation demanded more energy. All boded well for the future of Nocona Boot Company, but with growth came the need for expansion yet again.[31]

CHAPTER 4

In 1947, the company was producing 180 pairs of boots per day, and Enid was turning away new business because the factory could not produce more. The plant was crowded, and much of the older machinery needed to be replaced. Enid even worried that the factory had become a fire hazard. After a meeting with the board of directors, she announced, "It is the honest opinion of each director of this corporation that we absolutely must build a larger plant in order to meet the requirements in production to adequately serve our customers." Since its founding in 1925, Enid's factory had produced an astounding 300,000 pairs of boots, and in 1947 the company's annual payroll totaled $250,000. The decision was made to build a larger factory, and the next big question became "Where?"[32]

Enid was considering two possibilities for a new location. The first was purchasing town lots across the alley to the west of her factory, and the second was buying an empty downtown building owned by the McCall family. The building would have been another short-term fix, and Enid admitted that it "wasn't big enough for the future but it would have helped out for the time being." When she consulted C. S. McCall, he had an unexpected idea. As president of the Farmers and Merchants Bank, McCall had backed Enid's original venture in 1925 with a $5,000 loan, and now he had a plan for her new factory. The property was on a small hill just east of town on the north side of US Highway 82, a two-lane highway that bisected Nocona as it ran east-west across the top of Texas from Texarkana to Lubbock, then southwest to the Texas–New Mexico border. McCall, who was the family's longtime friend as well as banker, drove Enid to the proposed site, and when she expressed reluctance, he told her, "Here's an ideal site. Quit piecing up that old building and let's build a nice building here."[33]

Enid offered two objections to McCall's suggested location. The first was, "Why, I don't believe I could buy that property for love nor money. It's in the Jordan Estate." (Ranchers D. C. Jordan and William Broadus were Nocona's founders, having donated land for the original townsite and railroad right-of-way.) Her second objection had to do with the appearance of the tract: "Mr. McCall, that is a terrible looking place . . . the railroad runs right back of it . . . and there are oil wells right across the railroad tracks." To counter Enid's argument, McCall touted the visibility of the location: "Coming up Highway 82 from the east you come up a hill and round a curve and you just come right on to this building."³⁴

McCall must have been convincing, and with his encouragement, Enid contacted Calvin Dodson, who oversaw the Jordan estate about purchasing the land. "I decided it wouldn't hurt to ask, so I called him.... I told him I'd like to buy the property and build a nice factory on it." His answer was unexpected: "Enid, I'll sell it to you but no one else. I know you'll build something the town will be proud of." Enid purchased the Jordan land, bound on the south by the highway and on the north by the MK&T track. Ironically, the plot was only a few hundred yards west of a branch of the Chisholm Trail that continued north to cross the river at Red River Station. Enid reminisced, "I've always thought how appropriate it was that the new factory was built there, near the trail that gave Daddy Joe his start." The building site was quickly dubbed "Boot Hill."³⁵

Plans were soon underway for a new, modern factory. In February 1947, Enid and employee Virginia Johnson traveled to the Midwest, where they visited a number of shoe manufacturers to get ideas for the new plant. Among their numerous stops were the International Shoe Company in Hopkinsville, Kentucky, and the Nunn-Bush Shoe Company in Milwaukee, Wisconsin, but Enid was most impressed by the Trim-Foot Company in Farmington, Missouri. She described it as one of the newest and most up-to-date plants she had seen, and she planned to incorporate some of their innovative ideas in her new factory. Their final stop was Omaha, Nebraska, where they visited two competitors: Dehner Boot Company and Kirkendall Boot Company.³⁶

With the knowledge she gained from touring other factories, Enid was ready to begin construction of her new plant. She hired Lubbock architect S. B. Haynes to design the building that she intended to be "the most modern and efficient boot factory in the U.S." *The Nocona News* reported that when the new factory was complete, production was expected to increase from the current 180 pairs to between 350 and 400 pairs a day.³⁷

Ground was broken for the new factory on July 29, 1947, with over a thousand people braving one of the hottest days of the year to attend the ceremony. Years later, Enid fondly remembered riding to the event in the back of a truck with her employees, all of them waving their shovels as they paraded through downtown Nocona. The high school band

CHAPTER 4

Architect's rendering of the new Nocona Boot Factory completed in 1948. (Courtesy of the Enid Justin - Nocona Boot Company Collection, University of North Texas Special Collections.)

provided music to entertain the sweltering crowd gathered on "Boot Hill." Enid, along with Associate Justice Earl P. Hall of the Second Court of Civil Appeals in Fort Worth and many boot company employees, turned the first shovels of dirt. Enid wanted her employees to participate in the groundbreaking because she credited them with making the new factory possible through their loyalty and hard work.[38]

Justice Hall delivered the main address followed by speeches from a number of other dignitaries. Mayor Mack Thrasher offered his gratitude that Enid was "not thinking of greener pastures." And Chamber of Commerce President Claud Wallace echoed that sentiment by saying how much Nocona appreciated Enid and the fact "that she could see the possibilities here instead of elsewhere." Twenty-two years after the fact, town folk still seemed to have hard feelings about Justin Boot's departure from Nocona.[39]

Under the direction of Dallas contractor Wallace Burford, construction began on the new factory. Enid spent hours at the site watching the building take shape. The factory was completed in less than a year at a cost of $250,000, and just as McCall envisioned, the new building that crowned the hilltop was a stunning sight to behold. *The Nocona News* described a perfect Texas setting: "The landscape from the building is enchanting, with oil wells right up to the property lines on north and east, cattle grazing on the pastures, and wooded hillsides in the background."[40]

The grand opening, held on June 9, 1948, truly lived up to its name. One newspaper declared, "It was boot day in the boot town, and what a day!" Mayor Thrasher declared it an official town holiday, and many local businesses closed for the day to take part in the celebration. An estimated seven thousand people, including a number of dignitaries and representatives from Nocona Boot suppliers all over the United States, attended the event.[41]

The entire day was filled with activities. Visitors were treated to tours of the new plant where all 105 bootmakers, each wearing a red carnation, were at their posts to answer questions about the manufacture of boots. According to Enid, many visitors "were astounded by the size" of the new plant. The offices were filled with flowers, and *The Nocona News* that week swelled with congratulatory ads from all over the country. One newspaper reported, "Miss Justin was the busiest person in the plant as she attempted to greet friends and well-wishers, read telegrams of congratulations, pose for photographers, and answer innumerable requests for information."[42]

The crowd was delighted when Bill Tandy, a friend and owner of Tandy Leather Company in Tulsa, Oklahoma, flew his biplane over the factory trailing a huge banner that read, "Congratulations Miss Enid." The formal dedication ceremony was held that evening with music provided by the Flying X Ranch Boys and the Nocona Boot Company Employee Chorus. After a number of civic leaders spoke, Enid dedicated the new factory to the memory of her father and announced that the first pair of boots produced in the new factory would be a gift to Governor Beauford Jester. Radio broadcasts carried the excitement to listeners in Wichita Falls and Fort Worth. There were souvenirs and refreshments that included boot-shaped cookies and vanilla ice cream topped with a chocolate boot. In recalling the grand opening, Enid admitted, "I've always been accused of having a pretty big ego, of being strong-willed, aggressive and a staunch

CHAPTER 4

The grand opening of the new Nocona Boot Factory, with Bill Tandy's biplane overhead pulling a banner reading "Congratulations Miss Enid." (Courtesy of the Enid Justin - Nocona Boot Company Collection, University of North Texas Special Collections.)

businesswoman. I plead guilty to all of the above. And if my ego was ever bigger than it was as that new building was going up, I don't know when it was."[43]

Enid had every right to be proud of her new state-of-the-art factory. The striking mid-century modern building was constructed of cream-colored brick with abundant windows. The one-story structure was embellished with a two-story tower that framed the entrance. The interior of the factory was equally impressive. The offices and showroom were air-conditioned, an intercom system allowed communication between offices, and a public address system provided factory-wide broadcasts of announcements, music, and even football games. This pleased many of Enid's employees who were ardent football fans. The factory proper was cooled with outside air ventilated by a "monitor roof," a raised roof structure that ran along the ridge of the main roof with louvered sides to allow air to circulate through the building. The plant was not air-conditioned because, experts believed, it would cause leather to mold. In the winter, the building was heated by steam heat, and the entire factory was lit with fluorescent lights.[44]

New automated machinery was added to many of the departments, thus speeding up production in almost every step of the boot-making process. In the cutting department, for example, a new machine automatically cut out the intricate patterns used for inlaid designs. With the building's 33,000 square feet, the new factory had the capacity to produce 500 pairs of boots a day. According to Plant Superintendent J. W. Lunn, that volume of business would require hiring an additional forty-five people, bringing the total number of employees to 150. After years in the overcrowded downtown building, Enid remarked, "the new factory made things run a lot easier."[45]

Enid was fifty-four years old when the new factory was completed—she had been running her own boot business for twenty-three years. Even with her obvious success, she "never slowed down or took anything for granted," and her daily routine did not change when she moved to the new facility. She got up at 5 a.m., dressed, and had breakfast before heading to the post office to pick up the mail. She was at the office by seven, opened all the mail, and had it sorted by the time her employees arrived at eight o'clock. From her inlaid walnut desk Enid managed every dealer order, oversaw purchases, paid invoices, and "stayed on top of the collections end of the business, too." Every day she spent time in the factory with the workers, and she knew most of them by name. "It was always a pleasure to see a person who had no skills when hired, grow into a skilled worker," Enid recalled, "and to see them raise their families, to share their happiness as well as their sad times." She was truly sincere when she said, "The factory and the employees were always my family."[46]

Enid spent a good bit of time traveling to promote Nocona Boots, attend trade shows, and meet her dealers, many of whom became friends over the years. And she frequented state fairs, stock shows, and rodeos where her boots were exhibited and sold. Enid often took employees with her on those promotional trips. Secretary Luciel Leonard fondly remembered accompanying her boss to the rodeo in Cheyenne, Wyoming, and from there to the Colorado Springs Rodeo, and on to New York City for a radio interview. "I've always done everything I can to promote the

CHAPTER 4

Enid observing her employees at work in the spacious new factory. (Courtesy of the Enid Justin - Nocona Boot Company Collection, University of North Texas Special Collections.)

boot business both for Nocona Boots and the industry in general," Enid recalled, and she was tireless in that respect.[47]

Those who had not met Enid may have had an image in their minds of the lady bootmaker—most probably they were mistaken. Enid did not wear boots or sport a cowboy hat, unless a special event required it. She referred to herself as "rather feminine," preferring high heels to boots. "I've loved boots all my life. I just never wore them much," Enid confessed. "I just always preferred traditional feminine clothes, frilly things if you will. Just because I loved boots and made my living from them didn't dictate that I had to wear them."[48]

Enid was an enthusiastic supporter of the cattle industry and cowboys, but you would never see her on a horse. She once told an interviewer, "I'm one of the world's best rodeo fans, but there aren't enough people around to get me on a horse." To prove her point she added, "I remember one time years ago when I was asked to lead a rodeo parade in Big Spring, Texas. The parade officials came for me with a horse they wanted me to ride. I

Enid proudly poses with a display of Nocona Boots, c. 1950. (Courtesy of the Enid Justin - Nocona Boot Company Collection, University of North Texas Special Collections.)

explained to them real fast that a car would be just fine, and I led that parade in a convertible. In fact, I led a lot of parades all over the nation but I always asked for a car."[49]

Shortly after the new factory was completed, Enid moved into a new home. She sold the small red brick house in which she had lived for several years and moved into a spacious new pink stucco home with a pink cowboy boot weathervane adorning the roof. Enid's new home shared its

CHAPTER 4

Enid with cowboy movie star Ken Maynard, a Nocona Boot customer, and his white stallion Tarzan at the Fort Worth Stock Show in 1941. (Courtesy of the Enid Justin - Nocona Boot Company Collection, University of North Texas Special Collections.)

hilltop location with another home owned by a cattle raiser, and the site became known as "B and B Hill," the initials standing for boots and bulls. In recalling Enid's new house, niece Marsha Taylor noted, "It was easy to give directions to her house. You just go down the highway, and when you see the pink house, that's it." The house became a Nocona landmark—everyone knew where Miss Enid lived. Pink was always her favorite color, and for years she drove a pink Cadillac with the license plate E J BOOT.[50]

Life was good for the lady bootmaker. Her business was thriving, and she had succeeded in building a state-of-the-art factory with plenty of room for future production, or so she thought. But within a short time, even that expansive new building would not be sufficient to accommodate the growth of Nocona Boot Company.

CHAPTER 5

I'VE ALWAYS BELIEVED YOU'VE GOT TO WORK HARD TO BE "LUCKY" IN BUSINESS. AND I ALWAYS WORKED HARD.

—ENID JUSTIN[1]

Enid's new factory was humming as its bootmakers turned out some 300 pairs a day in 1950. The austere brown and black of the depression and war years had been replaced by "fancy boots" with colored leathers, elaborate stitching, and intricate cut-outs for inlaid patterns. "The competition of other boot companies was stiff," Enid recalled, "and I wasn't about to let Nocona Boots stay behind, so we developed fancier boots every year."[2]

The rapid growth of the cowboy boot industry was an unexpected boon. Back in 1921, a dozen prominent boot manufacturers met to discuss the future of the industry. Their conclusion: "Boots, like buggy whips, are on their way out." As the automobile rapidly replaced the horse, these leaders predicted the market for boots would quickly vanish. Enid's brothers bought into this forecast of doom and, to hedge their bets, began producing shoes as well as boots. But Enid never wavered in her belief that there would always be a market for cowboy boots, and she proved prophetic. Three decades later, the boot business in America had multiplied fifty times over. By the early 1950s, more than a million pairs of cowboy boots were manufactured in the US each year, the great majority Texas made.[3]

Enid shows off the elaborate boot designs of the 1950s. (Courtesy of the Enid Justin - Nocona Boot Company Collection, University of North Texas Special Collections.)

Boot historian Tyler Beard asserts that "boot art reached a pinnacle" in the 1950s. A western-wear fad was sweeping the country, fueled by popular interest in the nineteenth-century American West, and boots reflected that trend with extravagant designs. The "cowboy style" that became so popular was inspired by western movies featuring stars like Hopalong Cassidy, Roy Rogers and Dale Evans, and Gene Autry, a Nocona Boot customer. With an increasing number of televisions in American homes, shows like *Gunsmoke* and *The Lone Ranger*, whose star Clayton Moore also wore Nocona Boots, furthered the trend. "Westerns" became the most popular television genre of the fifties—in 1959 thirty different western-themed programs aired during primetime. Their influence on fashion was bound to be felt.[4]

Western wear became popular all over the United States. Ken Hand, business editor for the *Dallas Morning News*, wrote, "The remarkable thing about the footwear industry these days is not so much that the

CHAPTER 5

Fancy Nocona boots from the 1950s, described in the catalog as "a riot of color." (Courtesy of the Nocona Boot Company Collection, Tales 'N' Trails Museum, Nocona, Texas.)

vogue of cowboy boots is on the increase in the West and Southwest, but that sales are booming in such unlikely spots as New York, Pennsylvania and Delaware." Mail-order catalogs made western wear widely available

THE LADY MAKES BOOTS

across the country. Nocona Boot Company had been producing richly illustrated catalogs for years and had a successful mail-order business, but to take full advantage of the western-wear craze, Enid opened an on-site retail store shortly after her new factory was completed.[5]

The retail store handled a full line of western clothing for the entire family. A large sign fronting the building invited the public to tour the factory and visit the western-wear store. The *Fort Worth Star-Telegram* reported that Nocona Boot Company was "well on its way to being the headquarters for all western apparel. Not only the people of Texas are taking advantage of this new shop, but tourists are finding this the best place to outfit themselves." A guest book with signatures from most of the states and several foreign countries attested to the distance customers were willing to travel for western duds. They also could be measured for custom boots, and their measurements were placed on file to accommodate future orders. The cost of custom fittings at the retail store was two dollars. The new venture was so successful that in summer 1952 the store was tripled in size.[6]

In the midst of this boot craze, on June 15, 1950, Nocona Boot Company celebrated its twenty-fifth anniversary. One hundred fifty employees and their spouses were treated to a Southern fried chicken dinner at the First United Methodist Church and, as part of the program, Enid read poems she had composed for each employee. She then presented each of them with a copy of their poem and a bonus check. "I was always interested in the workers, individually and collectively," Enid recalled. "And I always did all I could to help them." For example, she provided her employees with life, accident, and hospitalization insurance. She reasoned, "I've always figured people have enough to worry about without adding to the everyday problems, so insurance was one way to eliminate problems for the employees."[7]

In addition to providing generous company benefits, Enid planned fun events for her workforce. There were bus trips to the Ice Capades in Fort Worth and the rodeo in Oklahoma City, and every year an elaborate Christmas party was held in the Nocona High School gym, the only place in town big enough to entertain the approximate five hundred guests. The employees were treated to "a sit-down Texas-style dinner" provided by Jettons, a company Enid called "the best caterer in the state." She once told an interviewer, "Someone said to me one day you have LBJ's [Lyndon Baines Johnson's] caterer, and I said, 'Thunder I do, I had him before he'd ever heard of him.'" In addition to a delicious dinner, guests received service awards and gifts and were treated to "the best entertainment" Enid could find.[8]

Another tradition of the Nocona Boot holiday season was the broadcasting of Christmas carols from the company office. The carolers included employees and anyone from the community who wanted to join in the singing. The carols were broadcast from loud-speakers on both the new and old Nocona Boot buildings. *The Nocona News* reported, "The carols can be heard for several miles around," and everyone looked forward to this "manifestation of the Christmas spirit." The unusual program even stopped traffic on Hwy 82 as travelers pulled over to the side of the road to listen to the caroling.[9]

As Enid did her best to provide some fun for her employees, the everyday work of building boots continued. There were always unexpected challenges to be dealt with, and this time it was the threat of another lawsuit initiated by Enid's brothers over the use of the Justin name. The two companies owned by Justin siblings continued to get mixed up, and the Justin brothers believed the confusion was due to Enid's liberal use of the family name. The 1938 incident with the *Wichita Daily Times* that became such a bone of contention between Enid and her brothers was just the beginning. In July 1946, a Burkburnett, Texas, newspaper article confused Nocona and Justin boots, prompting Earl Justin to write to the editor requesting a correction. Again, in 1948, *The Denver Post* made a similar mistake that led to a Justin representative's demands for a retraction:

> We have a copy of the June 11th *Post* that shows Miss Enid Justin stitching a pair of "Justin" boots. This is naturally a blow to the real manufacturers of Justin Cowboy Boots, our client, H. J. Justin & Sons, Inc. The Justin boys, John, Earl, and Sam, have worked hard all their lives in their father's factory building up the famous reputation of Justin Boots. To these men who have spent their time, effort and money in building up a nationally known name, it is somewhat disconcerting to have another firm given front page credit as the maker of famous Justin Boots.[10]

The letter went on to explain that Nocona Boot Company was not connected in any way to the Justin company, but the Justins had "a hard time convincing folks of this because Miss Justin uses her maiden name, rather than her married name, in all her business transactions." The letter continued, "A great many people have been misled into believing that Nocona Boots, made by Miss Justin, and genuine Justin Boots, made by the Justin Boys in Fort Worth, are one and the same." The Justin representative maintained that this confusion caused problems with both retailers and customers.[11]

The Justin brothers had a valid complaint. Enid did push the envelope with her use of the family name, and there was value in the name. In 1944, Ramon F. Adams authored *Western Words: A Dictionary of the Range, Cow Camp and Trail*, and his cowboy vocabulary included the following definition for the word "Justin's":

> Any cowman knows that this word is synonymous with good cowboy boots. From the day in 1879 when Joe Justin settled at Old Spanish Fort on the Texas side of the Red River and made his first pair of boots, down through the years to the present modern factory in Fort Worth, Texas, run by his three sons, Justin has set the style in cowboy boots. A few men have left their names to enrich permanently the vocabulary of the Westerner through the excellence and popularity of a necessary product. Among these are Colt, Stetson, Levi, and Justin. Even Easterners by now know what these names represent.[12]

In a decision that defied convention, Enid chose to keep her maiden name after she married. She was proud of her family name, but she also knew that the Justin name, with its known connection to quality boots, would be an asset to her company. "She never called it [Nocona Boot Company] the Justin Boot Company," John Justin Jr. recalled, "but all of her sales literature and ads carried the words, 'Enid Justin, President,' and she made sure that the Justin name was always a lot bigger than the Nocona name." In Enid's defense, while her name was not always in larger type, it was always prominently displayed. That "liberal use" of the Justin name, along with the resultant confusion of the two companies as evidenced in newspaper articles, led the Justin brothers to file a lawsuit to curtail Enid's use of the family name. They hired prominent Fort Worth attorney Sidney Samuels to represent them, and he felt they had a good case against their sister.[13]

According to John Justin Jr.'s account of the events surrounding the lawsuit, Enid "came down and pleaded with her brothers to drop the suit." In telling her side of the story, Enid made no mention of "pleading" her case in Fort Worth and instead argued that the Justin name was her birthright, "the name my father and mother gave me." She kept a boot company in Nocona where she believed her father intended it to stay, and although she could not keep the company name, she felt she had every right to use her own surname. The Fort Worth Justins decided to drop the suit before the case went to court—whether as a result of Enid's "pleading," or because they determined they had no real grounds for the suit, is open to question.[14]

The possibility exists that the Justin brothers initiated the lawsuit because they found their company falling behind their Nocona competitor. Justin biographer Irvin Farman wrote that years of conflict among the three Justin brothers had resulted in "a power vacuum in the company's top management," and by 1950 "H. J. Justin & Sons was floundering, losing ground in the marketplace." In the fall of that year, thirty-three-year-old John Justin Jr. took over leadership of the company after buying his Uncle Avis's (Samuel Avis Justin, also called Sam) stock. John Jr. knew there would be objections to the stock transfer from some of the shareholders, especially his Aunt Enid who would be most unhappy that Avis was leaving the company. "Avis had been Enid's grapevine into the Justin Boot Company operations," John Jr. explained. "She'd come down to Fort Worth and visit with him or he'd go up to Nocona to visit with her and he'd tell her everything that was going on, what every customer was doing, where we were getting the leather, what every customer was paying, what we were doing new." Avis may have been keeping his sister informed, but it is highly likely that Justin Boot Company had its own grapevine in Nocona as "competitor research" has always been a common practice among rival firms.[15]

When John Jr. took over leadership of H. J. Justin & Sons, he admitted, "Some of our competitors had gotten ahead of us, making more boots, making more popular boots, doing a better job than we were doing. So we were really playing catch-up, and that's a pretty tough way to play."

Leon A. Harris Jr. and models from Dallas's popular A. Harris Department Store show off their western finery and custom-designed Nocona Boots at "Texas on the Riviera" in Nice, France. (Courtesy of the Enid Justin - Nocona Boot Company Collection, University of North Texas Special Collections.)

John Jr. would go on to resurrect Justin Boot by eliminating shoe production and concentrating on the manufacture of cowboy boots. In the meantime, Enid's company had gained the advantage, as demonstrated by the special recognition she received and the special events she was invited to participate in throughout the 1950s.[16]

It was a heady time for Nocona Boot Company, with Nocona claiming the title "The Boot Capital of the World," a title the Fort Worth Justins surely refused to recognize. *The Nocona News* reported, "Miss Justin has glamorized cowboy boots," and it doesn't get more glamorous than the French Riviera. When A. Harris of Dallas's popular A. Harris Department Store decided to sponsor "Texas Week on the Riviera," he began looking for products manufactured in Texas, including "Old West" attire. He chose Nocona Boot Company to provide cowboy boots for the weeklong event to be held in July 1952. Enid's company made nine pairs of boots, seven for the models and two for A. Harris executives who were hosting the event. The boots were custom designed to match western outfits created by the Frontex Company of Dallas. They were elaborately decorated with a variety of inlaid designs and hand-embroidered in silver and gold thread.[17]

The Semaine du Texas was conceived to show off designed-in-Texas, made-in-Texas fashions from eighteen different manufacturers. Co-sponsored by A. Harris and the French Regional Tourist Committee in Nice, the occasion was a whirlwind of fashion shows and galas that promoted all things Texas. One party, given by Abilene oilman Jimmy Radford, took that concept to a new level. While a miniature oil derrick spouted French cognac, guests wore live horned toads on their shoulders, much like corsages. (Radford had imported one hundred of the critters from West Texas. Probably in shock from the trip, the reptiles sat obediently wherever they were placed.) Radford's shindig was described by *New York Herald Tribune* columnist Art Buchwald, who attended the Riviera event. In a lengthy column, Buchwald seemed to view the event, or perhaps Texas, as somewhat provincial—he referred to Texas as "a very valuable piece of real estate, since it is the only connecting link between the two great states of Louisiana and New Mexico." Despite his obvious disdain, Buchwald ultimately concluded that the week could be "chalked up as a success."[18]

The unique extravaganza drew the interest of media across both the US and Europe, and that publicity contributed to the growing reputation of Nocona Boot Company. Enid filled more than one scrapbook with newspaper clippings, correspondence, and magazine articles about the event. *Time*, *Life*, and *Newsweek* covered the story, and newsreel and television cameras filmed the revelries. A new morning program on NBC called *Today*, hosted by Dave Garaway, produced a segment on Texas Week. TV viewers watched as the models paraded through Cannes in their cowgirl outfits to the delight of cheering spectators who lined the streets. The publicity from the event proved to be invaluable. *The Nocona News* reported, "To Miss Enid goes the credit for doing something with cowboy boots that few, if any, other manufacturers have done. She has glamorized them and this glamorization has spread in advertising from coast to coast and several foreign countries."[19]

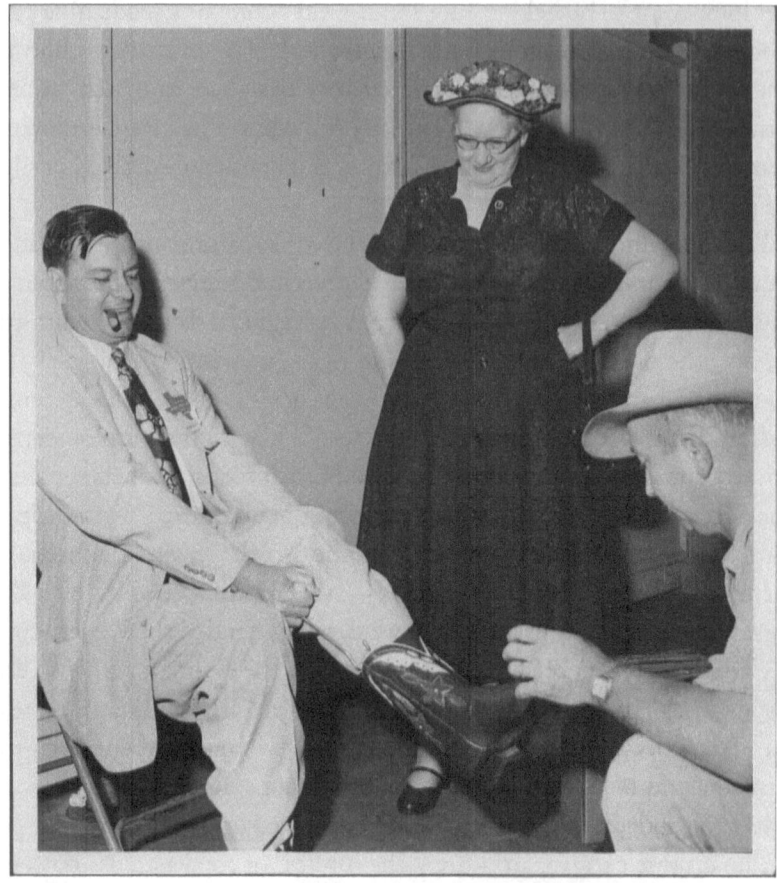

Governor Herman Talmadge of Georgia tries on his Nocona Boots at the 1952 Governor's Conference in Houston. (Courtesy of the Enid Justin - Nocona Boot Company Collection, University of North Texas Special Collections.)

Another honor came Enid's way that same summer of 1952. Nocona Boot Company was chosen to make boots for all the nation's governors when they met in Houston for the annual governors' conference. It was the first time Texas had hosted the gathering, and Governor Allan Shivers planned to welcome the attendees with a number of Texas-made gifts. Shivers invited all the bootmakers who were members of the Texas Manufacturers Association to submit a design for the gift boots, and Nocona won the honor. *The Nocona News* boasted, "Top gift will be a pair of cowboy boots and out of all of the boot companies in Texas, Noconas were chosen." Two Fort Worth companies were also chosen to

CHAPTER 5

make gifts for the conference. H. J. Justin & Sons provided belts for the governors, each hand-tooled with the names of their states, and Tandy Manufacturing Company made hand-tooled belts for the governors' wives. Enid and her retail sales manager Bill Pribble flew to Houston to personally fit each of the governors in brown boots with red and white butterfly inlays and red flowers. The company had obtained each governor's shoe size, but one hundred pairs of the specially designed boots were shipped ahead to Houston's Shamrock Hotel to assure that each governor's boots were a perfect fit.[20]

Years later, in recounting the story of the governors' conference in her memoir, Enid remembered how upset she had been when Adlai Stevenson, then governor of Illinois, said he didn't like the boots and didn't want them. "That really burned me down," Enid recalled. "He could have just taken them and kept his mouth shut since they were free." As it turned out, Stevenson's son called Enid wanting the boots, and she ultimately gave a pair to both Stevenson sons. But she vowed, "I'll guarantee you one thing, Adlai Stevenson couldn't have gotten my vote for dog-catcher after that."[21]

The accolades and honors for both Enid and her company just kept coming. In 1953, the Texas Legislature passed a resolution commending "Miss Enid Justin, President of Nocona Boot Company, for her various industrial and civic contributions to her community and the state." That same year, the Corpus Christi Chamber of Commerce presented Enid with its "Texas Women of Distinction" award as an "outstanding example of distinguished womanhood." And for two consecutive years, 1953 and 1954, the Nocona Boot Company won the blue ribbon at the Dallas Fashion Arts annual awards dinner held in the Cactus Room of the Adolphus Hotel. The prize meant that Nocona Boots would be used exclusively for modeling Texas-made attire at the State Fair of Texas held in Dallas in October. With the number of prestigious awards coming its way, it could certainly be argued that Nocona Boots had won out over the competition to become the best in Texas for both quality and style. And the competition was formidable. The principal competitors in Nocona's price range were the Tony Lama Company, a bootmaker with a rich history located in El Paso, and, of course, Fort Worth's H. J. Justin & Sons. Those competing companies, Nocona, Justin, and Tony Lama, made up the "big three" Texas boot manufacturers.[22]

Nocona Boot was not just competing in Texas; the company was giving bootmakers all over the country a run for their money. A map on the office wall of factory superintendent Weldon Lund showed Nocona boots being sold in every state in the United States and much of Canada, with the most distant dealer located in Bangor, Maine. Boot prices ranged from $23 to around $115 depending on style, intricacy of design, and type of leather. Leather had come a long way since the original cowhide boots. Varieties included kidskin, calfskin, elk, sheepskin, seal, alligator, shark, water buffalo, and kangaroo. An Australian government official sent an order from Canberra for a pair of kangaroo Nocona Boots. He planned to put the boots on display at the new United Nations in Lake Success, New York, to advertise the Australian leather. The most expensive leather choice was gold or silver kidskin that the company purchased by the inch instead of by the foot like other leathers. The boots were fancier than they had ever been, but styles were beginning to change in other ways.[23]

Gene Keller, a longtime Nocona Boot employee who held the position of assistant superintendent in the 1950s, remembered the decade as a time of drastic style change. According to Keller, production at the plant was actually slowed while fashion trends were in flux. Toe styles were changing—the traditional sharply pointed toe was giving way to a more rounded toe. Although both styles would ultimately be produced, the rounded toe became the more popular style. And boot tops became taller, with the traditional ten-inch top losing favor to a twelve-inch top. Heel styles had also changed, with customers preferring a lower walking heel to the traditional high heel. Under Enid's leadership, the company adjusted to the demands of the changing marketplace while continuing to focus on producing a quality product. In 1958, Enid told *The Nocona News*, "I felt back in the 20's that I owed my father a loyalty to his expert workmanship. I hope that I have fulfilled that loyalty." Enid explained that a boot has fifty-four parts, and no one part is attached to another before proper inspection to ensure "that the same quality workmanship of Joe Justin is woven into today's boots."[24]

Two Justin family members came to work for the Nocona Boot Company in the 1950s. Both came from Fort Worth's Justin Boot Company, and both proved to be important in the history of the Nocona factory, but for very different reasons. The first to arrive was Enid's nephew, Joe Justin. Joe was the son of Avis Justin, Enid's brother and former "informant" at H. J. Justin & Sons. Joe grew up in Fort Worth, and through high school and college he worked in the factory run by his father and uncles. Joe recalled that he started in the cutting department, and "over the years I pretty well went all the way through the plant in the various departments." By 1954, at age thirty he held an office job and served on the board of directors, but company leadership had changed. Earl had died, and Avis had retired from the company. John Justin Sr. still served as chairman of the board, but John Jr. was now president. There had always been a competitive rivalry between the two cousins, and when John Jr. took control of the company, Joe decided he needed to make a change. He recalled, "I could see my opportunities for movement in the company were going to be limited because there was that jealousy a little bit." Joe called his Aunt Enid to see if she might have a job for him.[25]

In September 1954, Joe started his new job as assistant manager of Nocona Boot Company, a title that quickly changed to vice president and sales manager. Enid welcomed the new addition to her staff, and she was especially pleased to have another Justin at her factory. Family had always been important to Enid, but she may also have derived some satisfaction from the fact that Joe left rival Justin to come to work for her. Joe brought new ideas, and his stated goals were to improve plant efficiency, maintain consistent quality control, and increase production. Enid did not always agree with Joe's methods, and by the end of his first year, the two were experiencing difficulty working together. He blamed the problems on Enid's "strong will," while she accused him of trying to grow the company too fast. She always feared losing control of the company if it became too big.[26]

Years later, in recalling his accomplishments at Nocona Boot, Joe took credit for resurrecting a struggling company. He claimed the company lost money for two years before his arrival in 1954. "I think combined it was $48,000," he recalled. "I changed that thing around from September 1st until the end of June that first year and showed a $12,000 profit." No evidence has been found to support those losing numbers for 1952 to 1953, but Superintendent Gene Keller said that production slowed in the '50s to adjust to style changes. Sales also may have decreased due to downturns in the economy. The country suffered mild recessions in 1949 and

1953, and longtime employee Luciel Leonard recalled that during that time the company "had to lay off about twenty employees." She added, "I don't remember just exactly how long it was before they were able to start calling them back. It seems like after that the volume of sales started to increase."[27]

Enid's nephew may have had a positive impact on Nocona Boot's bottom line in the early fifties, but his claim that he accomplished that feat by changing the company from "straight time" to "piecework" production is questionable. "I went up there, and there was so much to do," Joe recalled. "She [Enid] was working on straight time, all of them were on straight time.... I was familiar with Justin's operation. They had everybody on piecework. So I got up there, and I put everybody on piecework. We were able to increase production by 40%." The problem with Joe's assertion is that Enid had had her employees on piecework for years. Luciel Leonard refuted Joe's statement: "We always had piecework and straight time work." And when asked what changes Joe made in the company, Leonard replied, "I don't think he made a lot of changes because she [Enid] was still in control."[28]

Joe remained in Enid's employ for three years, but their relationship continued to deteriorate, and their heated arguments were often overheard by factory employees. In July 1957, *The Nocona News* announced Joe's departure, reporting that he would "sever his connections with the company this weekend to become associated with the Amsco Steel Products Company at Wichita Falls." But his resignation would not be the end of his association with Nocona Boot Company. Because he was family, he would return to run the company twenty years later when Enid's health was failing and she needed a successor, but that tenure would prove equally contentious.[29]

The second member of the Justin family to come to work for Nocona Boot Company was R. S. "Ruff" Lemon, the husband of Enid's sister Anis. Before coming to Nocona in 1958, Lemon was vice president of H. J. Justin & Sons for thirteen years, and he became a valued longtime employee for Enid's company. Known as an innovator in the boot-making process, he was responsible for a number of advancements in boot construction during his tenure as vice president and general manager in Nocona. In 1959, he introduced the Thin-Line Cushion Shank, an invention that the

CHAPTER 5

company patented. Called revolutionary, the steel rib embedded in a rubber cushion and bonded to the insole strengthened the shank of the boot and increased comfort. Another innovation, introduced in 1962, was the Seamless Saddle Side, a design that eliminated the vertical seam on the saddle side of the boot to increase both comfort and durability. A year later, the Flex-Line Sole, also patented, doubled the thickness of a seamless sole to increase foot comfort. And in 1964, a construction feature called the Needle Toe Cushion enhanced protection of the outer leather on sharp toes. Lemon's innovations helped ensure that Nocona boots continued to be "the better boot," as Enid boldly advertised. Ruff Lemon worked for Nocona Boot Company until his death in 1971.[30]

Much like Lemon, many Nocona Boot employees spent their careers working for Enid. She cared about her employees and treated them well, but she expected loyalty in return. Twenty years earlier she made that expectation brutally clear when she fired workers who demanded increased pay for a shorter workweek. Now she was presented with an even more serious labor dispute when factory workers voted to join the Boot and Shoe Workers' Union, an organization affiliated with the American Federation of Labor. Encouraged by a union organizer who came to Nocona and held meetings in the city park, the workers voted to unionize by a slim margin. Enid, devastated by the vote, described her reaction: "That really hurt me. I took it personal." She felt she had given her employees "every benefit in the world . . . much more than the union requires." She added, "You know, it just makes you mad when you're doing everything for your employees you can and someone from the outside sticks their nose into your business."[31]

Union officials told Enid she would have to collect employee dues and send them to the organization. Her reply: "I told the union I wasn't doing anything of the kind and I never did. . . . In a year, the union was voted out by the employees. It wasn't a close vote this time." After the union was voted out, Enid talked to her employees over the plant loudspeaker. She told them that what they had been through with unionization was like a football game with Nocona Boot being the football. "Now the game is over," she said, "so don't be mad at your fellow workers who have been on the opposing team. Everybody has a right to their own opinion. We are all settled now, so let's get back to being friends like we always have been." Plant workers never again attempted to unionize.[32]

An excellent source of revenue for Nocona Boot Company was that celebration of cowboy bravado called rodeo. Rodeos had always been a major market for boots, and Enid traveled to those cowboy contests all over the West to promote her brand and sell boots. She rode in countless rodeo parades, often serving as grand marshal. As always, she refused to ride a horse, and after surviving a runaway buckboard when she served as marshal for the Pageant Parade of the Rockies in Colorado Springs, she was through with horse-drawn conveyances altogether. After that experience, it was an automobile or nothing.[33]

Stock shows, often held in conjunction with rodeos, were another important venue for boot sellers. Enid's company created elaborate displays that were used at livestock shows to showcase the latest boot styles. She could often be found at Nocona Boot Company's booth at stock shows across the Midwest and West, where she personally greeted customers and friends, pointed out the superior construction of her boots, and answered the frequently asked question, "How is it that a woman makes cowboy boots?"[34]

Enid rarely missed an opportunity to advertise and promote Nocona Boots. Her company was the first to sponsor a telecast of the Fort Worth Rodeo in 1953—some fifteen years earlier Nocona Boots had been the first to sponsor a radio broadcast of that "legendary" event. The Southwestern Exposition and Fat Stock Show, originally held at Fort Worth's North Side Coliseum and later at Will Rogers Memorial Coliseum, was one of the four most highly respected livestock shows in the country in the 1950s, the others being held in Chicago, Kansas City, and Denver. By sponsoring that nationwide television broadcast, Enid's company gained valuable exposure. "We have observed that the telecast of the rodeo brings many visitors to Nocona," Enid told a reporter for *The Nocona News*. "All through the year we have people drop in at the factory and express their appreciation for our sponsoring the rodeo telecast." Most of those visitors probably went home with new boots.[35]

In 1952, the Nocona Rodeo Association was organized so the town would have its own annual rodeo. Enid was instrumental in founding the local event, dubbed the Chisholm Trail Roundup, and she was elected first president of the association, a position she held for ten years. In reporting on Enid's election to head the new organization, *The Nocona News* opined,

CHAPTER 5

Enid as Grand Marshal of Nocona's Chisholm Trail Roundup rodeo parade in 1954. (Courtesy of the Enid Justin - Nocona Boot Company Collection, University of North Texas Special Collections.)

"It is believed that she is the only woman president of a rodeo association in the country." The only woman bootmaker now claimed another "first," but for Enid it was not about titles or being a woman. It was more about getting things done. She was willing to put in the work necessary to achieve her goals, whether it was building boots or organizing a rodeo.[36]

On a May evening in 1954, friends gathered at Enid's home for a private screening of "Texas in Review," a weekly television series sponsored by Humble Oil and Refining Company. This particular episode spotlighted Nocona as a center for the manufacture of leather goods. Over the previous twenty years, the town's leather industry had expanded to such an extent that Nocona had become known as the "Leather Goods Manufacturing Center of the Southwest." The show would take television viewers inside the town's four major leather goods factories: Nocona Boot Company, Justin Leather Goods, Nocona Leather Goods, and F & E Leather Company. Workers from each factory were featured in the broadcast, and excitement surrounded the show that would air statewide and bring welcome publicity to Nocona. As an example of the show's popularity, in Dallas it aired in the primetime spot between *The Burns and Allen Show* and *I Love Lucy*.[37]

As might be expected, the "Texas in Review" spotlight on Enid and her Nocona Boot Company caused some animosity with her brothers in Fort Worth. In a letter to Enid, a friend in Fort Worth wrote that she heard through "the grapevine" that there was "some static about the program" from "the other company." She added:

> You no doubt realize part of the trouble is family envy and jealousy, while a lot of disappointment came to them for not getting in on the deal, but thru no fault of yours. You have achieved your place so if any brickbats are tossed your way, duck and keep going. There is a place for both of you in the business world and there really should be no envy. Competition, yes, and a lot of it.

The letter went on with praise: "As one woman to another, who realizes that a woman has to be good to make the grade, for the odds are against us in some respects, I want to compliment you on your progress and your standing, and that of your company, all are remarkable. And that's not applesauce." The friend's advice and obvious admiration meant a lot to Enid, who saved the letter in her scrapbook.[38]

The Humble broadcast promoted the industry that was the backbone of Nocona's economy. The town was touted as a center for leather goods manufacture as early as the 1930s, and by the late forties, according to the *Wichita Falls Record News*, more leather was cut there than in any other town west of the Mississippi River. Another newspaper wrote, "Although the recent flurry of oil discovery . . . has brought new life to aspirations of future growth for Nocona, old-timers still feel that the hub of their universe is leather." The town's foremost industry began with boots and evolved into the production of a wide array of leather products. The leatherwork tradition began with H. J. Justin in 1887, and when Enid's brothers moved the original boot factory to Fort Worth, Enid carried on her father's work in their hometown. By that time, Justin Leather Goods, established in 1919, was successfully producing purses and a variety of small leather items, and in 1926, one year after Enid founded her boot company, another leather manufacturer that would have a storied history entered the picture.[39]

The Nocona Leather Goods Company, founded by Cadmus McCall and T. B. Wilkes with a capital investment of $35,000, originally produced women's steerhide purses. When the popularity of those handbags declined, the company branched into a variety of small leather items: billfolds, key cases, cigarette cases, desk sets, and other novelties. The products sold well, and the company moved from a rented building to its own newly built brick-and-concrete factory. In early 1929, capital stock was increased to $50,000. Then the stock market crashed, and virtually overnight the bottom dropped out of the market for the products manufactured by the young company.[40]

During the height of the depression, as the company struggled to redefine itself, Robert E. Storey, McCall's son-in-law, became president of Nocona Leather Goods. Storey, who had played baseball at Rice University, turned to the manufacture of baseball gloves to offset the decline in sales of small leather goods. The gamble paid off, and within six years the company had redirected its entire production to sports equipment, becoming the only manufacturer of leather sporting goods west of the Mississippi. In addition to baseball gloves, production included footballs, basketballs, volleyballs, leg guards, body protectors, catcher's masks, football helmets, shoulder pads, blocking pads, training bags, and other related athletic equipment. During World War II, the company's entire production went to the armed forces: the initial order from the War Department was for 2,500 basketballs, 21,000 fielder's gloves, and 1,004 baseball catcher's masks. *The Nocona News* reported, "Only the rejects, or seconds, were available for domestic sales."[41]

Believing that children should have good sports equipment, Storey pioneered the manufacture of junior ball gloves that were equal in quality to "big league" gloves. Another first was the introduction of brightly colored gloves to match team uniforms. Those were especially popular with girls' softball teams. The company's display room preserves an interesting array of sports equipment, but a favorite is the 1909 football that Nocona Leather Goods reproduced for *Jim Thorpe–All American*, a 1951 Warner Brothers movie that told the story of the Olympic gold medalist considered one of the most versatile athletes of modern sports. Another interesting item was a special football helmet the company made for Jack Crain, Nocona's All-American. Crain, a running back for the University of Texas, wore the white rawhide helmet in the Texas-LSU game in 1942.[42]

The company name was changed to Nocona Athletic Goods in 1956, and there are conflicting stories about why Nocona (with a "c") Athletic Goods products are branded Nokona (with a "k"). According to a 1952 edition of *The Nocona News*, the company is named for the town of Nocona and its products are named for Peta Nokona, famous Comanche Indian chief. That is a good story, but it lacks credibility since the chief's name is also most often spelled with a "c." The other, less colorful, reason for the letter change is that in 1934 when the baseball glove was trademarked, the United States Patent and Trademark Office would not allow the name of an incorporated town to be registered. The Nokona brand became widely respected for superior workmanship, and by the mid-forties, annual sales reached $1 million. In the 1950s, the company occupied a 60,000-square-foot factory and employed up to 150 people with an annual payroll approaching $200,000. Much like Nocona Boot Company, Athletic Goods personnel were "home trained," and many of them stayed with the company for years.[43]

Nocona's forth major leather goods company, F & E Leather, opened in 1945. Owners Floyd and Ethel Garner met in 1927 while working at Nocona Leather Goods. They married a few years later, and both continued to work in the leather industry while planning to someday open a leather goods business of their own. The couple worked for a variety of leather manufacturers across north Texas, including the Olsen-Stelzer Boot Company in Henrietta. As they moved from job to job, they bought used equipment whenever they found it, and in 1945 they returned to Nocona to open F & E Leather. Their company specialized in watchbands, purses, and belts, all made of hand-tooled leather. Tooling involved using an assortment of specialized tools to apply a decorative design to the surface of leather. Floyd and Ethel could hand tool 100 watchbands an hour, and it soon became evident that the couple had found a niche market. Hand-tooled leather items were popular accessories for western wear, and company growth surpassed the couple's expectations. By 1951, the business had outgrown its space in their Main Street home, and the couple built a new plant next door.[44]

In 1952, F & E products were sold in thirty states, and the company had acquired a number of famous customers. When a young boy came to the plant asking for a belt like the one Roy Rogers wore, he was delighted to learn that he could have the exact belt the Garners had made for the cowboy star. Singing cowboy Gene Autry was also a customer. The couple created all their own designs, and they also developed a coloring process for leather that was "strictly a secret." In another innovation, their watchbands were lined with leather that was specially treated to resist perspiration, a process the couple developed to prolong the life of the band.[45]

Shortly after they built the new factory, the Garners were approached by representatives from Tandy Leather Company of Fort Worth, who wanted F & E to cut leather for craft kits. Originally a supplier of sole leather and other shoe repair materials, the Hinckley-Tandy Leather Company began producing craft kits for the armed forces during World War II. When Charles Tandy, son of founding partner Dave Tandy, returned from the war and joined the business, he wanted the company to continue producing leathercrafts. Partner Norton Hinckley disagreed, and the partnership was dissolved. Hinckley continued in the shoe repair supply business, and the Tandy Company focused on leathercrafts. Under the leadership of the younger Tandy, the company opened its first two retail stores in 1950 and contracted with F & E to cut leather for its craft kits. The Garners purchased more than four dozen dies to cut the variety of shapes required for the kits. Tandy offered to pay the Garners in stock in order to keep cash flow at a minimum as his company expanded. Floyd Garner graciously declined the offer, telling Tandy just to pay when they could. It was a decision the Garners later regretted, as Tandy became a leader in the leathercraft industry, and company stock prices soared.[46]

Over the years, a number of smaller leather companies sprang up in the "Leather Goods Manufacturing Center of the Southwest." Products ran the gamut of items that could be manufactured from leather. In 1948, Howard Paine Saddlery began producing hand-tooled saddles. According to *The Nocona News*, "Howard began working with leather as a hobby and became an expert at it." He carried on a tradition that began with William H. Wilson, Montague County's first saddle maker, who patented the Wilson stirrup in 1897. Paul Haggerton opened the Nocona Sandal Company in the mid-forties to produce a variety of sandals with special hand tooling, and the Nocona Belt & Novelty Company was organized in fall 1929 to manufacture belts and other items like brief cases and pistol holders. That small factory was run by John Drake, "a leather worker of many years' experience."[47]

Another startup company, the Nocona Baby Shoe Company, had a brief tenure in the late 1930s, but it ran afoul of Enid, who objected to the company's use of the name "Nocona" for a shoe manufacturer. She had trademarked the name for both boots and shoes. (Interesting timing: Enid applied to the U.S. Patent Office for that trademark in June 1937, one month before *The Nocona News* announced the opening of the new baby shoe company. Her patent was registered in September of that year.) Enid hired the law firm of C. A. Snow & Co. in Washington, DC, specialists in patent law, to try to prevent the new company from filing a charter. In a letter to the attorney she asked, "Can he call his company "Nocona Baby Shoe Company" when we have Nocona patented for footwear? Of course he is trying to steal the reputation we have and I hope very sincerely this can be stopped."[48]

W. R. Smallwood, supervisor of the new company whose product would be soft sole infant shoes, contended that he had no intention of infringing on Enid's trademark. His company name was Nocona Baby Shoe Company, but his trademark would be "Little Texan." The office of the Texas Secretary of State found no problem with the name and granted Smallwood's company a charter to incorporate. Enid's attorney advised, "If they make no effort to advertise their products as "Nocona" products we do not think you would have any cause for action against them. As their business is located in Nocona they of course have the right to use the name "Nocona" as a part of their business name so long as their business name is not identical with yours." Despite their charter from the state, it appears that the Nocona Baby Shoe Company never produced

CHAPTER 5

more than a few dozen samples. At one point, Enid attempted to discredit Smallwood by referring to him as "not a good moral risk," and intimating that he was low class, but if the baby shoe company's failure was a result of Enid's interference, no evidence has been found to support that supposition.[49]

The long-established reputation of Nocona's leather industry encouraged the proliferation of leather manufacturers. Some were short-lived, but others were successful and lasted for years. The contention between Nocona Boot Company and Nocona Baby Shoe Company was the exception rather than the rule. More often, the leather community worked together to support each other and promote the town's main industry. As an example, F & E's watchbands were distributed by Justin Leather Goods. In an article about Nocona's leather companies, the *Fort Worth Press* wrote, "They all make leather goods. They're all friends. It's as near a perfect set-up as one could hope to find." In another article about the leather manufacturing center, the *Dallas Morning News* described Nocona as "an outstanding example of how highly specialized industries can get along together, learn from each other, and prove that a high-quality product will attract customers from near and far."[50]

There were other cities and towns in Texas that had significant leather fabricating factories. In 1963, El Paso, San Antonio, Dallas, San Angelo, and Fort Worth all had leather plants that employed 100 or more people, but none of those larger cities matched the scale of Nocona's leather industry, where the combined plants employed close to 400 people. In an article about Nocona's leather manufacturers, the *Wichita Daily Times* noted, "One might safely assume that at least one out of every three working persons in the city is directly dependent upon the leather industries there for his livelihood." The availability of skilled leather workers was a primary factor in the growth of Nocona's major industry. Noconans were proud of their leather tradition, and one reporter wrote, "Many youngsters grow up in Nocona with the full expectation of living and working with leather—boots, sporting goods, specialty articles."[51]

Another small Texas town presented a challenge to Nocona's title of "Leather Goods Manufacturing Center of the Southwest." Yoakum, a South Texas community located on the Lavaca–DeWitt County line, claimed the title "Leather Capital of the Southwest." Like Nocona, the town bordered the Chisholm Trail, and in the 1880s it became a meat-packing center when refrigerated boxcars made it possible to ship hanging beef to northern markets. As mounds of cowhides grew on the outskirts of town, Carl Welhausen, a young saddle maker, began Texas Hide and Leather Company in 1919. The small tannery and leather manufacturer originally specialized in saddles, harnesses, and horse collars. The company later expanded its product line to include belts, billfolds, and holsters, and in the 1940s it was renamed Tex Tan. The company's popular products were marketed across the United States and in Mexico and Canada. Tex Tan Western Leather Company was acquired by the Tandy Corporation in 1956.[52]

Much as did Nocona, Yoakum's leather industry attracted like concerns and eventually grew to include some ten additional leather manufacturers. The town's leather production consisted primarily of saddles, bridles, harnesses, and small personal items, but Tex Tan did have a small boot factory in Moulton, Texas, some twenty miles north of Yoakum. In the 1970s, when Nocona Boot Company was desperate for room to grow, Enid would purchase that factory from the Tandy Corporation. Over the years she had gotten to know the Tandy family, whom she called "some of my very best friends." She added, "Charles [Tandy] tried for several years to buy my Nocona Boot Company, but I just didn't want to sell.... I said, 'Charles, if I ever do sell, it will be to you.' That is the way I felt about the family." If there was rivalry between Nocona and Yoakum it was friendly rivalry, and it appears that Texas was big enough to have both a "Leather Center" and a "Leather Capital."[53]

Yoakum was also home to the most successful tannery in Texas, but it was small by northern standards as the industry was dominated by large tanneries in the Northeast and Midwest. Enid may have purchased leather from the Yoakum tannery, but she preferred the tanneries up north. "We bought most of our hides from the northeast because that's where the best tanneries were. We bought regularly from tanneries in Philadelphia. I insisted on buying the best leathers because if you don't start out with quality material, you don't have a chance of ending up with a quality product." In searching out the best leather for her boots, Enid personally visited many of the tanneries, and she was especially impressed with one plant in Hoboken, New Jersey, where fresh eggs were used to tan leather.

CHAPTER 5

She also frequently attended leather shows where tanneries wholesaled their products. Although Enid was involved in buying leather, just as she was in every facet of Nocona Boot production, she had a leather "buyer" whose job was to shop for leather and purchase the number of hides needed for each boot style. W. O. Cooper was Enid's leather buyer for over fifty years because "he demanded the best in materials and he got it." Through the years, Nocona Boot also bought leather from countries around the world—exotic leathers like python, kangaroo, and elephant. "The snakes, lizards and such are beautiful skins," Enid opined, "but they'll never replace the tried and true leather known as cowhide."[54]

The other materials used in Nocona Boots were also of the highest quality. "There are basics in a boot that make it good and those basics don't change," Enid explained. One of those is the steel shank that strengthens the boot and supports the foot; Nocona's patented Cushion Shank, invented by Ruff Lemon, took that technology to a new level. Hardwood pegs, used to hold the shank in place, are another important element in boot manufacture. A quality boot has one or two rows of pegs running along the sole of the boot at the instep. Wooden pegs will not fall out when the boot gets wet because they expand and contract much like the leather sole. Lesser quality boots are made with nails, which often rust when they get wet, causing the leather around them to rot. Nails can also work through the boot into the foot—an obvious impediment to boot comfort. A quality boot has at least twenty hardwood pegs. "Pegs got so scarce one time I had to go to Massachusetts to find a supply," Enid recalled, "but I wouldn't compromise quality. Nocona Boots always had hardwood pegs."[55]

Quality was always the number one ingredient in Enid's boots: quality leather, quality materials, and quality workmanship. It was a value she learned from Daddy Joe many years earlier, and she never stopped demanding it. As she entered her fourth decade in the boot business, her quality products would continue to bring unprecedented growth to Nocona Boot Company, growth that would necessitate factory expansion to the very limits of Boot Hill.

CHAPTER 6

I'D RATHER WEAR OUT THAN RUST OUT.

—ENID JUSTIN[1]

"At a time in our industry when both tradition and innovation are equally important key elements of a common business ethos, Miss Enid Justin is an icon of both qualities." With that single sentence, *Western & English Today*, a trade magazine for western lifestyle retailers, may have hit upon the very formula for Enid's phenomenal success. Through the years, she produced a product that embodied the romance of the "Old West" while it continually evolved to meet changing styles and incorporate new technology. That formula led to ever-increasing demand for Nocona boots. Despite her fear that she would lose control of the business if it grew too fast, Enid simply could not contain the growth of Nocona Boot Company if she met product demand. By the early 1960s, the factory that seemed so massive when it was built in 1948 had been enlarged twice. The first addition of 5,000 square feet was followed by another of 15,000 square feet, resulting in a total 53,000 square feet of factory space where some 300 employees manufactured 400 to 450 pairs of boots each day.[2]

In 1965, Enid was seventy-one years old and showing no signs of slowing down. She was described as "a remarkably active, interesting, and charming lady." Photographs show a woman with short, neatly styled silver hair, bright eyes behind metal-framed glasses, and a wide smile. One journalist provided a unique description: "'Miss Enid,' as her employees call her, weighs 180 pounds. These are compactly but proportionately arranged below her 5-foot, 8-inch ceiling. She wears smart clothes, and at least one diamond dazzler is a regular part of her costume. She admits to a definite weakness for diamonds (her only real extravagance), but her career is her principal passion."[3]

Pat Keck, a longtime boot company employee who grew up across the street from Enid, corroborated her fondness for diamonds. According to Keck, Enid shared her storm cellar with the neighborhood, and when ominous clouds gathered, she would climb down the cellar stairs clutching her jewelry and her driver's license, afraid that she would not be able to replace either if her house blew away.[4]

Enid still worked full-time, and she often said, "I work, I don't just sit." She was in her office five days a week, unless she was traveling, and she made office visits on Saturday morning and after church on Sunday to take care of weekend mail and get a jump on Monday's work. She marked invoices with due dates, calculated discounts for early remittance, and paid all the bills, always before they were due—with one exception. An office worker arranging some papers inadvertently moved a bill, and it wasn't discovered until the second notice was received. "I lost twenty-six cents discount on that one," Enid admitted, "but it's the only time." She also supervised customer orders, and with a glance at a dealer's order tag, she knew the city and state where that dealer was located. She knew many of her dealers personally as she occasionally traveled with her salesmen to visit the retail stores. In discussing those visits, she told a reporter for the *San Francisco Examiner*, "Everyone at home calls me Miss Enid, but they call me 'Boots' on the road. I have a lot of fun."[5]

Her daily routine also included interaction with factory workers. Every day without fail she left her office to walk through the factory and visit with her employees. "I spent a lot of time back in the factory with the workers." Enid explained. "I was always interested in them and the work they were doing." Her personal interest in her employees worked to her benefit. The company's employee turnover rate was low, and one family even boasted three generations of workers at the factory. "The most gratifying thing to me," she told an interviewer, "is that we give employment to so many people." Enid's visits to the factory floor were intended to be social, but they also included supervision. She had grown up stitching boot tops, and she was not above sitting down to show a new employee how the job was done. She also was not above correcting an employee if she observed something she did not like. Stitching supervisor Darla Linn recalled the day she dropped empty wooden thread bobbins on the floor by her sewing machine. "Young lady," Enid chastised, "these bobbins are a nickel apiece. We don't waste them."[6]

With her boot business thriving, Enid decided to venture into apparel manufacturing. It was not the first time she had demonstrated a willingness to diversify. In 1930 she had purchased McChesney Bits & Spurs and operated the company successfully for nearly twenty years. Her main criterion for acquisition was a "western" connection, and Texas Togs, Inc., met that requirement. In spring 1965, Nocona Boot Company purchased the San Antonio–based apparel manufacturer from Henrietta and Nathan Fisher. The venture seemed a natural progression for the boot company, as Enid was doing well with retail sales of western apparel in the company store, and for years she had worked with Texas apparel manufacturers on promotional events for the industry. Through promotions like "Texas on the Riviera" and Dallas Fashion Arts shows, Enid had gained valuable knowledge of Texas's apparel industry.[7]

The industry had grown steadily in the postwar years, and by 1963 it was the fourth largest manufacturing industry in Texas in number of employees and size of payroll, eclipsed only by the manufacture of machinery, transportation equipment, and chemical products. Dallas was the hub of the industry, but Fort Worth, El Paso, and San Antonio had significant apparel manufacturing enterprises. Companies like Haggar and Lorch in Dallas, Williamson-Dickie in Fort Worth, Finesilver and Santone in San Antonio, and Farrah in El Paso contributed to the state's success in apparel manufacture and enabled Texas to successfully compete with manufacturers in New York and California. Construction of the $15 million Dallas Apparel Mart in 1964 was a major boost to Texas's apparel industry. The enormous building housed a wholesale fashion market that allowed buyers to visit hundreds of manufacturers' showrooms under one roof. Industry growth was also encouraged by fashion-minded retailers—stores like Dallas's Neiman-Marcus created fashion demand that led to the expansion of upscale garment producers.[8]

Enid's new company was known for producing high-end western wear that included shirts for the entire family and a wide range of apparel for women and girls. According to *The Nocona News*, "Texas Togs western wear has for many years been sold to Neiman Marcus in Dallas and has been a traditional Christmas gift purchased from the store by Princess Grace for Prince Rainier of Monaco. The factory keeps his sizes and specifications on hand at all times." The *News* added that the "high styles of Texas Togs" were also popular with rodeo queens. At the time of the purchase, the upscale brand was sold only in Texas, but Enid planned to grow the company and market the apparel nationwide through retailers who sold her boots. When asked about the acquisition, Enid explained, "In purchasing a garment factory, we have diversified our position in the Western Wear Industry." The purchase price of $72,000 included 300 shares of common stock, machinery, inventory on hand at the time of the purchase, and assignment of "right, title, and interest" to any trade name or copyrighted name used by the company. Those labels included Texas Togs, Inc., Sportswear by Nat Fisher, Texas Ranchwear, and Texas Western.[9]

The San Antonio company was a relatively small manufacturer with twenty-six employees. Ten of those craftsmen agreed to relocate to Nocona to facilitate the start-up of production in the company's new home. In addition to factory workers, Enid hired a designer and a patternmaker. Sam and Kathleen Crain, formerly from Nocona, returned to town to manage the plant. The Texas Togs factory was installed in the west end of Enid's old downtown boot factory with an entrance on Willow Street. The machinery arrived in late June, but remodel of the building delayed the opening until the end of July. On Friday, July 30, Enid invited the town to attend an open house at the new factory "to acquaint Nocona citizens with the facilities and operation of the factory which now employs thirty-one persons." Over four hundred visitors toured the new factory, where employees demonstrated each phase of the assembly line process, from cutting room to stitching and embroidery rooms, and finally to the shipping department. In true "Enid style," refreshments were served to all who attended.[10]

The factory, which operated as a subsidiary of Nocona Boot Company, had a successful start, and less than a year after it opened, it was announced that Texas Togs "is outgrowing its present facilities and will expand into the remainder of the company building which at present houses *The Nocona News*." In what appeared to be a friendly eviction, the *News* told readers it was "seeking a new location as a result of growing pains by Texas Togs, Nocona's newest manufacturing concern." Three years later, a magazine article about Enid noted, "Nocona Boots and Texas Togs are continually advancing in production and sales with this dedicated lady setting the pace." That article was written in spring 1969, but by the end of that year the Texas Togs factory had been shut down. In January 1970, *The Nocona News* announced that Action-Line, Inc., a Dallas-based clothing manufacturer, had purchased Texas Togs' machinery and other equipment and leased the building where the former company operated. Enid made no public statement about the closure, but longtime employee Luciel Leonard speculated that Texas Togs was not as profitable as "they had expected it to be." She added that "they made some colorful clothing" while they were there.[11]

The failure of Texas Togs seems not to have affected the profitability of its parent company. Because Nocona Boot's earnings were at an all-time high, Enid's attorney Otis Nelson suggested that the company was "paying so much in taxes to the government that could be distributed, set up as profit-sharing for the employees." Enid and her board of directors liked the idea, and she enlisted Nelson's help in setting up the plan. She recalled, "I couldn't believe there were so many rules and regulations to discourage an employer from setting up such a program. But the attorney stayed with it and my employees got a profit-sharing program." Personnel who had worked for Nocona Boot a minimum of three years were eligible for the program and received a yearly check for a percentage of company profit. "I figured they deserved it better than I did." Enid explained. "They were the ones making the boots which in turn made the money for the company." Joe Justin later recalled that the plan was good incentive: "The employees could actually see yearly what they had made over and above what they earned." He also speculated that the profit-sharing plan discouraged unionization because the employees received more benefits from the company than they would gain from paying into a union. Years later, a retired employee described the plan as "wonderful." She participated in it for over twenty years, and it provided "a lot of nice retirement money."[12]

Both Nocona Boot Company and H. J. Justin & Sons were successful businesses, but their individual success did not stop their ongoing rivalry. For several years, a conflict had been brewing between Enid and John Justin Jr., president of the Fort Worth company, and in 1964 that conflict culminated in a lawsuit. John Jr. told his version of the "family feud" in Irvin Farman's *Standard of the West: The Justin Story*, while Enid's side of the story can only be surmised from court records. The tiff began when Enid, who still owned her original stock in H. J. Justin & Sons, wrote to John Jr. requesting as a shareholder "a detailed audit report of the company for the last four years, giving detailed expense accounts, salaries, etc." John Jr. replied that he regretted Enid had not attended the annual stockholders' meetings for the last several years, but he added that company records would be open for her inspection during business hours.[13]

Rather than attend Justin's annual meetings, Enid sent her lawyer from Wichita Falls to represent her. According to John Jr., the attorney disrupted the meetings with allegations aimed solely at causing trouble among stockholders. "All of my aunts and all these other people who owned stock would be there," John Jr. remembered, "and this lawyer would try to stir things up." At one of the meetings, Enid's attorney asked John Jr. if he charged personal alcoholic beverage purchases to the company, an assertion that offended his nondrinking aunts. "I would look over at my aunts, who had never taken a drink in their lives," John Jr. declared, "and they would be absolutely horrified." This harassment, as John Jr. called it, went on for some time, and he finally decided to take action. "I thought about it a great deal," he recalled, "and I came to the conclusion that if I owned some stock in Nocona Boot Company, it would make a big difference in equalizing things." After a lengthy search of Nocona Boot stockholders, he was able to purchase nineteen shares from a brother and sister who had inherited the stock from their father. With nineteen shares of Nocona Boot Company stock out of a total 400, he was a long way from having any control, but he was in a position to return the harassment. His next step was to register the stock in his name, and that required a visit to Nocona. John Jr. was apprehensive about confronting his Aunt Enid, a testament to her formidability, so he took his attorney along for support. When they arrived at Enid's office, she was obviously taken by surprise. She tried to delay the stock transfer with flimsy excuses, but ultimately she had no choice but to fill out a new certificate in John Jr.'s name, sign it, and stamp it with her corporate seal.[14]

Over the next few days, Enid called her nephew numerous times while attempting to convince him to sell his stock to her, but he refused. He later added that "wild horses" couldn't have gotten that stock away from him. Enid's next step was a legal maneuver intended to keep John Jr. from acquiring more stock in Nocona Boot Company. She sent a letter to all her stockholders, including her nephew, advising them that a recent amendment to the corporation bylaws, voted on by majority stockholders, specified that the stock could no longer be sold to anyone other than Enid Justin or Nocona Boot Company. Each certificate had to be stamped with a legend stating the new requirement, and stockholders had sixty days to have their certificates stamped or their stock would be voided. John Jr. questioned the legality of the new bylaw and decided to challenge Enid with a class action lawsuit.[15]

The suit was filed in the District Court of Montague County, Texas, on September 8, 1964. In a petition to the court, John Jr.'s attorney, Atwood McDonald, argued that the restriction on the sale of Nocona Boot Company stock "violates the constitutions of both Texas and the United States, that it is contrary to public policy, that it impairs the vested contractual rights of the stockholders of said company, and that it impairs the market value of all of such stock." The petition went on to state that stockholders would "suffer irreparable damage" unless the court declared the subject bylaw to be unlawful and invalid.[16]

In answer to the plaintiff's petition, Otis Nelson, attorney for Enid and Nocona Boot Company, argued that all the stockholders had not agreed to be a part of Justin's class action suit, and those stockholders might be willing to accept the subject bylaw. He further argued that the amended bylaw was legal under terms of Article 222 of the Texas Business Corporation Act. And he offered to add an additional amendment to the bylaw stating that it would not apply to any stockholder who objected to the provision. Lastly, he argued that the defendants denied that the plaintiff had suffered any loss in the market value of his stock.[17]

Judge Louis Holland heard the arguments in the picturesque Montague County Courthouse. After hearing the evidence of both parties, Holland presented his succinct judgment in open court. He declared the subject bylaw invalid and "not binding upon any stockholder of Nocona Boot Company, Inc." The judge also ruled that John Jr. was entitled to damages, and he asked the plaintiff to name the amount. John Jr. waived his right to damages, but Enid Justin and Nocona Boot Company were ordered to pay court costs. John Jr. obviously won that round, but the rivalry and contention did not end with that lawsuit.[18]

John Jr. described his aunt as "a tough competitor with a flair for self-promotion" and added, "She was really good at getting publicity for herself and her company." In a statement that was obviously not meant as a compliment, he claimed that his aunt was "extremely adept at playing up the 'woman's angle' years before the feminist movement became a force, working assiduously to enhance her self-proclaimed image as the 'Queen of the Boot Industry.'" Enid fueled John Jr.'s rancor by continuing to advertise Nocona Boots as the "world's biggest producer of quality Western boots." Justin biographer Irvin Farman wrote that Enid's claim really "galled her nephew," as it was a claim that "H. J. Justin & Sons considered only applicable to itself." Enid's advertising also touted Nocona Boots as "the better boot," another claim that angered John Jr. She insisted, "I thought we made a better boot than Justin Boots, my own flesh and blood. But we did make better boots. . . . I know about those things." And the rivalry continued. Interestingly, there is no record of Nocona Boot Company facing lawsuits or similar contentious incidents with other competitors in the boot industry. The family rivalry was so intense that it led to unreasonable actions and subsequent retaliation on both sides, and neither company profited from the petty feuds.[19]

One of Enid's business strengths was her ongoing effort to keep her company abreast of the latest technology. "I've always tried to keep up with the best machinery," she asserted. "I used to go to St. Louis and take my equipment man with me to see the new machines. If there was a machine that would increase production or make production easier, I'd buy it . . . in fact, I'd buy several." In 1969, Enid told an interviewer, "They have new types of machines all the time, like that new machine that turns the boot. It is made wrong side out and turned right before they put the soles on. That, to me, is a marvelous piece of machinery." A strange-looking machine, called a "revolving shoe tree," was designed by Nocona's innovative vice president, R. S. Lemon. Used as the last step in

CHAPTER 6

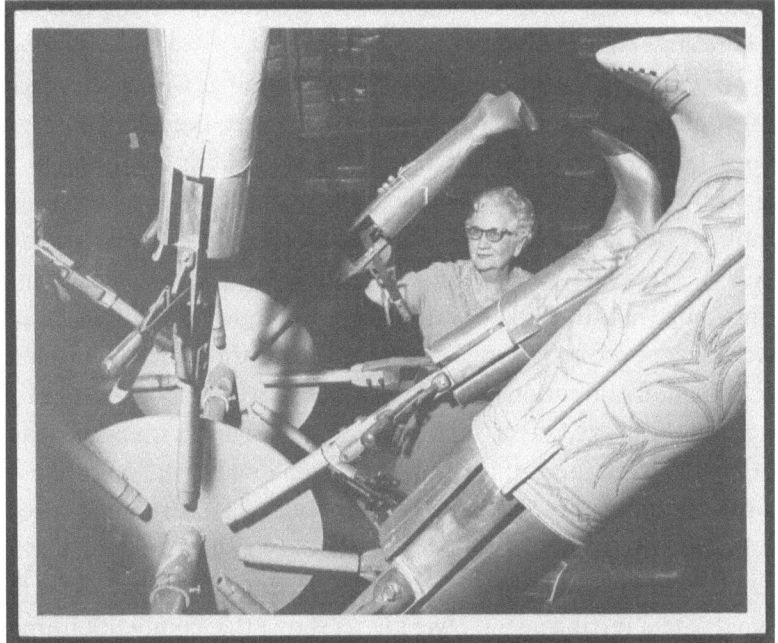

Enid observes the "revolving shoe tree" invented by long-time employee R. S. Lemon for the final stretching and finishing of Nocona Boots. (Courtesy of the Enid Justin - Nocona Boot Company Collection, University of North Texas Special Collections.)

the manufacturing process, the unusual machine that looked like a miniature Ferris wheel for boots helped ensure a properly shaped boot. Enid always maintained that the main change in boot-making over the years was the rate of production—technology had really sped up the process.[20]

The office staff also benefited from the latest technology as the company's first computer, made by NCR, was installed in 1969. When asked what the computer would do, Enid replied, "Everything. . . . It's going to be a marvelous thing." She expected the computer to be especially helpful in recording each employee's piecework and determining their pay for that work. That particular accounting function required "checking and double checking" to avoid mistakes, and the computer would eliminate that time-consuming process. Enid also improved factory working conditions with the installation of a year-round heating and air-conditioning system. When the factory was originally built in 1948, it was believed that air-conditioning would cause leather to mold. That notion had since been dispelled, and plant workers could now work through the hot Texas summer in relative comfort.[21]

Innovative technology applied to the boot itself as well as the machinery that made it, and thanks to Lemon's ingenuity, Nocona boots incorporated technological advances that made them both comfortable and long wearing. That other companies wished to incorporate those innovations is evident in a letter to Nocona Boot Company from attorneys for C. H. Hyer & Sons, a bootmaker in Olathe, Kansas. Hyer enlisted a firm of patent attorneys in Kansas City to request the patent number as well as a "photostatic copy" of the patent for the Thin-Line Cushion Shank. Lemon's invention, a steel rib embedded in a rubber cushion and bonded to the insole, was called revolutionary because it strengthened the boot's shank while increasing its comfort. Perhaps Hyer & Sons wanted to incorporate the innovative shank in their boots if Enid's company could not produce the patent or, if Nocona Boot did produce a patent, perhaps Hyer planned to "invent" a similar shank, altering the design just enough to avoid patent infringement. Hyer's letter shows that competition among bootmakers was stiff and extended beyond Texas borders.[22]

Boot style was equally as important as boot construction, and styles were continually changing. Fashion trends dictated toe shape, height of the boot top and heel, and types of leather. In 1969, Enid told an interviewer that her company was currently making "lots of turtle," and her sales manager was in Mexico looking for good turtle skins. She added that the variety of leathers being used was "unbelievable." Armadillo and ostrich were popular, but Enid opined, "You take a good ol' kangaroo leather for dress wear, it can't be beat." She added, "We're making a beautiful boot now. We take little pieces of leather and cut diamond shapes and combine different colors in the leg. It's a beautiful boot." Embossed leather, calf skin incised with a variety of patterns, was also popular. A *Fort Worth Star-Telegram* reporter wrote, "Miss Justin knows her leather, too, and can spot imitation alligator a mile away." Readers of the *Standard-Times* in New Bedford, Massachusetts, must have been surprised when they read that, according to Miss Enid Justin, owner of Nocona Boot Company, the latest thing in cowboy boots was whale skin. "Cowboys love the whale skin boots," Miss Enid declared, then quipped, "Whales are more skeptical."[23]

CHAPTER 6

Ladies Nocona boots in the 1969 catalog feature a bone kidskin boot with diamond-shape turtle skin inlays, a style that Enid described as "a beautiful boot." (Courtesy of the Nocona Boot Company Collection, Tale's 'N' Trails Museum, Nocona, Texas.)

By 1970, Nocona Boot was again experiencing growing pains. The company had some four thousand dealers working in every state in the continental US, Alaska, and Canada and employed eighteen salesmen to call on those dealers. "We've stopped taking any new dealers right now because we can't supply the demand," Enid stated. "We're four months behind on orders right now, so I believe in taking care of the people who have taken care of us. We need more room, we're training more people all the time and installing more machines. We just need to produce more boots, but we're doing the best we can, so it doesn't look like there's any stopping."[24]

Nocona Boot Company's capital stock was still $40,000, a surprisingly small amount for a corporation with sales exceeding $4 million, and Enid still held the majority of that stock. Over the years, she was able to control the amount of capitalization, but she could not control company growth. In what may have been an acknowledgement that she no longer had total control, Enid conceded, "I said all the time I wanted to keep it as small as I could so I could keep my finger on it, but it's grown, the operations and all, beyond that, but I still know a lot about it."[25]

Enid's business was booming, and in fall 1971, the *Wichita Falls Record News* reported that the firm's retail store was attracting so many customers seeking custom-made boots that the Nocona airport facilities were being improved to accommodate them. That same year, Nocona Boot received an Industrial Expansion Award from Governor Preston Smith and the Texas Industrial Commission. The award was presented to twenty-five Texas industries that "were making the most significant contributions to their community economies." Enid traveled to Austin to personally accept the award at a luncheon at the Municipal Auditorium. The recognition was well deserved: In 1970 the boot company averaged 238 employees with an annual payroll of approximately $1,270,000, a sizable contribution to a town with a population of just under 3,000.[26]

The popularity of cowboy boots seemed to have no limits. As a fashion trend, boots were being worn with all types of clothing by both men and women. Stanley Marcus, iconic founder of Neiman-Marcus, believed the fad began with the popularity of blue jeans in the mid-1960s. The "blue-jean phenomenon" resulted in the addition of "traditional accessories—cowboy boots, shirts, and hats," and by the 1970s western attire had become "a major international fashion." Tyler Beard, author of *The Cowboy Boot Book*, wrote that "the western look took a backseat for a while" in the 1960s, but by the seventies, western wear as a fashion statement was back—even "rock bands were wearing cowboy boots." Beard added that once again "there was no getting away from our American history and the influence of the cowboy."[27]

Enid agreed with both Marcus and Beard: "Couple our country's trend towards nostalgia with the denim and blue-jeans craze and you've got a natural—almost a must—for western boots to complete the western look." She added that she could not recall "any period of time comparable to this when the interest in and demand for western boots has been as great as it is today. Many Americans are discovering that you don't have to own a horse or live in Texas to enjoy cowboy boots." More women were wearing cowboy boots because they were fashionable, but Enid also credited "women's lib" for the increase in boot popularity among women. Recalling when "women wouldn't wear pants, much less boots," she added, "women are finally coming to their senses and are dressing comfortably and practically." She also credited the rounded toe, as opposed to the traditional pointed toe, for increasing boot popularity because it was "an attractive companion for the most tailored business suit, as well as for women's slacks and pant suits." Nocona Boot had offered a rounded toe for years, but it was now a style trend. In discussing the increasing popularity of cowboy boots, Enid remarked, "It's good to know who's wearing the boots in the American families these days—everybody."[28]

Nocona Boot added a new style to its 1972 catalog for an unusual reason: the boot was designed to serve a practical purpose in the rodeo arena. "One of the most important factors in a successful bucking event ride in rodeo is constant spurring of the mount by the rider," a boot company executive explained. "Rodeo athletes discovered that wearing white boots made it easier for the judges to see their spurring efforts and often resulted in higher scores." To help rodeo cowboys win the prize money, the Nocona Boot Company created the "Gold Nugget," a dressy style with a vamp of bone-colored kid. The flashy boot was sure to catch the judge's eye.[29]

In spring 1972, Enid told a writer for a trade publication, "The boot explosion in the east has been good for all cowboy bootmakers, and Nocona has tripled production over the past few years." The company was turning out 1,200 pairs a day in early 1972 but was still four to five months behind in delivering orders. The decision was made to enlarge the factory for the third time. Mel Chapman, vice president and general manager, explained the urgency of the situation: "We must increase our production in order to take care of our customers." A year earlier, Nocona Boot had purchased the land directly east of the factory, site of the Chief Drive-in Theatre, with thoughts of future expansion. Just as Enid had done in 1947 when planning her new plant, Vice President Mel Chapman and Production Manager Sam Campbell visited some ten factories to search out the latest innovations in footwear manufacturing. The men then consolidated ideas from all of them to design the plant expansion. Plans were drawn for a 26,268-square-foot addition to the east end of the building that would expand the factory area and add a new retail store.

It was estimated that the expanded factory would allow production to increase by 500 pairs a day.[30]

The addition would preserve the building's original architecture, and the entrance to the new retail store would house a small museum. Display cases on either side of the foyer would feature the hand tools that Daddy Joe used when he began making boots in Spanish Fort as well as other boot company memorabilia and examples of Nocona Boots through the years. A building contractor was hired and given 120 working days to complete the project. New machinery was ordered so that it could be installed immediately when the addition was complete. Construction began in April, and the new space was finished and operational by mid-August. With the completion of the new addition, the factory totaled almost 80,000 square feet. One reporter wrote, "Even in Texas that's a lot of square feet."[31]

The newly added space contributed to production almost immediately, but the factory still could not produce enough boots to fill orders on a timely basis. In February 1973, Sales Manager Dick Petrie announced that the company again would "hold the line" on opening new accounts. In an effort to improve delivery to existing customers, Nocona Boot would not take new dealers until the current backlog of orders was cleared. Petrie speculated that the moratorium might last a year. "The new factory addition has given us the room to grow to meet the demand," he stated, "but we plan to bring the first benefits of this growth to the dealers who've been Nocona customers for years."[32]

In May 1973, less than a year after the factory expansion was completed, Enid purchased Tex Tan Boot Company in Moulton, Texas. "We just needed more production," she explained, "and that's why we bought the Moulton plant." Enid was able to purchase the small factory from Tandy Corporation because it was phasing out boots from its Tex Tan line of leather goods. The small community in Lavaca County was some 350 miles south of Nocona. The boot factory was the only manufacturing plant in Moulton, population 900. The factory had around thirty employees and was expected to increase Nocona Boot's production by 300 pairs a day. The plant would produce only boot bottoms, while boot tops would be made in Nocona and shipped to Moulton for assembly. Twice weekly, trucks transported goods between the two factories.[33]

CHAPTER 6

The Moulton factory had some skilled bootmakers. Paul Mosier, "a highly qualified bootmaker of 27 years' experience," was named plant manager. Ramon Valadez, a plant supervisor and chief mechanic, had been making boots for twenty-five years. He learned the art of handcrafting leather as a teenager in his brother's boot factory in Matamoros, Mexico. Both men spent two weeks learning "the Nocona art of boot-making" so that they could maintain the same quality standards with Moulton production. The South Texas factory attracted Enid for two reasons: Moulton's experienced bootmakers were capable of producing the quality product that she required, and the small plant was an operating boot factory that could contribute to Nocona Boot's production almost immediately. The new satellite plant provided an effective short-term boost to production, but the distance involved in transporting goods between Nocona and Moulton would eventually cause the company to look for production locations closer to home.[34]

Enid was 79 years old in 1973. In an interview with the *Wichita Falls Times*, she told the reporter that she had twenty-three letters in her files with offers to buy her company for a sizable profit. "I won't sell and have made arrangements to see the company always stays here. Some big company might come in and do anything they wanted with the employees." If she indeed had a plan for her company when she was no longer at the helm, she did not reveal it to the reporter. When asked if she was considering retirement since she was almost an octogenarian, she answered, "I'm not about to retire. I'm enjoying every minute of my life." Enid truly did not seem to be slowing down. In April, she and Vice President Mel Chapman flew to New York City to accept the American Shoe Designer Award of 1973 for the best line of cowboy boots. The prestigious award, presented by Leather Industries of America, recognized designers and manufacturers who combined American artistry, technical know-how, and American tanned leathers to create high-quality footwear. While in New York, Enid was interviewed by the *New York Daily News* and WNBC Radio.[35]

Enid was tireless when it came to promoting Nocona Boots. In fall 1973, accompanied by various employees, family members, and guests, she attended an array of apparel shows, parades, roundups, and rodeos—a schedule that would have been difficult even for a younger person. Her first stop was Frontier Days in Cheyenne, Wyoming, followed by participation in the Pageant Parade of the Rockies in Colorado Springs. Then from Denver she flew to New York City, in a new DC-10, for an interview with the National Broadcasting Company. She returned home briefly before heading to the Western Apparel Show in Las Vegas, Nevada, accompanied by her general manager and sales manager. After the show, the men returned to Nocona, but Enid continued on to Pendleton, Oregon, where she served as one of the judges for the American Indian Beauty Pageant. While in Pendleton, Enid granted three different interviews. Known for her accessibility, she rarely turned down an interview. Enid enjoyed talking about her company, her history, and her boots, and because she was the world's only lady cowboy bootmaker, her unique story had widespread appeal. Her interviews were often picked up by wire services and circulated to newspapers across the country.[36]

Over the years, countless photos were taken of Enid presenting boots to dignitaries, politicians, award winners, and persons worthy of recognition or commendation. She truly enjoyed encouraging and rewarding success, and she was always generous with Nocona Boots. All the better if her generosity also publicized her company. In February 1973, the front page of *The Nocona News* featured a photo of Enid presenting a custom-made pair of boots to the retiring president of the Texas Hereford Association, an organization she had supported for over twenty years. Enid understood the connection between the cattle industry and her boot business. As far back as 1925, when her brother had predicted a dying market for cowboy boots, Enid had countered, "Why, Earl, we'll always eat meat and the cowboys will always have to ride the range." She considered that to be simple common sense, and for all her years in the boot business, she actively supported the livestock industry. The Hereford Association made her an honorary lifetime member for her "unselfish service and support." The boots she presented through the years to each outgoing president at the organization's annual banquet were an exclusive design—the elaborate boot tops featured the appliqued face of a Hereford bull. She did not limit her patronage to Hereford breeders, however, as she also supported the Texas Angus Association.[37]

Enid's support of the livestock industry included local organizations like Future Farmers of America, an organization that uses agricultural education to encourage student leadership, personal growth, and career success. Each year she presented boots to the high school student honored

CHAPTER 6

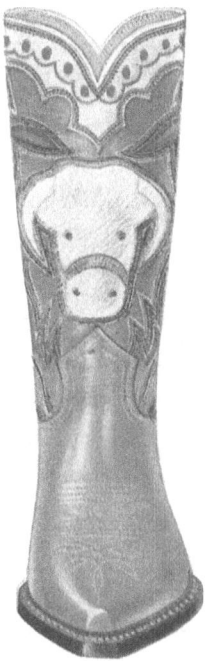

For many years, Enid presented a pair of "Hereford" boots to the retiring president of the Texas Hereford Association. The Hereford face was made of white hair on calf. (Courtesy of the Nocona Boot Company Collection, Tales 'N' Trails Museum, Nocona, Texas.)

as outstanding FFA farmer. In spring 1972, for the first time in the history of the chapter and "possibly of the entire state," a girl received the award. *The Nocona News* headline read "Girl Named Star Chapter Farmer at FFA Banquet." When Enid presented boots to Melanie Hayes, a senior at Prairie Valley High School, she exclaimed, "It sure is a lot of fun seeing a girl win these boots." Enid's civic involvement and promotional activities were so numerous that it is hard to imagine how she found time to run a boot company, but she managed to do it all.[38]

In December 1973, Enid received a special honor when she was named one of three new trustees of the National Cowboy Hall of Fame and Western Heritage Center in Oklahoma City. She was nominated for the position by actor Joel McCrea, a star of Western films. The two became acquainted when they attended some of the same rodeo performances. The Cowboy Hall of Fame was founded in 1955 to honor the cowboy and promote and preserve the legacy of the American West. The museum contained an extensive western art collection along with gallery exhibits focusing on the working cowboy, ranching, the American rodeo, and Native Americans. Hall of Fame trustees had a number of responsibilities, foremost among them choosing the recipient of "The Wrangler," an award presented annually for outstanding contributions to Western heritage. Enid's fellow inductees were Joe Story, editor of *Arizona Highways* magazine, and Colorado artist Arthur Roy Mitchell. Mitchell, a western artist and illustrator, was given a special "Honorary Trustee Award" for being "the man who has done the most for southwestern history" through his collective art. Enid proudly added her framed certificate to her wall, and when asked about it over the years, she would often say that it reminded her of her friend Joel McCrea.[39]

The boot company threw a party for Enid on her eightieth birthday. On April 8, 1974, over 300 employees, family members, and friends helped her celebrate the milestone. Flowers, cards, and gifts arrived from all over the United States. The *Western Outfitter* magazine recognized the special occasion with a small article that noted, "The energetic octogenarian plays an active role in the daily management and operations of the company she founded nearly fifty years ago." The company that Enid started with a $5,000 loan was now a $7 million enterprise that employed around 350 people. "We're adding employees so fast that I don't even know them," Enid acknowledged, then hastily added, "But, I will." She still spent her twice daily fifteen-minute coffee breaks on the factory floor visiting with employees and hearing the latest news of children and grandchildren. There were twenty-six people working in the front office, with eight of them assigned to computer operations. The original computer had been updated to an NCR Century 101 in 1972, and according to Enid, the "giant computer did all the jobs she and assistants used to toil over for long hours." Handling the mail was still her special domain, and she managed to make a game out of it. On her calendar, she recorded the number of letters that crossed her desk each day, and at the end of the month everyone guessed the final number. The employee who came closest won a small prize from a stash that Enid kept in a special office closet. She considered her employees to be her friends, and she tried to add some fun to their workday.[40]

Enid still insisted she had no intention of retiring. "I don't plan on letting the rocking chair get me," she told a Salt Lake City reporter. "Besides, I've got too much to do to be worrying about myself." In June 1974, a writer for the *Las Vegas Sun* described Enid as a "powerhouse of energy and conviviality" and added that she was "peppy, full of ideas, and healthy as can be." Enid was still the moving force behind her company, but at age eighty, she surely realized that she could not go on forever. It seems she still considered her retirement to be "down the road." In her memoir, she recalled hearing rumors around town that she was ready to quit. Her reply to those rumors was emphatic: "There are a lot of people thinking the old lady's getting older and they think they are going to move in, but they're not moving in and I'm not even considering retiring." She added that there would not be any "mergers or sales of this company," certainly a reaffirmation that she would not let her business fall into the hands of her Fort Worth rival, the newly named Justin Industries, Inc.[41]

Despite her strong statements, there were indications that Enid had begun to feel insecure about the future of her company. The resignation of longtime vice president Mel Chapman, who left for personal reasons, may have contributed to her concerns. At some point, Enid may have considered Chapman for her successor; he had that important Justin family connection because he was married to Enid's niece Zana. But when Zana died after a long bout with cancer, the relationship between Enid and Chapman deteriorated, and he left the boot company to run Nocona Belt Company, a business he had started several years earlier.[42]

After Chapman's departure, Enid asked nephew and former employee Joe Justin to come back to work for her. It was a clear sign that she was considering her vulnerability and pondering the succession of her company. Joe, now forty-nine years old, owned a successful steel company in Wichita Falls where he had moved when he left Enid's employ in 1957. According to Joe, "Enid came to me and said, 'Joe, I need you back. I really need you.'" He replied, "Auntie, we've been down this road before. I'm doing well, and I just hate to turn loose of what I've got here. . . . I just think you'd be unhappy with me again." Enid countered his objection, "We'll get an attorney, and we'll draw up some papers where you'll know what's expected of you and you'll know what's expected of me, and that's the way it will be." Joe agreed to his aunt's proposal, and her attorney Otis Nelson drew up a work contract spelling out Joe's duties and the extent of his authority with provisions for job security.[43]

With the contract in place, Joe believed he was Enid's heir apparent. "She couldn't get rid of me short of theft or something like that," he touted. "I had to perform and produce, but I had a total say over what went on. . . . She couldn't sell the business without my approval, so I really had all the bases covered." On July 1, 1974, Joe became vice president and general manager of Nocona Boot Company. A contractual clause allowed him to retain his ownership of Amsco Steel in Wichita Falls, with the specification that he would divide his time 65/35 between the boot and steel companies. Enid was pleased to have Joe back in her employ—four pages in her scrapbook attest to that fact. After all, he was Daddy Joe's grandson and namesake, and family had always been of the utmost importance to Enid. She took pride in the Justin family name, and there was no doubt that she wanted a Justin to carry on her legacy.[44]

"Joe's knowledge of boot-making is an inheritance," Enid explained in announcing her nephew's return, "and Nocona is very fortunate to have a man of his experience and capability assume this very important position." She added, "He grew up in a boot factory and he knows quality. This background, coupled with his thorough knowledge of business management, will be a valuable asset to The Nocona Boot Company and to its customers throughout the nation." Joe's enthusiasm was more restrained, as he described his new position as "a challenge." He added, "I'm really glad, though, to get back into the boot business. I have a strong heritage in this business, and I am glad to be a part of it. It's like coming home again."[45]

Joe's return to Nocona was timely. Plans were already underway for the boot company's fiftieth anniversary that would be celebrated in the

CHAPTER 6

coming year. In December 1974, the company newsletter announced that the boot line for 1975 would include an unheard-of thirty-nine new styles that would be introduced at winter markets in Denver, Dallas, Las Vegas, and Sacramento. "Normally to introduce eight or ten new boots in one year was considered record-setting within the boot industry," Sales Manager Dick Petrie explained, and this new line was one more reason that Nocona Boot "continued to be a pace-setter among western boot manufacturers." Joe added, "We know the public wants variety, something different, something new," and this line provided all those things in large measure. One of the new styles attested to the fact that Nocona Boot Company still catered to real cowboys as much as to "drugstore cowboys." Style #238, "for the wrangler or ranch hand who really gives his boots a workout," was a rugged work boot made of black Troutbrook, a leather that was tanned twice and impregnated with oil for a more water repellent finish.

In addition to the new designs, the line retained thirteen "favorites" for a total of fifty-two styles that would grace the pages of Nocona Boots' anniversary catalog. Those "stock styles" made up the lion's share of production, but the company also turned out around two hundred individual custom orders each day. For over twenty years, custom orders were the purview of Marguerite Holcomb, a petite lady with bright eyes and a big smile. "We get requests for all kinds of things in here," she explained. "Things never get dull." Over the years, she handled many unusual "make-up order boots," but her favorite came from a Texan who owned a chain of hamburger eateries and wanted an image of the popular sandwich appliqued on the sides of his Nocona Boots. "By the time our leather craftsmen were finished," Holcomb recalled, "those hamburgers looked good enough to eat."[46]

Among the countless styles Nocona Boot produced over the years, Enid had a personal preference. "The favorite of all my creations was a boot that featured a Texas bluebonnet and a California poppy on silver leather. They were really beautiful boots. I wore them a few times to special events." In her memoir, Enid told the story of what became of those special boots. She was dining at a Dallas restaurant and noticed shabby boots on her waitress, who wore a cowgirl's outfit. She called the waitress over and began talking boots with her. "I asked what size she wore, and it was the same as I wore, so I called home and told my folks to polish up that pair of boots and send them to her. She was one surprised waitress." Probably one of the best tips ever, those boots speak to Enid's love of people and her generosity.[47]

The town of Nocona was a frequent recipient of Enid's generosity. In a project that combined her love of her hometown with her love of children, she made the Nocona City Park into a kids' paradise. "I started out by buying one or two pieces of playground equipment for the park because I loved the children of this town. I guess I got sort of carried away because once I started, I couldn't quit. I'd find myself thumbing through playground equipment catalogs when I should have been working." When she could no longer find new equipment because "everything I see we already have," she bought a decommissioned jet plane for the children to play in. She acquired the plane for the bargain price of $100, the amount required to transport it to the park where it was permanently mounted with metal steps so children could climb inside and pretend to fly. She later added a retired Army tank to the playground equipment. In 1972, Enid observed, "The park is becoming crowded," so she purchased three adjacent lots and deeded them to the city for park expansion. The additional space made room for tennis courts and summer programs on Saturday nights that were free to everyone. The events offered live music and movies—one night showcased "Dewey Holcomb and his string band" followed by films featuring the comedy duo Laurel and Hardy. Enid later recalled, "I didn't anticipate the park growing so large in size or being so full of equipment, but it's nice and I'm very proud of it."[48]

But Enid was not finished with the park yet. To provide a stage for live music and other entertainment, she added a band shell in 1975. At a ceremony attended by some five hundred guests, she dedicated the new structure to her parents, Mr. and Mrs. H. J. Justin, pioneers of Spanish Fort and Nocona. *The Nocona News* reported that Enid "wasn't prepared for what followed." The citizens of Nocona had arranged an elaborate "This is Your Life" program that came as a complete surprise to her. A number of current and former employees, politicians, and other dignitaries presented praise and tribute to the longtime bootmaker for her business success as well as her generosity and public service. "It sort of scared me

CHAPTER 6

when they said, 'This is Your Life,' Enid confessed. "I thought they were going to tell everything."[49]

It was Enid's fiftieth year in the boot business, and the band shell dedication led off the celebration. On September 1, 1975, Nocona Boot Company observed its golden anniversary. The date fell on a Monday, which happened to be Labor Day, so the company announced that "the entire force will take a holiday." *The Nocona News* dedicated its weekly issue "to Miss Enid Justin and the Nocona Boot Company." The special edition included a lengthy history of the company, profiles of various employees, and pages of congratulatory ads. Many of the company's suppliers from all over the nation purchased ads, some taking an entire page, to offer their congratulations to Enid and her company. An ad placed by F. E. Schmitz Co., "Oldest Shoe Heel Factory in Texas," pictured two boot heels with the caption, "I only hope the two items I make for you have a little bittie part in making the Nocona Boot the Best Boot in the whole U.S.A." The special edition's front page featured a photo of Enid holding a custom-designed anniversary boot appliqued with the Nocona Boot logo. Below the photo, the editor wrote a congratulatory paragraph to "Miss Enid, known for her generous nature, her untiring interest in her employees, in young people and children and in the community as a whole.... The fact that she is also an unusually capable businesswoman is equally evident when one looks at the growth and progress of Nocona Boot Company during these fifty years."[50]

The "growth and progress" of Enid's company was remarkable considering its meager beginning in 1925 with a $5,000 loan and a handful of employees making boots in a 25 x 40-foot building. Fifty years later, the company was housed in a 100,000-square-foot factory—a 10,000-square-foot storage facility had been added to the existing 90,000-square-foot plant in July, and another 10,000-square-foot building would be completed before the end of the year. Enid noted that the new inventory storage space "allows us to speed our delivery schedule considerably." On its fiftieth anniversary, the company employed 350 men and women who made between 1,200 and 1,250 pairs of boots each working day. Those boots were marketed by eighteen salesmen across the United States along with four representatives in Canada who worked through an import company. "We were getting requests to go worldwide," Enid recalled, "but I wouldn't do that. . . . We could never supply the demand in the United States so why would I want to take on the whole world?"[51]

Although Nocona Boots were widely distributed in the United States and Canada, Production Manager Sam Campbell noted, surprisingly, that 50 percent of the company's total sales still came from Texas and Oklahoma. Boot prices in 1975 ranged from $39.50 to $275 for stock styles, with the most popular price range around $85. Prices for custom-made boots could go as high as $1,000, depending on what the customer wanted. Campbell added that automation and new technology had sped up the boot-making process over the years, but many of the two hundred steps involved in producing a boot were still done by hand—no machine had been designed to do them. "The development of machinery for the shoe manufacturing industry has been pretty good," Campbell explained, "but not much has been done in the way of special machinery for the boot-making industry." He credited Nocona Boot employees with creating production innovations. The company had its own machine shop, and some of the machinery that helped increase production was designed and made by employees.[52]

When new boot-making technology became available, Enid was quick to install it in her factory. The company had recently purchased four computer stitching machines, sewing machines guided by a computer that automatically did the topstitching on boot tops. That decorative stitching had always been a slow process, especially if the pattern was complex or the design called for more than one color of thread. One operator using a standard sewing machine could topstitch about six pairs of boots a day. Using the new computer stitcher, the same operator could produce twenty-five pairs in the same amount of time. "It's just amazing to watch the girl at the computer," Enid related. "She puts a card in—the design is all programmed—and the machine stitches it perfectly." Sole stitching was another slow process when done by hand, so automated sole stitching machines were another boon to production, as were British high-speed stitching machines. Enid welcomed new technology to speed production, but she still insisted that "boot-making is an art . . . much of the work must be done as it has always been done—by hand. Otherwise it wouldn't be a Nocona boot. At the same time, there have been innovations that my father never dreamed of." In its fiftieth year, Nocona Boot Company produced 306,250 pairs of boots.[53]

CHAPTER 6

Much of the credit for the company's success in the 1970s can be attributed to creative advertising. In 1973, Enid's advertising manager attended the National Finals Rodeo in Oklahoma City, and he used the occasion to contact Ackerman McQueen Advertising, Inc. about creating an ad campaign for the boot company. The agency, the oldest in Oklahoma, had been in the advertising business since 1939 and had a reputation for creative genius. The Oklahoma company took on the Nocona account, and the association proved to be profitable for both companies.[54]

Ackerman McQueen's first campaign for Nocona Boot, created by partner Angus McQueen, was based on the slogan "Let's Rodeo." The foundation of the campaign was a series of twelve ads depicting cowboys dealing with danger as though it were a minor annoyance. The first and most famous of the images featured only the cowboy's Nocona boots, one of which was stepping on the head of a rattlesnake while the cowboy's hand reached down with a large hunting knife. The fate of the snake was obvious. Another ad featured a Gila monster ineffectively biting into the side of the wearer's boot, conveying the message that Nocona Boots are tough and durable. Still another featured the cowboy's boot stepping on the gun-toting hand of a bank robber, preventing his escape with the loot. Not to neglect the women's market, one ad showed a woman's booted legs straddling a snarling timber wolf. The wolf appears ready to attack an unseen provoker. What happens next is up to the viewer's imagination.[55]

All the ads used the same theme, always featuring a beautiful pair of Nocona boots and a dangerous varmint, animal or human, that was destined to meet its demise at the hands of the cowboy, or cowgirl, wearing the boots. The face of the boot-wearer was never shown. "This allows the viewer to inject himself or herself into the drama," a spokesman for the agency explained. "The scene is left ambiguous so the viewer can complete the story on his own." The ads were visually stunning, with backgrounds that featured a Southwest landscape of cactus, sagebrush, and rocky desert terrain. The detail in the ads was painstakingly realistic: the weave of denim fabric, the beadlike scales of the Gila monster, the chipped and dirty fingernails of the would-be bank robber, and the exquisite leather of the Nocona Boots made the ads stand out against the competition. When

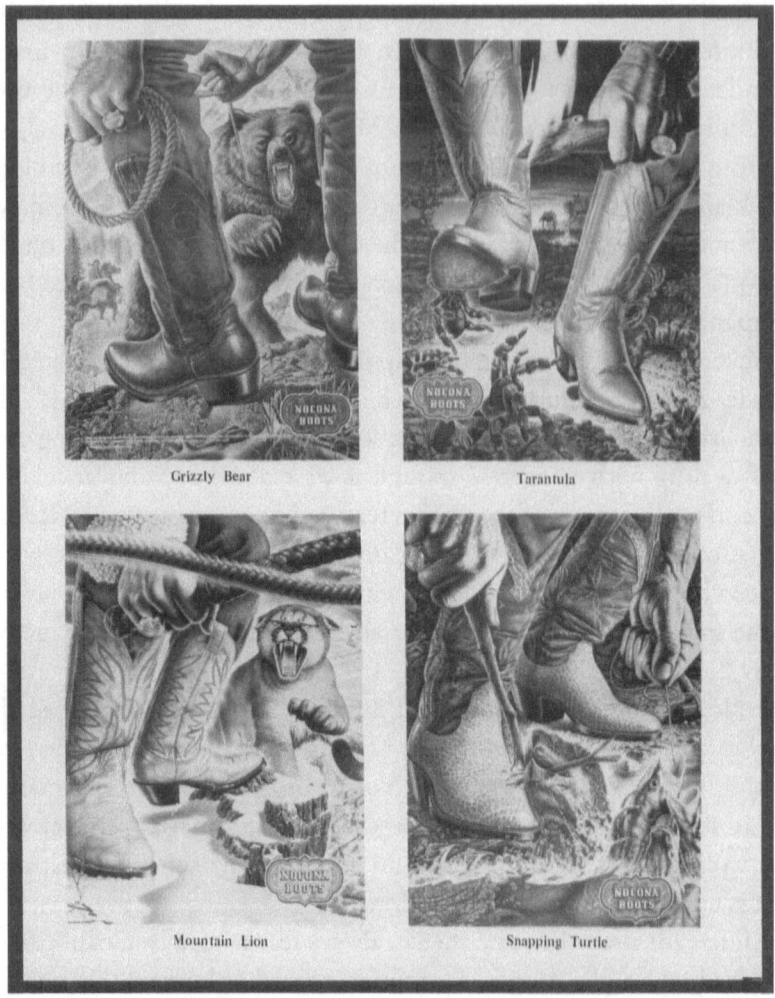

Four examples of posters, now popular with collectors, from Nocona Boot Company's "Let's Rodeo" ad campaign. (Courtesy of the Enid Justin - Nocona Boot Company Collection, University of North Texas Special Collections.)

asked about the Let's Rodeo ads, Enid's sales manager Dale Gordon commented, "Ninety-eight percent of the letters Nocona receives about the ads are favorable. The other two percent complain that the ads promote cruelty to animals."[56]

Ray Ackerman called the ads "a fabulous success." The campaign won more than 150 awards including a National Addy from the American Advertising Federation in 1981, and in 1983 the original painting of the ad featuring a scorpion was selected for inclusion in the Library of Congress exhibit "The American Cowboy." The campaign brought fame to Ackerman McQueen, and it boosted sales for Nocona Boot Company. According to Ackerman, "The two biggest killer boot companies at the time were Justin Boot Company and Tony Lama . . . we brought Nocona right up there with them."[57]

The Oklahoma agency also geared Nocona's advertising campaign to reach a broader market. The boot company's previous advertising media included Western publications, some radio, and "outdoor" that consisted of billboards and signs. That mix had successfully established a strong customer base with the 40-plus age group, typically a rancher or rodeo fan in a rural setting. To ensure Nocona Boot's future growth, Ackerman McQueen intended to reach the younger consumer as well as the more affluent older consumer. They especially wanted to attract the customer who didn't live on a ranch, the city slicker who would soon come to be called an "urban cowboy." The agency chose publications that reached a wider audience, like *Texas Monthly*, and in spring 1976, Nocona became "the first boot company ever" to advertise in the pages of that magazine.[58]

Enid described her new advertising agency as "absolutely out of this world," but when Ackerman McQueen placed ads in *Playboy* magazine, she objected. Ray Ackerman countered her objection with the usual defense of the publication: "Miss Enid, a lot of people read it." With the help of the Oklahoma agency, Nocona Boot took full advantage of the national boot craze. Ackerman described it as a time when "every man in America wanted a pair of western boots, you didn't have to be associated with the west, you could be on Madison Avenue, and you had to have western boots."[59]

The demand for cowboy boots got another boost when the nation celebrated its 200th birthday. Western wear, already trendy across the US, became even more popular on account of the bicentennial. The country was swept by a wave of patriotism and nostalgia for the nation's history. People were "very interested in everything American," Dale Gordon noted. "As a result they kind of discovered western boots." The history of the settlement of the West is uniquely American, and many people seemed drawn to the adventure and romance of that era and to the clothing that represented it. Gordon told *The Nocona News* that in the heavily

Nocona Boot Company's Bicentennial Boot featured a red top with white shooting stars and a white vamp with blue and red inlays on the toe. (Courtesy of the Nocona Boot Company Collection, Tales 'N' Trails Museum, Nocona, Texas.)

populated northeast the demand for boots had "dramatically increased," and western boots were "becoming quite a fashion item in New York City." He added, "We feel we can sell all the quality boots we can manufacture."

Among the new designs produced that year was a special bicentennial boot with the appropriate style number L76. The catalog description was vivid: "The patriotic-theme boot honoring America's 200th birthday makes "Old Glory's" red, white, and blue available for the step of every All-American woman and man." The red boot top was adorned with white shooting stars, while the white vamp ended with red and blue stripes on the toe.[60]

When the country's birthday celebration came to an end, Enid's boot company had tallied another record year, with gross sales of $8 million. Her sprawling factory, with some 375 employees, produced 1,400 pairs of boots a day with help from the Moulton plant. The company's yearly payroll approached $2.5 million. At age 82, Enid was still traveling to the customary rodeos and trade shows, and when she was in town, she was in her office each day conducting business as usual. She was grappling with the same problem that had defied solution for a number of years: "We need more production," she told a local reporter. In fact, plans were already underway for major expansion to be completed in the coming year to meet the increasing demand created by bicentennial enthusiasm for western wear.[61]

Incidentally, on Sunday, July 4, 1976, country & western singer Johnny Cash served as grand marshal of the Bicentennial Parade in Washington, DC. As an estimated 500,000 spectators waved and cheered, he led the parade down Constitution Avenue. Of course, he was wearing cowboy boots.[62]

CHAPTER 7

I AM WILLING TO WORK IN THE SUN WHILE I AM YOUNG SO THAT I CAN WORK IN THE SHADE WHEN I AM OLDER.

—ENID JUSTIN[1]

As the nation's bicentennial year ended, Enid reflected, "We're celebrating the end of a year of tremendous growth and good fortune and looking forward to an even better year in 1977." In a surprising announcement, she added, "Over the past year we've seen strong economic gains in our country which I believe is reflected in Nocona's growth. With our quality boots now being marketed in 50 states and Canada, we felt a challenge to expand our facilities and increase our production capacity. I'm pleased to report that with the completion of the new plant in Vernon, we will double our output."[2]

A satellite plant had been under consideration for some time, but in the last year the location was selected and plans were finalized for the new facility. The enormous Nocona factory could not produce enough boots to meet demand on a timely basis, and further expansion in the company's hometown was not an option because the available workforce was used up. "There weren't enough people there," Joe Justin explained. "We couldn't hire enough people to do what we needed to do." Several towns within a hundred-mile radius of Nocona, including Quanah, Jacksboro, and Mineral Wells, were considered for the satellite plant, but Vernon won out for a number of reasons. The county seat of Wilbarger County was ninety-seven miles west of Nocona on US Highway 287—major highways connected the two locations, facilitating transportation between factories. Equally important, the town had a sizable potential workforce. Vernon was considerably larger than Nocona, with a population approaching 12,000, prompting some Noconans to express concern that Enid might move her entire operation to the larger town. She reassured those citizens, "This will always be here. Nocona is my hometown."[3]

Vernon welcomed the new industry, and city fathers offered incentives to seal the deal. The Vernon Industrial Foundation agreed to finance construction of the factory at a cost of $325,000, and the completed building would then be sold to Nocona Boot Company. Vernon Regional Junior College would provide facilities for training "a new generation of Nocona bootmakers." The training program, created in cooperation with the Texas Industrial Foundation, allowed students to receive credits for boot-making courses offered as part of the college curriculum. To help fund the program, the college received a $16,000 grant from the "Texas First" job creation program, and Nocona Boot's training supervisor David Hellinger directed the program to ensure students were trained to meet Nocona standards. Initially, the Vernon plant would employ forty to sixty people, but when full capacity was reached, the plant could provide work for as many as two hundred.[4]

A cotton field on the northeast edge of Vernon became the site of the new factory. Groundbreaking ceremonies were held on October 13, 1976, and Enid's only disappointment was that she could not use the shovel she had used to break ground for her new factory in 1948. "I did want to use that same shovel," she told a reporter, "but we just couldn't find it." A highlight of the ceremony was the unveiling of the street sign—the new street that fronted the factory would be called "Enid Drive." Construction of the new facility progressed according to schedule, and by summer of the following year the plant had begun manufacturing boots. The official opening, however, was delayed by Mother Nature. "Thunderstorms dumped seventeen inches of rain over Vernon in May, and the plant was literally surrounded by a moat," Enid recounted. "For weeks we were unable to do landscaping work." Summer heat eventually dried the surrounding land, and on the afternoon of September 17, 1977, Enid cut the ribbon, officially opening the new 26,000-square-foot factory.[5]

CHAPTER 7

Enid and nephew Joe Justin at the groundbreaking ceremony for the new Vernon factory to be located on Enid Drive. (Courtesy of the Enid Justin - Nocona Boot Company Collection, University of North Texas Special Collections.)

The opening ceremony actually began in the early morning hours with the start of a small-scale reenactment of the 1939 Pony Express Race. Members of Nocona's Chisholm Trail Riding Club, about forty riders, staged a relay from Nocona to Vernon. The last rider arrived during the afternoon event, made his way through a crowd of about 350 gathered around the speaker's stand, and delivered a hand-tooled leather saddlebag containing a proclamation of the official opening to Vice President Joe Justin. A speech by Texas Commissioner of Agriculture Reagan Brown commended Enid and her company "for the scores of jobs they will create in Vernon." He added, "This new wealth will turn over many times in the area." Live music by two of Enid's favorite local bands and tours of the new plant rounded out the event.[6]

Nocona Boot executives estimated that by year's end Vernon would be producing 150 pairs of boots daily, and total production for all plants—Nocona, Vernon, and Moulton—would increase by 30 percent. But less than a month after the Vernon plant officially opened, the decision was made to close the Moulton factory. In a letter to the *Moulton Eagle* with the headline "Thanks Extended to Local Citizens," Enid wrote, "The main factor in closing this plant is the distance of at least two days from our parent factory in Nocona." She added, "I shall always cherish the memories of visiting your lovely town, and the kindness extended to me on each of those visits." It is doubtful that Enid's kind words soothed the anxiety felt by Moulton citizens on learning they were losing the town's only manufacturer along with its fifty jobs, but they only had to look to the adjacent column to allay their concerns. The announcement, "To All Employees of Nocona Boot Co.," proclaimed, "On January 1, 1978, we will begin operation under new ownership, under the name Moulton Boot Co., Inc. We expect to double our employment force very shortly after operations begin." The announcement was signed by Paul Mosier, former plant manager of Nocona's Moulton division, whose new title was president of the Moulton Boot Company. With the plant's experienced bootmakers, there was a good chance the new company would succeed.[7]

Nocona Boot's decision to pull out of Moulton begs questions. The small factory was running smoothly and producing 400 pairs of boots a day. The Vernon plant was on schedule to produce 150 pairs a day by the end of the year, but it would be months before the new factory ramped up to Moulton's numbers. At a time when Enid's company urgently needed increased production to fill existing orders as well as meet future demand, it is difficult to comprehend why the company would give up Moulton's production because of transportation costs. The decision to limit satellite plants to a 100-mile radius of Nocona indicates that the 365-mile distance caused problems with logistics as well as transportation expense.

CHAPTER 7

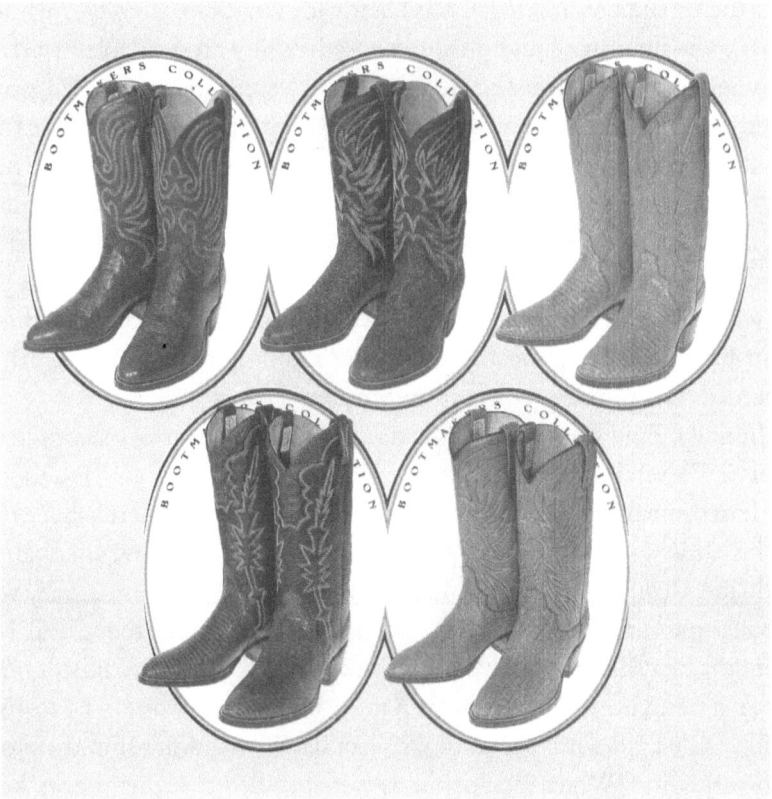

The "Bootmaker's Collection" showcased Nocona boots made in Spain from 1977 to 1981. (Courtesy of the Nocona Boot Company Collection, Tales 'N' Trails Museum, Nocona, Texas.)

But the Moulton plant had been operating successfully for five years, and it is surprising that Nocona Boot did not keep the plant open at least until Vernon's production increased. The answer may lie in a new manufacturing source engaged by Joe Justin.[8]

The new source was Spain. In spring 1977, Nocona Boot announced the "Bootmakers Collection," sixteen styles in a variety of leathers that would retail from $100 to $335. The company newsletter noted that the collection was produced entirely in Spain, "where fine leather work is a tradition passed on from one generation to the next for many centuries." Handcrafting distinguished the Spanish boot, as all critical steps in the production process were done by hand. "Spanish craftsmen teach their sons the art of boot-making just as Daddy Joe taught me," Enid explained. "This is the first time hand finishing and detailing are available in a large volume of boots." She added that the boots were made to the company's traditional standards and were constructed on Nocona lasts to assure "the famous Nocona fit." An ad campaign was created specifically for the new collection with the rugged New Mexico landscape serving as background for a pair of Bootmakers boots. According to the company newsletter, producing boots in Spain was "one more effort by Nocona to meet the growing demand for top-quality boots." The cost of the Spanish boots must have been the enticement, because shipping from Spain certainly exceeded transportation costs from Moulton, Texas.[9]

Initially, Enid seemed enthusiastic about the Spanish boots, but in an interview several years later, she told a different story. "I tell you, Joe almost got into some pretty serious trouble with a couple of Spaniards that came up here. He was going to have them make Nocona Boots over in Spain. I said, 'Joe, that is going to be a mistake.' Joe replied, 'Oh, Auntie, they will produce more, and they are good craftsmen.'" Enid agreed to the deal, but when the first shipment arrived, it was evident that the boots did not meet Nocona standards. "The first bunch that came over we wouldn't dare use," Enid recalled. "We put them in our seconds. We wouldn't ship them out as first quality." When the Spaniards were notified that their boots were unacceptable, they hired New York attorneys and threatened a lawsuit. Joe and production manager Sam Campbell met with those attorneys at the Dallas–Fort Worth airport hotel. No record of that meeting has been found, but the parties must have resolved the quality issues as the "Bootmaker's Collection" remained in the catalog for four more seasons. Although the collaboration had its problems, Nocona Boot "made a little money" on the deal, according to credit manager Chester Taylor. Enid was 83 years old when Joe made his deal with Spanish bootmakers; she voiced her reluctance but ultimately capitulated. She seemed to be making a conscious effort to turn over the reins to Joe and allow him to make critical decisions, but it is safe to say that Enid would not have initiated the Spanish deal.[10]

Despite the shaky Spanish collaboration, Nocona Boot Company was headed for another record year in 1978, with sales estimated to reach $15 million. The combined Nocona and Vernon factories were turning out

CHAPTER 7

1,400 pairs of boots a day. Those boots were produced by 450 employees whose annual payroll totaled $3 million, and the company was still looking for more workers. In March, *The Nocona News* reported that the original factory could use thirty to forty more employees. The company was currently operating one shift, but sales manager Dale Gordon noted, "We have the sales potential to run two shifts." The problem, he explained, was that the town simply did not have a sufficient labor force. The only solution was to attract workers from other areas and, according to Gordon, "the community must become more attractive to outsiders if the boot company continues to grow and run another shift." The shortage of local labor would soon necessitate another remote expansion similar to the Vernon facility.[11]

Nocona's Vernon plant was surpassing expectations. "Our new factory production is increasing rapidly," production manager Sam Campbell reported. "In January we were making approximately 100 pairs of boots a day; now we're up to 360 and the quality is excellent." The factory produced finished boots as well as stitched tops. The stitching department worked around the clock with three shifts operating twenty-four Automatic Control Stitchers, providing boot tops for both Nocona and Vernon. The plant's workforce had grown from forty employees to 113 in its nine months of operation. Campbell attributed Vernon's early success to its new plant manager, Tommy Roberts, who had twenty-three years' experience in the boot and shoe industry. He came to Vernon from rival Justin Boot Company, where he spent six years as plant manager and another six years as national sales manager.[12]

Always looking to expand its workforce, Nocona Boot Company had a remarkable history of hiring minorities. If a person could do the job, gender and ethnicity were irrelevant. Women had been an important presence on the factory floor since World War II, and as the town's Hispanic population grew, they, too, were employed. To help with the language barrier, Joe arranged for an instructor from Midwestern State University in Wichita Falls to come to Nocona to teach Spanish to plant supervisors. There were no Black people living in Nocona, but the boot company hired Black workers at the satellite plant in Vernon. In an interview in 1981, Enid was asked if she ever had any complaints filed with the Equal Employment Opportunity Commission, a federal agency that enforces laws against workplace discrimination. She replied emphatically, "We haven't had any," and she added, "We have some Mexicans working out there now." She welcomed anyone who was willing to learn a skill and work hard to produce Nocona Boots.[13]

As production increased at the Nocona factory, storage space again became inadequate. In March 1978, the company completed construction of another warehouse to store boots awaiting shipment to customers. According to Sam Campbell, the 1,600-square-foot building "will give us a facility for storing about 100,000 boots. This will give Nocona about 120,000 square feet of manufacturing and warehouse space." Shipping foreman Carroll Fuller explained that boots were shelved by style number and size, which "saves time in pulling inventory and helps get more shipments out each day." Around 1,300 pairs of boots were shipped out of the warehouse daily to dealers and customers across the nation and beyond. There seemed to be no catching up with the demand for cowboy boots as the western wear craze remained strong.[14]

The *Washington Post* reported on the phenomenon in February 1979 with an article that began, "It's hardly what you would call a stampede, but the cowboy look is leaving its mark on Washington, as cowboy boots, ten-gallon hats, yoked shirts and hand-tooled belts are finding a home on a range of customers." The *Post* went on to explain how the fad originated:

> Westernwear, particularly jeans and flannel shirts, became widely accepted in the 1960s by a generation seeking inexpensive, non-establishment clothes. It was not long until jeans shops picked up the western theme and filled out their stock with other western accessories.... But nationwide, the fastest-moving fashion in western chic is the cowboy boot—with $200 million in business this year alone. And Washington is no exception to the national trend. Cowboy boot sales are really booming in New York, where Billy Martin, the former manager of the New York Yankees, opened a westernwear shop that was proving so successful that he was considering selling franchises.

What's the appeal? Most wearers list comfort and the long-wearing quality of cowboy boots. But White House speechwriter Hendrik Hertzberg asserted that he wore boots because they made him feel close to being a movie star.[15]

CHAPTER 7

Enid agreed that the boot business was booming. "Not only were the cowboys buying and wearing them, folks on Fifth Avenue in New York were wearing them too," she marveled. "Boots were being worn everywhere, even with tuxedos. Boots were the 'in-thing.'" Some entrepreneurial Texans took advantage of the boot craze on the East Coast. Judi Buie, a fashion photographer in New York City who grew up in Itasca, began wearing cowboy boots with skirts in the late 1970s. When people began asking her to bring them boots from Texas so they could imitate her style, she decided to open a boot store—she named it "Texas." Located on Manhattan's East Side, the shop specialized in fancy boots and was frequented by an astounding mix of clientele. According to boot historians Sharon Delano and David Rieff, "Buie's intuition and taste shaped a look," and the fashionable Texan's influence was instrumental in promoting the trend for cowboy boots on the East Coast.[16]

Dallasites Al Martinez and Robin Steakley also took advantage of the boot craze in New York City. The two got the idea to "open a real Texas boot store" when New York friends visited Dallas to buy western boots they could not find in the Big Apple. After researching the market with encouraging results, the men got financing from a Texas bank, bought 500 pairs of boots, and moved to New York City. They opened "To Boot" on West 72nd Street in early 1979 and stocked the store with only Texas-made boots, including Noconas, along with some belts, hats, and western jewelry. They found they could barely keep the shelves stocked—on a good Saturday they sold one hundred pairs of boots. When a Nocona Boot salesman asked how many Nocona Boots they had sold since opening the store, Steakley replied, "I'm not sure. If you can find out how many you've sent us, that's how many we've sold."[17]

The decade of the '70s was a period of phenomenal growth for Nocona Boot Company. "We expanded to new markets on the East and West Coasts where only a few short years ago the sale of a pair of boots was a novelty," Enid remarked. "Over the past ten years, the entire Western wear market, particularly boots, has experienced a level of growth that even the most optimistic among us wouldn't have believed possible." The August 1979 issue of *GQ* (*Gentlemen's Quarterly*), a leading menswear magazine with a circulation of 330,000, was dedicated to "the Western look and its impact in the urban areas." The cover featured a handsome cowboy holding a Nocona Boot.[18]

With the growing demand for boots, Enid was quick to recognize a potential pitfall for boot manufacturers: the temptation to increase production by sacrificing quality. A trade publication noted that "some manufacturers in an attempt to meet demand are adopting production methods which sacrifice quality. It could be the proverbial case of curing the disease by killing the calf." Enid addressed the "quantity versus quality" issue in a newsletter to her dealers: "It concerns me that many bootmakers are losing sight of the real reason more and more people are buying cowboy boots. Their quality." She added, "Consumers, especially young consumers between the ages of 16 and 28, are nostalgic—they are looking to the traditions of the Old West. . . . The most important of those traditions is rugged dependability." Since founding her company, Enid had focused primarily on producing a quality boot, one that met Daddy Joe's standards. Throughout her fifty-plus years in business, she had never wavered from that commitment, and she was not about to lower her standards now. "When our customers receive a boot," she asserted, "we want to be sure that it is indeed a Nocona Boot, not just a cowboy boot with a Nocona label." She reassured dealers that Nocona plants were operating at full capacity, and every effort was being made to supply dealers with the boots they needed while maintaining the quality they were known for.[19]

In the late 1970s, Nocona Boot's popular advertising campaign, "Let's Rodeo," continued to entice customers to the brand. In addition to print ads in newspapers, magazines, and rodeo programs, the company announced that its award-winning radio spots would be aired during broadcasts of the Grand Ole Opry. The newsletter proudly proclaimed, "They've both been around for 50 years, The Nocona Boot Company and the Grand Old Opry, and in that time both have become *Great American Traditions*." Nocona Boot's radio spots would reach the thirty million listeners from coast to coast who tuned in to the Opry on Saturday night for "the best in country and western entertainment." In a similar vein but geared to a younger market, progressive country musician Jerry Jeff Walker became the face of "Let's Rodeo" ads in magazines across the country. "We believe young adults identify with Jerry Jeff Walker," Enid told her dealers. "He's a wanderer, a real independent guy who enjoys the rough and tumble life, and this makes him a natural attraction to the

CHAPTER 7

Country & western musician Jerry Jeff Walker, featured in a Nocona Boot ad campaign, tours the factory with Enid. (Courtesy of the Nocona Boot Company Collection, Tales 'N' Trails Museum, Nocona, Texas.)

younger set." Walker visited the Nocona factory, and Enid gave him a personal tour as she explained all the steps involved in making a boot.

Ads featuring Walker promoted round-toed, light-colored styles that were favored by young consumers. It is not surprising that Nocona Boot's competition was going after the youthful market—Justin Boot Company hired country musician Rusty Wier "to sell cowboy boots to youngsters who never even saw a horse, much less rode one." Wier promoted a Justin line called "The New Breed," designed specifically for young buyers.[20]

Enid used celebrities to advertise her boots, but over the years she had attained a celebrity status of her own. The "world's only lady cowboy bootmaker" was asked frequently to be a guest speaker, and she accepted those invitations whenever possible. Her first love was making boots, but if she had needed a second career, she could have been a motivational speaker. Throughout her years in business, she tried to inspire people to be the best they could be—her "Creed for Success" (see p. 203), written early in her business career, is a perfect example of her commitment to inspire others. Enid's encouragement had typically been gender-neutral, as she always valued men and women equally. She grew up in a home where sons and daughters were given the same opportunities, and that lesson of "equality" endured throughout her life. But in the late 1970s as the occasion presented itself, she began to take an active role in encouraging women as they sought equal opportunities with men.

What became known as "second-wave feminism" began in the early 1960s and lasted for roughly two decades. The aim of the new movement was to advance equality for women beyond the gains achieved by first-wave feminists whose activism began over a century earlier with the Seneca Falls Convention, the first women's rights convention, held in New York in 1848. That early movement focused primarily on suffrage and eliminating legal obstacles to gender equality, such as denying women ownership of wages, money, and property, and lack of access to education and professional careers. With the passage of the Nineteenth Amendment in 1920, women won the right to vote, and that victory is generally considered to be the end of first-wave feminism.[21]

The movement was sparked again in 1963 by Betty Friedan's bestselling book *The Feminine Mystique*. The author objected to mainstream media's portrayal of women as homemakers, arguing that the image limited women's possibilities and wasted their talent and potential. That same year, John F. Kennedy's Presidential Commission on the Status of Women, chaired by Eleanor Roosevelt, released its report on gender inequality, and freelance journalist Gloria Steinem became an influential figure in the movement after her undercover work as a "Playboy Bunny" led to publication of an article alleging that the Playboy Club was exploiting its waitresses. Second-wave feminism grew to encompass a wide range of issues including legal inequalities, workplace issues, sexuality, and reproductive rights. The National Organization for Women, founded in 1966, advocated for a "fully equal partnership of the sexes" and campaigned for an Equal Rights Amendment to be added to the US Constitution.[22]

In Texas, the women's movement boasted some unique accomplishments. The state's Equal Legal Rights Amendment, originally proposed in the 1950s, was approved by voters in November 1972 by a margin of 4 to 1. The amendment granted men and women equal legal rights and resulted in the passage of a number of state laws that halted discriminatory

CHAPTER 7

practices. That same year, six women were elected to the legislature, more than had ever been seated at any one time. Liz Carpenter, former press secretary for President Lyndon Johnson, was instrumental in the 1971 founding of the Texas Women's Political Caucus, an organization that promoted passage of the national Equal Rights Amendment. In a special session in March 1972, the Texas Legislature ratified the national amendment. The Texas ERA withstood a heated rescission effort, and ultimately Texas remained the only Southern state to ratify and stand by the national amendment.[23]

The national ERA failed to be ratified by the necessary thirty-eight states, but the women's movement accomplished some notable goals through a combination of legislation and legal decisions, including the Equal Pay Act of 1963 and *Roe v. Wade* in 1973, but its greatest success is generally considered to be the changing of social attitudes toward women. In 1975, *Time* magazine gave its "Man of the Year" award to "American women." The article proclaimed, "Across the broad range of American life, from suburban tract houses to state legislatures, from church pulpits to Army barracks, women's lives are profoundly changing." The article added that an immense variety of women were "altering their lives, entering new fields, and functioning with a new sense of identity, integrity and confidence."[24]

The modern women's movement in Texas had some high-profile leaders, like State Senator Barbara Jordan who went on to serve in the US House of Representatives, State Representative Frances "Sissy" Farenthold who made a bid for governor in 1972, and Lila Cockrell of San Antonio who was the first woman elected mayor of one of Texas's largest cities. But there were many women who were working in fields that had traditionally been the purview of men who were not actively engaged in the equal rights movement. The large majority of those women were broadening women's opportunities while going about their daily lives. Enid was one of those women. She did not start a boot company because she was a woman but rather in spite of the fact that she was a woman. Through her many years in business, she set an example for women entrepreneurs who came after her, and when asked by a reporter if she was a "women's libber," she answered, "I was a libber before the word and the definition were even invented." She credited that "liberation" to "a bad case of German independence" she inherited from Daddy Joe.[25]

THE LADY MAKES BOOTS

Although Enid did not take a leadership role in the feminist movement, she was always willing to speak at women's conferences where she believed she could benefit women by telling her own story. In November 1976, the *Denton Record Chronicle* reported that Enid "visited the campus of Texas Woman's University this week and shared a little of her wisdom with young women interested in business careers." In telling her story, Enid always credited her father with being the prime motivating force in her decision to found a boot company, and she told of the difficulties she had overcome in her early years in business. "Stick with it," she advised the students. "My father always said it was worry, not work, that killed people." In March 1977, Enid was keynote speaker at a secretaries seminar in Corsicana, Texas, and a month later she was a principal speaker at the second annual "Symposium on Women" at the University of Science & Arts of Oklahoma in Chickasha. Once again she related the struggle she faced in establishing Nocona Boot Company. "I guess it was during these times that my attitude about life really inspired me to try harder." She told attendees, "I have always looked for the silver linings in the clouds that have come my way."[26]

The feminist movement was certainly a motivating factor in the establishment of the National Cowgirl Hall of Fame and Western Heritage Center in Hereford, Texas. The Panhandle town launched the center in 1974 with the goal of honoring women who contributed significantly to the culture of the American West. "There's a lot to be said about the woman's role," Margaret Formby, project president, told reporters, "not only as a cowgirl, but as a pioneer woman, conquering the untamed land." The center was housed in the basement of the Deaf Smith County Library until a permanent museum could be constructed on land donated by the city. Each year new inductees were announced at Hereford's popular All-Girl Rodeo, and in 1978 Enid received that honor. The newspaper announcement described the lady bootmaker as "a legend in her time" and added that "no one has done as much for the boot industry as Enid Justin." She was presented with a plaque that she proudly displayed in the boot company entry, and her portrait, painted by Albuquerque artist Leona M. Turner, graced the cover of *Sidesaddle*, the Hall of Fame's magazine.[27]

Another famous Texan became the face of Nocona Boots in spring 1979. Football star Earl Campbell, nicknamed the "Tyler Rose" because

CHAPTER 7

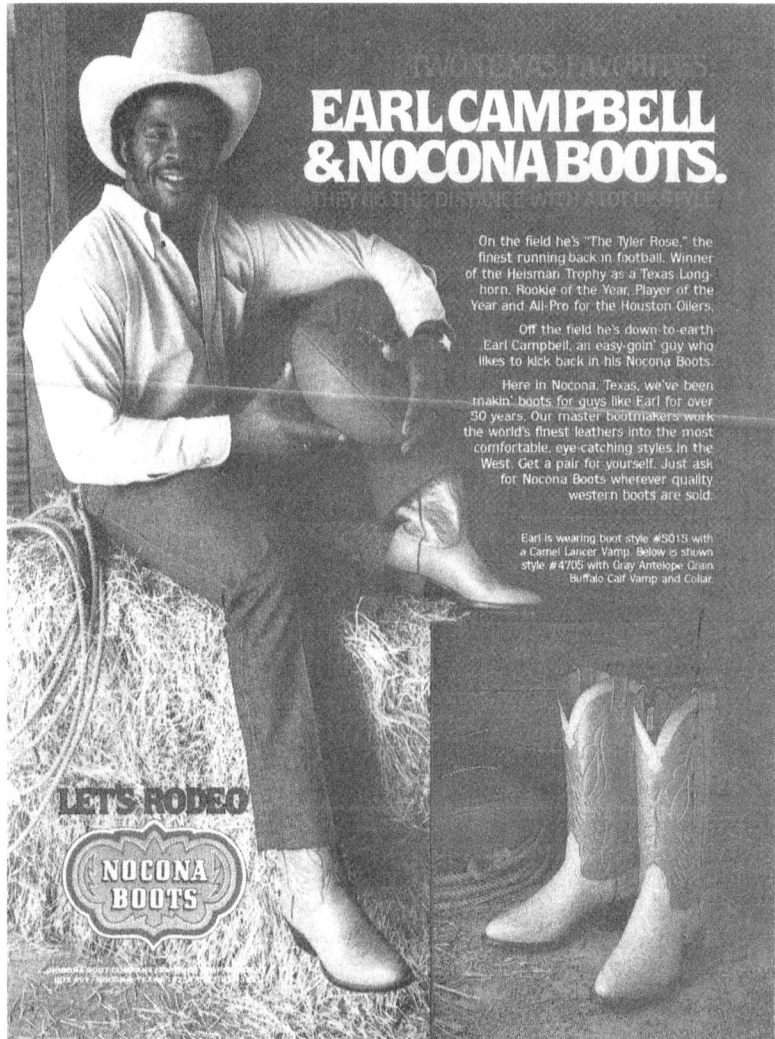

Football superstar Earl Campbell advertises Nocona Boots. (Courtesy of the Nocona Boot Company Collection, Tales 'N' Trails Museum, Nocona, Texas.)

his East Texas hometown was known as the Rose Capital of America, agreed to represent Nocona Boot Company in sales promotion and advertising during 1979 and 1980. A Heisman Trophy winner from the University of Texas, Campbell moved on to the Houston Oilers where he was named NFL Rookie of the Year in 1978. Enid held a "signing ceremony" for Campbell at Fincher's Western Wear Store in Fort Worth to publicize his joining the advertising team. Several years later she told a reporter about their meeting. Earl asked, "Miss Enid, may I kiss you on the cheek?" and she gave her permission. When the signing event concluded, he kissed her on the other cheek and remarked, "That's such a lovely fragrance." The perfume was Shalimar, and Enid had worn it for years. She sent a check to her salesman in Tyler asking him to buy the perfume and send it to Earl's mother. "She wrote the sweetest letter I ever read in my life," Enid recalled. "And he [Earl] had a beautiful wedding out in the rose garden. They invited me. She invited me to be a guest in her home." Enid truly cared about people, and that caring was often returned in kind.[28]

Campbell was the second National Football League star to appear in Nocona ads. The first was Tony Franklin, ironically a barefoot kicker for the Philadelphia Eagles. Born in Big Spring, Texas, Franklin played college football at Texas A&M, where he was awarded All-American honors three years in a row. Franklin was drafted by the Eagles in 1979, and when the kicker was on the sideline, he wore a specially designed Nocona Boot to keep his foot warm between kicks. Ads featuring Franklin appeared in *Texas Monthly*, *Professional Athlete*, and Eagles' football programs. With the expanding customer base, Nocona advertising was reaching out to new segments of the market. A decade earlier, the only sports fans courted by the boot industry were rodeo fans.[29]

As the boot market continued to grow, Enid's company was constantly striving to create new styles to keep pace with the demand for variety, and a new style often involved a new leather. Leather was Nocona Boot's biggest and most important investment, and each week tanneries shipped 75,000 to 100,000 square feet of leather to the Nocona factory for boot tops and vamps. (One pair of boots required 13 1/2 square feet of leather, not counting soles and heels.) The job of leather buyer, held by Berry Ritchie since 1976, was a complicated one. The leather market was always changing, and Ritchie had to know when and how much to buy while considering price and determining availability. "I try to keep a five weeks' supply on hand at all times," Ritchie explained, "and a seven weeks' supply on order." Some 200 different leathers were gathered from a variety of tanneries, both domestic and foreign, and in a single year, Ritchie was responsible for the purchase of around 4,000,000 square feet

CHAPTER 7

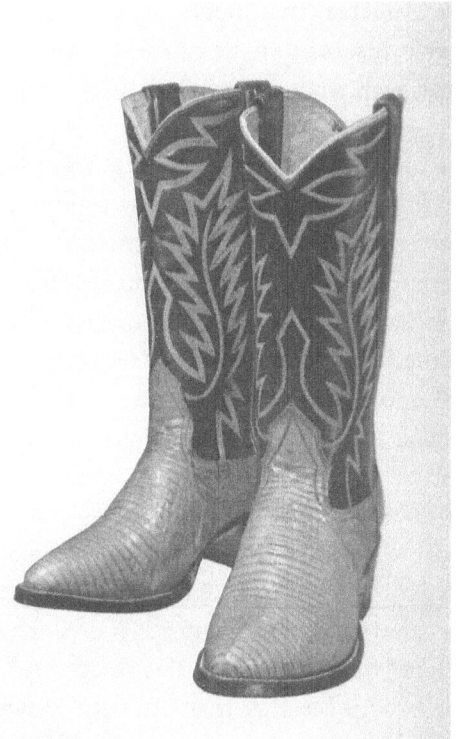

Late 1970s Nocona boot with a lizard vamp. (Courtesy of the Nocona Boot Company Collection, Tales 'N' Trails Museum, Nocona, Texas.)

of leather—enough to carpet more than 222 football fields.[30]

Exotic leathers continued to grow in popularity—in 1977, popular skins included sea turtle from Mexico and lizard, anteater, and snake from South America. "Some leathers, such as shark and elephant, are hard to get now," Ritchie explained, "while ostrich, raised on special farms in South Africa, is plentiful." But the market was always changing, and a year later, ostrich was difficult to find because a demand for plumes, bringing $300 a pound, made it more profitable for ostrich ranchers to pluck their herds than to turn them into hides. The fluctuating availability of exotic leathers prompted Nocona Boot salesman Lloyd Quigley to complain, "Just let something get scarce, and that's what everybody wants." Elephant hide could only be obtained from a "legal kill," defined as an animal that had died of natural causes or had to be euthanized for humane reasons, and anteater was no longer obtainable because of customs restrictions. When exotic skins were available, the import process was another challenge. Skins coming from overseas had to be cleared through customs according to regulations, and each shipment was required to have certification of point of origin.[31]

Always on the lookout for new leathers, Ritchie frequently traveled to shows and markets, but leather also came to him: salesmen, about a dozen a week, brought their samples directly to the factory. New leathers under consideration in 1978 included water buffalo from India, kudu and paradise snake from Africa, and a new species of shark from Mexico. "If it looks like something we might be interested in," Ritchie explained, "we make a pair of boots from a sample skin." Other skins that were used included rattlesnake, penguin, boa constrictor, kangaroo, caribou, and even walrus. Despite the popularity of exotics, however, they comprised only 10 percent of Nocona's leather volume. Cowhide, arriving from tanners as bundles of uncut hides, made up 90 percent of leather used for Nocona Boots. Ritchie spent much of his workday in the "leather room" where employees carefully checked shipments of skins for quality, color, and thickness before "weighing out" leather to cutters.[32]

Bull Hide was a rugged leather that had been growing in popularity for several years. The name is misleading, as Bull Hide is made by a process that brings out the natural grain texture of leather, regardless of the sex of the bovine. During tanning, the hide is thoroughly wetted then allowed to dry naturally. The resultant shrinkage brings out the natural grain pattern that comes from fat wrinkles, stretch marks, and the flexing of the hide on the animal. When the process is complete, each hide has a distinctive and individual pattern. The graining process had the additional advantage of allowing the leather to retain both softness and durability. Most grained leathers were produced by printing or embossing the hides, a process that involved soaking the leather, stretching it, and running it through a press. The method resulted in an artificially grained leather that was stiff and rigid with reduced strength. Bull Hide was obviously a superior leather, but the drawback to the natural graining process was the cost—not only was it a time-consuming process, but the resultant shrinkage reduced the tanner's yield. Domestic tanners quit producing Bull Hide because of its cost, and for years the product had to be obtained from foreign tanneries.[33]

CHAPTER 7

In fall 1976, Enid announced that her company had secured a domestic source for the popular leather. "In the past few years, we've seen an increased demand for Bull Hide boots," she stated. "Because of this interest, we felt it was necessary to make special arrangements for a reliable source for this attractive yet durable leather. Now with that source secure, we are able to produce these boots in the quantity their popularity demands." The fall catalog introduced five boot styles made from Bull Hide, and when those garnered "overwhelming response from dealers and customers," three additional styles were added in the 1977 catalog. Probably for competitive reasons, Enid did not reveal which tannery she had a "special arrangement" with. The rugged beauty of Bull Hide continued to attract customers and became a staple in the Nocona Boot catalog. Another leather, touted as "a new breed" in Nocona ads, was horsehide. Unlike Bull Hide, horsehide was just what its name implied.[34]

The economy remained strong in the late '70s, and consumer spending was on the rise. Nocona Boot Company's newsletter informed dealers that "people are spending more money on all types of retail items including western clothes." Dealers were encouraged to "stock up," as there seemed to be no end to the boot craze. "We had more business than we ever dreamed we would," Enid told an interviewer, but then an unexpected event in the form of a major motion picture propelled boot sales to new heights.[35]

In summer 1980, Paramount Pictures released *Urban Cowboy*, a modern American Western about the relationship between a young oil field worker named Bud, played by John Travolta, and a girl named Sissy (actress Debra Winger). The two met at Gilley's, a "honky-tonk" on the outskirts of Houston where patrons in western duds danced the night away to the latest country & western hits. A box office success, the film greatly increased the popularity of western wear, and people who had never worn boots were buying them for the first time. An Associated Press article reported on the phenomenon: "On the dance floors across the United States, in Europe and wherever else disco flourishes, cowboy boots are pounding out the frantic rhythm of the current craze." The article quoted Lloyd Quigley, a salesman for Nocona Boot Company for twenty years, who noted that with the "urban cowboy" fad, "orders have come in so rapidly and are stacked so high that the company is as much as two years behind in filling some of them." Enid supplied a remarkable statistic: "Sales were up 700 percent in Manhattan alone," a fact she attributed to the movie's influence. Nationally, western boots had become a $550 million industry.[36]

Nocona Boot took full advantage of the movie's popularity by sponsoring the "Great American Honky Tonk Queen Contest" at Gilley's soon after the movie's release. The contest was held in conjunction with a concert tour featuring country music stars Michael Martin Murphey and Hank Thompson. Ten contestants vied for the title of Honky Tonk Queen, and the winner received a $1,000 check and a pair of Nocona Boots. Murphey and Thompson were also given boots, prompting Thompson to tell the crowd that "Noconas are the best boots in the world." Joe Justin and sales manager Dale Gordon, both insisting "it was work," attended the event to present the boots. The company newsletter quipped, "Joe said he attended to make sure the barbeque dinner and the presentation of boots to Murphey, Thompson, and the queen were done right. Dale said he went to help Joe." The promotion was successful in drawing publicity for the Nocona brand.[37]

Another modern-day Western, the television series *Dallas*, did its part to promote the sale of cowboy boots. Set on the Ewing family's Southfork Ranch on the outskirts of Dallas, the story revolved around oil, cattle, and a longtime rivalry between the Ewing and Barnes families. Cowboy hats and boots were typical attire for the show's male characters, the most prominent being the "full of swagger" J. R. Ewing. The series first aired in 1978, and by 1980 when the season ended with the "Who Shot J. R." cliffhanger, the popular show reportedly set viewing records domestically and globally. Jim Schutze, a columnist for the *Dallas Times Herald*, recalled, "Dallas hated *Dallas* at first. It was everything that Dallas felt that it was not. The boots, the hats, the ranching, the oil. That was all Houston." It was not long before Dallasites changed their attitudes. The society photographer for the *Herald* called Schutze one night from the Crystal Charity Ball and said, "Schutze, you're not gonna believe it. People are showing up in cowboy boots. They are dressing like they're on the show."[38]

By the next year, the combined facilities of Nocona Boot Company were producing 1,700 pairs of boots a day, and the company grossed over $27 million, a significant increase over the previous year's $19.5 million.

CHAPTER 7

The combined plants had 532 employees—the Vernon factory had grown from its original 40 employees in 1977 to 150 in 1981. Between 1969 and 1979, the company increased production by 180 percent, but even at that level, expansion again became essential, and this time the company looked to the east. In a fitting coincidence, they chose the town where Daddy Joe had worked as a cobbler when he first arrived in Texas just over 100 years earlier. An existing building in Gainesville became the second Nocona Boot satellite location. The town, slightly larger than Vernon, was only thirty-eight miles east of Nocona on US Hwy 82, and because Nocona Boot leased the building, the new facility was less costly than the Vernon plant. In addition to minimal remodeling, all that was required to make it operational was to install the machinery and hire and train employees. The Gainesville factory began operation in September 1981 and was expected to produce 400 to 600 pairs a day by early 1982. With the addition of the third plant, Joe noted, "That pretty well saturated our need and our demand for production."[39]

As the 1980s began, Enid thanked her dealers and customers for making "the decade of the 70s the best one yet for Nocona Boot Company." She added, "It's an exciting industry, constantly changing and improving, building upon its traditions and strength. I'm glad to be a part of it." She was 86 years old, and she had been at the helm of Nocona Boot Company for fifty-five years. Her business could not have been better, but in her memoir she wrote, "My health wasn't anything to brag about." After a stroke in 1975, she recovered reasonably well and returned to work, but in early 1980 a second stroke left her partially paralyzed. She talked about her physical condition with the same courage that had gotten her through other difficulties in her life: "I'd had a stroke that left me paralyzed on my left side and pretty much tied to a big easy chair at home. But I tried to keep up with the business by phone and by visiting the factory when I could. I'd go over and tour the plant in my wheelchair . . . it was so good to visit with the employees."[40]

Despite her physical impairment, Enid continued as president of the company. She had very capable managers and production supervisors, all under Joe's leadership, and the company continued to perform well. Enid gave much of the credit for Nocona Boot's ongoing success to her employees, many of whom had been with her for years. "I think the old hands are the strength of Nocona because they are continually teaching new people how to do the job," she stated. "I have seen lots of employees come and go, but the main crew—like me—has been here a long time." Winstead O. Cooper, a buyer, had joined the company in 1934, and production supervisor Gene Keller had been reporting to the factory every workday for 37 years. "In the cutting room we have a man that's been here 47 years," Enid added, "and there's an employee in fitting that's been here 38 years." And there were others. Those longtime employees provided stability that helped to keep the company on an even keel when its president was no longer there on a daily basis.[41]

The future of Nocona Boot Company was weighing heavily on Enid's mind, and a collision of events, or perceptions of them, led her to make some unexpected decisions. In June 1980, she contacted Thomas Florsheim, president of Weyenberg Shoe Manufacturing Company in Milwaukee, Wisconsin. She told him she was considering selling the boot company and asked him to come talk with her if he was interested. She had known Florsheim for some time—he had visited her in Nocona several years earlier, possibly with the intent of acquiring her company. She decided to contact Florsheim that June because his company manufactured a quality product, and, as always, quality was her number one requirement for Nocona Boots. Weyenberg Shoe Company produced a broad line of men's dress shoes along with some work shoes and boots. Enid did not discuss her sudden decision to sell or her overture to Florsheim with anyone in the company. She was accustomed to making decisions on her own, noting, "I'm president and chairman of the board and own the stock."[42]

Obviously interested in hearing Enid's proposition, Florsheim arrived in Nocona on June 23. He met with Enid at her home, and during their meeting, she called Chester Taylor, her credit manager, to handle "some specific questions" that she could not answer. Enid offered the Wisconsin manufacturer her controlling interest, 153 shares, for $25,000 a share. When their meeting concluded, she gave Florsheim a personal tour of the factory, and as a "courtesy," sent him to Joe's office to meet her vice president. Florsheim left Nocona with the promise to get back in touch with Enid when he returned from an upcoming trip. As the old saying goes, "the cat was out of the bag," and word quickly spread that the company was for sale. Enid remarked, "Of course, Joe was upset about it." A justifiable reaction considering the work contract and "irrevocable" trust signed by Enid in 1974 that gave Joe controlling interest in the company upon her death.[43]

Enid's decision to negate her agreement with Joe and sell her company to someone else came about because she "was very unhappy with some of the things that had been going on in the management of the company." Her grievances were all related to Joe. He was not spending enough time at the company, and when she needed him, he was not there. He was not doing what she asked and was not keeping her informed. She was especially unhappy about the deal to manufacture boots in Spain. Enid also worried that Joe was spending too much money—he had borrowed $400,000 from a Fort Worth bank to purchase leather and equipment, and he had purchased a new station wagon against her wishes. Joe recalled, "She had gotten off of me again. I mean she hated my guts, she really did, and we had some hard words back and forth." Enid's animosity toward Joe had apparently led her to reach out to Florsheim.[44]

To further complicate the story, on the day before Florsheim visited Nocona, Enid called her nephew John Jr., president of Justin Industries in Fort Worth, and told him she was "thinking about selling her company." John Jr. replied, "Well, if you're interested in doing something with the company, Auntie, I'd be glad to talk to you." Enid explained that she was meeting with Florsheim the next day, and they agreed to talk again after that meeting. When John Jr. called the following afternoon, Enid was upset. She had heard a rumor that Joe told Florsheim that she was not mentally competent to run her business. That rumor may have cemented her decision to break her contract with Joe, and she asked John Jr. to recommend an attorney who might be able to help her undo the contractual agreement with her other nephew. John Jr. agreed to ask his attorney, Dee Kelly, to recommend "somebody that would handle a case like this." It appears that Enid had dismissed the idea of selling to Florsheim at that point and was considering a merger with Justin Industries. The idea to contact John Jr. had come to her in the middle of the night when she could not sleep, and she "thought maybe that would be an avenue to take." The advantage of Justin over Florsheim was obvious—a merger with John Jr.

would keep her company in the family with the Justin name, and that aspect had always been important to her.[45]

On Dee Kelly's recommendation, Enid contacted Fort Worth attorney William Brown to help her dismantle the agreement with Joe. It did not take long for Brown to find an escape clause in the "irrevocable" contract—item 1b of the "Agreement of Employment" stated that the "employee shall manage the company affairs under the supervision of the president . . ." According to Enid, Joe had violated that clause, giving her grounds to terminate his employment and revoke the trust, and on July 10 she notified her nephew of his termination by certified mail. On the same day, she signed an agreement with John Jr. granting Justin Industries a one-year option to buy her controlling interest—153 shares she owned plus 68 shares she held in trust for her nieces and their children.[46]

In discussing the merger (Enid preferred "transfer of stock"), John Jr. assured his aunt that the factory would remain in Nocona and operate much as it had been doing, with the same personnel; he did not intend to bring new management from Fort Worth. "I told her I would like for her to remain as chairman of the board," he recalled. "She seemed very pleased with that." The two talked at length about the details of the acquisition, and John Jr. agreed to most of her requests regarding the future operation of Nocona Boot Company. The option agreement was especially attractive to Enid because the transfer of stock was a tax-free transaction. The price of that stock would be negotiated, based on market value, at the time the option was initiated. John Jr. stated, "She seemed to think that it was a very good deal, as did I."[47]

The good deal for John Jr. was a bad one for Joe. When Enid fired Joe, she broke the good faith agreement the two had signed six years earlier when she "realized she needed help running the factory." Joe had since sold his steel company in Wichita Falls to devote his full attention to Nocona Boot Company. He may have done things that angered his aunt—the two had a contentious history—but evidence indicates he was a good general manager. Under Joe's direction, company sales grew from $8 million to $20 million, and only six months earlier, Enid had authorized both a raise in salary and a bonus for her nephew. Her recent dissatisfaction with Joe seemed to stem from the fact that she was no longer able to observe the day-to-day operation of her factory, and she felt she had lost control.

Despite being confined to a wheelchair, she tried to visit the plant twice a week with assistance from a full-time nurse, and she made frequent phone calls to discuss business with various employees, but her participation was far from what it had been a few years earlier. With that limited access, she may not have gotten a complete picture of all that was taking place at the factory, and rumors did not help. "Things kind of worried me, because I'd hear this and that," Enid admitted. "You know, people will say things. And I couldn't be over there all the time." After fifty-five years at the helm of Nocona Boot Company, it was frustrating, to say the least, for Enid to no longer have total control, but her dismissal of Joe on grounds that he was not following her directions was both unwarranted and unfair.[48]

Just when it seemed that the future of Nocona Boot Company was settled and the merger with Justin Industries would go forward, another turnabout occurred. Joe, along with his wife Pat, implored Enid to change her mind about merging with Justin Industries, and their arguments were convincing. Enid reversed her decision, telling John Jr. she had changed her mind. "I decided that I did not want to sell to anybody," she asserted, adding, "I changed my mind one night when I couldn't sleep and thinking about I was letting my children down—I call them my children—my employees. I was letting them down to do it [sell the company], because I knew that it would not be run like I run it." Enid reinstated Joe as vice president just over a month after she had fired him. She intended to ignore the option agreement she had signed with Justin Industries and continue with the corporate structure that was in place before her initial decision to sell. That is when the lawsuits began.[49]

On August 20, 1980, Justin Industries filed suit in Tarrant County to uphold the option contract that Enid signed with John Jr. The suit alleged that Enid "wrongfully sought to repudiate the option and avoid her obligations thereunder." Prior to that filing, Joe initiated a lawsuit in Montague County to enforce the employment agreement and trust signed by his aunt six years earlier. The reinstatement of Joe's contracts would make the option agreement with Justin Industries "void and unenforceable." Having finally chosen Joe to be her successor, Enid supported his lawsuit, and according to court documents, "upon reflection and refreshing her memory as to the events . . . acknowledged that she acted incorrectly in attempting to revoke the trust. She further stated that Joe Justin had accepted proper supervision and was wrongfully discharged."[50]

But Enid was willing to go a step farther to have her way regarding the future of her company. In an oral deposition on October 8, she alleged that her Fort Worth attorney, William Brown, had tricked her into signing the option with Justin Industries by telling her, "It's an option that you will not sell to anyone for a year." She testified that Brown did not read or explain the option to her and did not leave her a copy of it. She also stated that it was Brown's idea to terminate Joe, and she accused the attorney of "double-crossing" her by secretly working for "her opposition." In short, she perjured herself regarding events surrounding the signing of the option with Justin Industries. Obviously, she believed she could get out of the agreement by claiming an unscrupulous attorney had deceived her by misrepresenting the contract.[51]

Enid's deposition testimony was uncharacteristic. She did not have a history of lying—by all accounts she had been honest and trustworthy in both business and personal life—but she did have a history of getting her way. It appears she decided the means justified the end in this case as she was determined to control the future of her company. Perhaps she thought the witnesses to the option signing who worked for her would support her story, but she was mistaken. Even Chester Taylor, her credit manager and husband of her niece, refuted her testimony while trying to defend her in the process. Taylor was deposed by John Jr.'s attorney Dee Kelly, who asked if Enid was a strong-willed woman. Taylor replied, "To say the least." Kelly then asked, "Is she accustomed to having her own way?" to which Taylor simply relied, "Yes." Kelly followed up by asking, "Does she resent it if people resist her in the course of action she has determined?" Taylor replied, "Don't we all." He added that Enid's employees did not question her decisions, "You just don't do that to Miss Enid."[52]

When asked if Enid was a good businesswoman, Taylor answered, "Yes. For her to succeed in a man's world and done [*sic*] what she's done, yes." He went on to explain that because of her age and physical disabilities, she was "not as sharp as she was," but she was still capable of understanding the business. Taylor added, "Mr. Kelly, she's 86, and that's the reason she has me and Charles Rogers and Joe and Sam. . . . There's no one that can do all this. When I came up 20 years ago, and we had 62 employees, sure, you could keep your thumb on it all. But as we have grown from less than one million to twenty million and from 62 employees to close to 475, then you have to expand and delegate it out." Kelly continued to question Enid's mental competency, causing Taylor to reply, "I'm never going to say that she doesn't have all of her faculties. I think her mind is fine." Kelly established that Enid was of sound mind and capable of entering into a contractual agreement, and when the remaining depositions were taken, it was evident that Enid's account of events surrounding the signing of the option agreement was untrue. Now the final decision on who would acquire Nocona Boot Company lay in the hands of the court.[53]

On behalf of Justin Industries, Kelly obtained a writ from the Court of Civil Appeals in Fort Worth prohibiting the case in Montague County from going forward until a verdict was reached on the option contract case in Fort Worth. The writ was granted in order to "prevent a multiplicity of suits," because the Tarrant County suit "would afford complete relief to all parties." When District Judge James Wright handed down his decision in *Justin Industries, Inc. v. Enid Justin, et al.*, Enid did not get her way—Justin Industries prevailed, and Enid was required to honor the option contract. As a result of that verdict, the case in Montague County was dismissed, and negotiations began on the transfer of stock. When a price was finally agreed upon, Justin Industries would acquire all of Nocona's outstanding stock through exchanges for Justin Industries stock.[54]

Justin originally offered around $4.5 million for the Nocona company, but Joe argued the purchase price was "too low." He told a reporter for the *Fort Worth Star-Telegram* that he "figured the company was worth as much as $12 million." Joe participated in the negotiations and was instrumental in obtaining a better deal for his aunt. "John Jr. tried to steal it at first," Enid recalled, "but we got a good price." When all was finally settled on June 12, 1981, Nocona Boot Company formally merged with Justin Industries in an exchange of stock valued at $8,950,000. According to the terms of the merger, Nocona Boot Company remained a separate entity within the Justin corporate family structure, maintaining its own identity, brand name, style of boots, and management. Enid continued as president, and Joe retained his position as vice president and general manager.[55]

Enid knew that her employees were worried about the future of the company and the stability of their jobs, so she went to the factory and personally told them about the merger. "They had been disturbed. They didn't know what was going on," she recalled. "In a little town, you know, you can hear all kinds of things. Some things are true and some are not." From the factory floor, she announced, "I am going to tell you, and this comes right from the horse's mouth, I have finally consented to merge." She assured them that it would be business as usual, and added, "We are going to have our Christmas party, too. Don't think we are not." The employees "all hollered" their approval.[56]

At the time of the merger, Texas's big three bootmakers were led by Tony Lama Company of El Paso followed by Justin in second place and Nocona in third. Tony Lama had recently acquired Hyer Boot Company, a well-known manufacturer in Olathe, Kansas, whose founder was a contemporary of Daddy Joe. With the acquisition of Nocona Boot Company, Justin's boot production was expected to surpass that of Tony Lama. Justin had recently opened new factories in El Paso and Cassville, Missouri, and the combined Justin and Nocona factories, six in total, were expected to produce 6,000 pairs of boots a day. An Associated Press article reported, "A family quarrel that lasted six months and wound up in court has finally been resolved, and the solution may make Justin Industries the largest bootmaker in the nation."[57]

Publicly, Enid put a brave face on the merger, telling dealers, "I am pleased that the members of the Justin family are together again in the boot-making business; as I'm sure you've heard, Nocona Boot Company has merged with Justin Industries, Inc., bringing the histories of the two companies full circle.... I gave the merger much thought and am pleased it has taken place. It ensures the future of Nocona Boot Company and that the company will remain a family-owned, small town company which benefits the employees." She made similar statements on other occasions. "The merger has suited me perfectly," she told *The Nocona News*. "I don't feel I'll ever have any regret that I've merged with them." But in her memoir, published four years after the merger, she revealed the emotional toll the merger had inflicted:

> I can't tell you how much it hurts to let something go when you'd rather not. But there are many decisions in life that must be made for the benefit of others rather than for yourself. It doesn't hurt any less when you

CHAPTER 7

make such a decision, but you make it and live with it. I have so many memories, so many good memories about that company ... but the time came when I had to get out and make way for the future. I didn't want to see my company fail or even go downhill ... and I didn't want to see the workers hurt in any way. After all, the workers are the ones who made Nocona Boots what it is ... and they made me look so very, very good in the business world.[58]

As promised, Enid continued as president and chairman of the board, but her participation was limited by her physical condition. She told an interviewer, "I get over there as often as I can," and when asked what she did at the factory, she replied, "Sit in my office and look out the picture window. There is a picture window between my office and the big office, and it is just full of girls working." Enid's nurse often pushed her through the factory in her wheelchair, where she enjoyed talking with her employees, noting, "They are all my friends." As one might suspect, Enid did not totally give up her "say" in company business. She observed day-to-day operations just as she had done for over five decades, and when she saw something she did not like, she confronted management about correcting the problem. "I get after them about things," she asserted. "They don't run over me altogether."[59]

Enid described her first dividend from Justin Industries as "pretty substantial because I had a lot of stock," but during merger negotiations John Jr. had promised her a "nice bonus." She explained, "He was tickled to death to get my name in that industry.... I hadn't thought of a bonus, didn't expect one, but he said it." She called her nephew to remind him, "I got my dividend, but I haven't gotten the bonus." When John Jr. replied, "What bonus?" Enid was quick to remind him of his earlier promise. She had plans for that money. The town was raising funds for a new library, and Enid noted that with her bonus, "The library will be built pretty soon."[60]

Less than a year after the merger, Enid suffered a heart attack that further debilitated her physical condition, and in September 1982, at age 88, she resigned as president and chief executive officer. She was named honorary chairman of the board and continued to serve as a consultant. Displaying her characteristic positive attitude, Enid told *The Nocona News*, "I'm looking forward to having more time to travel." A month after her resignation, she attended the Cow Palace Rodeo in Las Vegas. Enid enjoyed Las Vegas, especially the slot machines, and she once told an interviewer it was "her only vice." She added, "I like to play those silly slot machines. I really do. That's my weakness." Steve Pickens, who later became president of Nocona Boot, laughingly recalled that Enid only remembered how much she won, not how much she spent for those winnings. Enid would say, "I won $3,200," and her nurse would say, "but she put in $6,000." Clearly, the joy was in winning despite the cost.[61]

Nocona Boots had been worn by countless celebrities and politicians over the years, but in winter 1983 a special presentation made Noconans particularly proud of their leather industry. Todd Fore, a senior at Nocona High School, was headed to Washington, DC, to participate in the Washington Workshops Congressional Seminar, a weeklong event that allowed high school seniors to learn about the three branches of government. Fore, obviously destined to be a politician, asked Nocona Boot Company and Nocona Belt Company "if they might be interested in presenting President Reagan with some tokens of Nocona's craftsmanship in celebration of the president's 72nd birthday on February 6." Both agreed it was a superb idea. The boot company had the president's size on file and quickly decided on "a pair of truly Texas boots" made of armadillo. The belt company produced a matching belt with a buckle adorned with a piece of armadillo shell. Texas congressman Charles Stenholm arranged for Fore to personally make the presentation to President Reagan. After Fore, boots, and belt all passed security clearance, the young man, along with Stenholm, met with the president in the Oval Office. Reagan graciously accepted the gifts, telling Fore that "he had a pair of Noconas that were 25 years old and kind of worn out and he needed a new pair." *The Nocona News* opined that now "President Reagan was dressed the way Nocona wants everyone dressed."[62]

After Enid's resignation, Joe took over as president of the company, and under his leadership, Justin Industries' newest acquisition continued to grow. Nocona Boot's three factories produced more than 1,750 pairs of boots a day in 1982. The market for western wear remained strong and sales forecasts were optimistic. Joe stayed with the company for three years after the merger. "I could see some changes coming that I was not going

CHAPTER 7

The fun-loving side of this staunch businesswoman is evident in this photo. (Courtesy of the Enid Justin - Nocona Boot Company Collection, University of North Texas Special Collections.)

to be happy with," he explained, "so I began to think maybe I ought to retire." He did not expound on what he foresaw in the company's future, but in June 1984 at age 60, he announced his retirement. John Jr. accepted his resignation and, in Joe's words, "He was glad, and I was glad."[63]

A different story of events surrounding Joe's retirement was told by others on the management team. According to their account, John Jr. and J. T. Dickenson, chief operating officer of Justin Boot, made a visit to the Nocona factory for the express purpose of "letting Joe go." Joe left the next day—obviously, he had been given the option to retire. Also obvious is the fact that there was no love lost between the two cousins, but Joe's termination appears to have been based on perceived ineffective leadership rather than personal enmity. Steve Pickens, who would later replace Joe as Nocona Boot president, described him as "a personable guy," but his management style was not "strong enough to run the company. The company was just running basically on its own." Nocona Boot continued to sell record numbers of boots, but there were indications that company leadership was no longer functioning as efficiently as when Enid was at the helm.[64]

Enid still visited the factory as often as she could, and "girls" from the office frequently came to her home and caught her up on the latest news. She was determined to remain active despite her wheelchair, and she once declared that "folks had better not invite her to anything if they didn't want her there." At home in her pink stucco house, she spent much of her time in a recliner. A side table held catalogs, notes, phone books, a bell to call her nurse, and a police scanner—she liked to know "what's going on around Nocona." Requests for interviews came frequently, and she rarely turned one down. She enjoyed talking about her company and its history and, always the promoter, she hated to miss an opportunity for publicity. She confessed that while her memory about things that happened many years before remained good, she "didn't remember a lot of things that happened yesterday." Her blue eyes still sparkled when she recalled a favorite experience that happened to her—she had so many stories to tell.[65]

CHAPTER 8

I'VE BEEN BLESSED TO HAVE BEEN IN THIS BUSINESS WITH THESE PEOPLE RIGHT HERE IN NOCONA, TEXAS. WHAT MORE COULD I HAVE ASKED FOR?

—ENID JUSTIN[1]

Throughout the 1980s, the demand for cowboy boots continued to grow, and in spite of faltering leadership, Nocona Boot Company continued to prosper. Because of indications that the company had management problems, John Jr. broke his promise to Enid and sent "outsiders" to Nocona to join the executive team. First to arrive in 1983 was financial analyst Steve Pickens, who eventually replaced Joe Justin as president of the company. During his tenure as president, Pickens made significant changes and updates to the overall operation of the company. In a major modification to production, he began manufacturing boots strictly to order. "We no longer manufactured to put it in the warehouse," Pickens explained. "It was cheaper for us to have an ostrich skin in stock than to have four ostrich boots sitting over there that aren't selling because of the wrong size, the wrong heel, or the wrong toe." With the goal of modernizing operations, he began using barcodes to track boots through the factory, deliver customer orders on a timely basis, and speed up the inventory process.[2]

In a more controversial decision aimed at reducing overhead, Pickens closed the satellite factories in Gainesville and Vernon, believing that the

Nocona factory alone could meet production demands by operating more than one shift. He was warned that Nocona people would not work a second shift—a long-held understanding that led to satellite plants in the first place. Despite the skepticism, Pickens added a night shift that paid twenty-five cents more an hour, and he recalled, "I had trouble getting people for the day shift because everybody wanted to work the night shift." It was not so much the additional money as the convenience for some employees. That late shift, from 5 p.m. to midnight, was especially popular with mothers because they could be with their children all day and go to work in the evenings when their husbands were at home. At that time, approximately 40 percent of Nocona's workforce was women. With two shifts, the Nocona factory alone was able to meet production demands. The closure of the satellite plants, although a decided negative for their hometowns, eliminated the cost of operating two additional factories as well as transportation costs involved in moving goods between factories.[3]

In addition to cutting production costs and reducing overhead, Pickens oversaw the introduction of two popular fashion boot styles as well as innovations in advertising and marketing. He was aided by John Tillotson, also sent to Nocona by John Jr., to take over as vice president of sales and marketing. Tillotson held that position for three-and-a-half years before moving on to become president of Lucchese Boot Company. Under their leadership, Nocona Boot introduced a ladies' flowered roper. The roper, a less expensive boot with a ten-inch top, had been made by both Nocona and Justin for years, but in the mid-eighties the style "just took off." To take full advantage of the trend, Nocona Boot introduced a ladies' roper in a variety of bright colors with a single flower embroidered on the vamp. Dubbed the "wildflower roper," the popular seller remained in the catalog for three years until a surprising new fad hit the market.[4]

Fashion had always dictated changes in Nocona Boot's product line, but in 1987 an unexpected series of events proved to be a windfall for the company. It started with a Guess jeans advertisement. The advertising agency for the popular fashion line was traveling around Texas shooting magazine layouts and happened upon two old pairs of Nocona shoe boots in a western-wear store in Big Spring. Shoe boots, described by a Nocona Boot employee as "cowboy boots that look chopped off at the ankle," first

CHAPTER 8

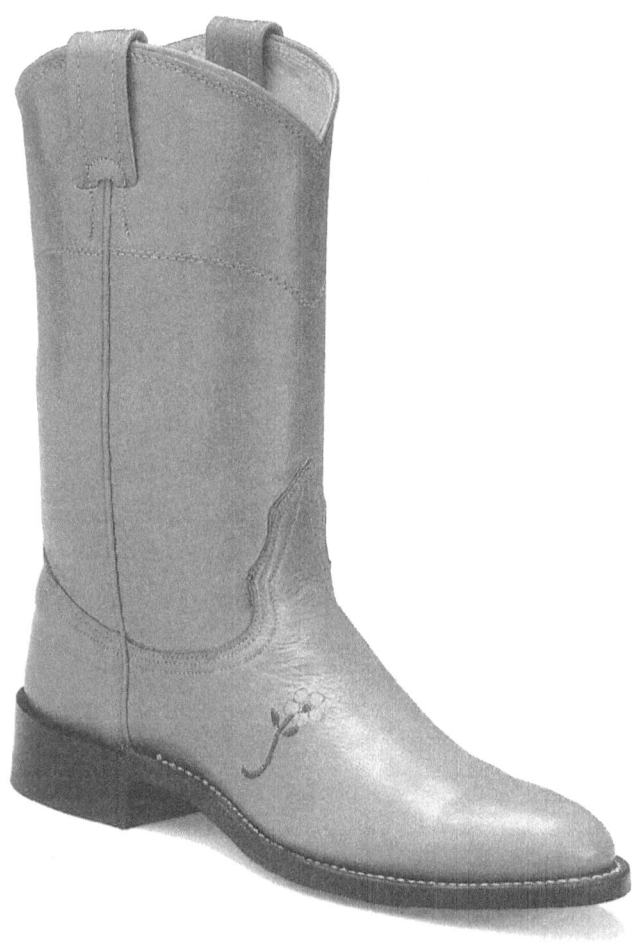

In the mid-1980s, the Ladies Wildflower Roper, offered in a variety of bright colors with a single flower embroidered on the vamp, was a best seller. (Courtesy of the Nocona Boot Company Collection, Tales 'N' Trails Museum, Nocona, Texas.)

appeared in Nocona Boot catalogs in the 1930s. The agency produced an advertisement featuring a model wearing those vintage boots with her Guess jeans, and when the ad hit the market, public demand for the shoe boot was immediate. People began calling Guess from all over the

The shoe boot, made popular in a 1987 Guess Jeans advertisement. (Courtesy of the Nocona Boot Company Collection, Tales 'N' Trails Museum, Nocona, Texas.)

country wanting to know where they could buy the unusual footwear. The demand was so great that Nocona Boot Company reintroduced the style to its product line and ultimately became the largest producer of shoe boots in the country. According to *The Nocona News*, the shoe boot was a "plus" for the company in two ways: it brought in new customers who traditionally had not worn boots, and it allowed Nocona Boot "to get its foot, literally, in the door of some of the exclusive retail outlets in the country." In 1992, at the height of the trend, yearly production of shoe boots topped fifty thousand pairs.[5]

Shortly after Pickens arrived in Nocona, Enid invited him and his wife for dinner, and over his years at the helm of the boot company, the two became friends. "She and I always got along," Pickens recalled. "If I had a question, I'd go talk to her and ask her about it." He respected her knowledge. "She was one of those that could go out there and make a pair of boots—she knew that much about the assembly process." He wanted Enid to continue to be a part of the company that was "her baby." When the National Finals Rodeo was held in Las Vegas for the first time in 1985, the boot company invited some forty employees to attend the event, and Enid and her nurse were included in the trip. Pickens also made sure that

Enid visited the factory on special occasions. "We brought her back for her birthday and wheeled her all through and let her talk to all the employees," he reminisced. "She was just beaming from ear to ear."[6]

In 1985, Nocona Boot took advantage of the company's enormously successful advertising campaign by launching the "Hero Boot Box." Twelve of the original ads depicting cowboys confronting dangerous critters were reproduced in full color on the company's boot boxes. The most famous of the "hero" ads, featuring a rattlesnake about to meet its demise at the hands of a Nocona boot-wearing cowboy with a Bowie knife, had become the third highest-selling poster in the country, surpassed only by *Star Wars* and Farrah Fawcett. "People loved those boxes," Pickens recalled. Dealers recounted stories of customers buying Justin boots and asking if they could have a Nocona Boot box. "No matter whether they're wearing our boots or not," Pickens added, "if they've got one of our boxes, that's advertising for us."[7]

Business was good, and company executives decided to jump into the western belt market. The company had been selling Nocona brand belts for some time, but they were produced by Justin Belt Company. Now the company would manufacture its own brand of exotic leather belts. Pickens explained the reasoning behind the decision: "We had so much exotic scrap . . . it didn't make sense for us to be selling it for twenty cents a pound. We'll just make exotic belts to complement our line." The company leased the former Piggly Wiggly grocery store building and began manufacturing belts with around a dozen employees. The advantages were twofold: Nocona Boot produced belts at a lower cost by using leftover leather, and customers could purchase a belt that exactly matched their boots. In addition to belt manufacture, the building housed a newly created boot repair facility, long requested by Nocona Boot's retail dealers. Plans also were being finalized for a 40,000-square-foot "finished products warehouse" that would be built on the east side of the plant. The warehouse would free up existing factory space that could be used to expand production. In summer 1988, *The Nocona News* reported that some ten employees had been added to the workforce, and "existing employees have been called upon to increase weekly production quotas, and in some instances work overtime . . . an indication of a strong market."[8]

In a tribute to the founder of the town's famous company, the Nocona City Council voted to rename in Enid's honor the park that the lady bootmaker had so enthusiastically equipped with an imaginative array of playground equipment. The fifty-year-old park underwent an extensive facelift before the official renaming. The park, originally part of a Civilian Conservation Corps camp established during the Great Depression, was beginning to show the ravages of time and constant use, and Enid asked that the refurbishing be done. She financed the restoration while her niece Marsha Taylor and the latter's husband Chester oversaw the project. The dedication ceremony, held on October 1, 1988, was preceded by a parade, and Enid agreed to ride on a float. The newspaper reported, "She was lifted onto the float by a lift connected to the back of a truck and said she liked riding it more than an elevator." At age 94, Enid had obviously not lost her fun-loving spirit and was still holding true to her often-espoused advice: "Stay involved; it keeps you young."[9]

Nocona Boot continued to have record years in the late 1980s in spite of a recession that gripped Texas, Oklahoma, and Louisiana. Falling oil prices triggered the downturn that ultimately led to real estate foreclosures and bank failures, but Nocona Boot's nationwide market remained strong, cushioning the effect of the regional crisis. In 1989, Nocona Boot Company, operating as a division of Justin Industries, had its best year ever. The factory set a new all-time production record of 343,000 pairs of boots. Enid must have been proud and perhaps reassured that she had made the right decision in merging with her longtime rival.[10]

Enid died on October 14, 1990, at age 96. Her funeral was held at St. Joseph's Catholic Church, where she had donated the carillon bells that rang out in her honor. Mayor Mary Lee Nix issued a proclamation asking the community's businesses to close on that day "in remembrance of Miss Enid." And in a final tribute, members of the Nocona Boot Company Riding Club, wearing green leather chaps designed and made at the boot company in the 1950s, "posted colors" for the funeral procession at each intersection along Pine Street leading to the cemetery where the lady bootmaker was laid to rest. The town mourned her passing; it was hard to imagine Nocona without Enid Justin. "I would hate to think what the city of Nocona would be if she hadn't been here," Steve Pickens mused. "If she had joined her brothers and gone to Fort Worth, would Nocona have dried up and blown away way back then?" Several years earlier, two reporters from the *Wichita Falls Times* had visited Nocona and proclaimed it "the town that Enid Justin built." They concluded, "We decided then and there that this town's biggest asset is and has been that dynamic builder of cowboy boots. Every community should have an Enid Justin."[11]

The Texas House of Representatives also paid tribute to the "lady bootmaker" with a resolution that listed her business accomplishments as well as her civic contributions and finally proclaimed "this exceptional woman was a true embodiment of the Texas spirit."[12]

The lady bootmaker led the company she founded for fifty-seven years, and with her vision and under her leadership Nocona Boot Company grew to be a multimillion-dollar corporation. Recalling the company's early years, Pickens reflected, "Here she was, a woman in a man's world, making a man's product and selling it to men! I can't even imagine what that mountain looked like back then." Enid was obviously a strong and determined woman, but there was also a certain simplicity, perhaps even naivete, about her. She saw things in black and white—there was no gray. She once told an interviewer, "Listen, things are either right or wrong. There is no in-between with me." Retired boot company employee Clara Beth Speights provided an interesting example of this decisiveness: "She wouldn't abide cohabiting by members of the opposite sex before marriage. They had to get married or they didn't have a job."[13]

"She was a strong woman," Joe Justin recalled. "She ran a business with a tough hand. And she was good to her employees as long as they were good to her. But when they weren't, they were gone. She was quite a gal." Joe often used the term "tough" to describe his aunt; it was a word that Enid used to describe herself. "At times," she said, "I've had to be sort of tough to keep from being stepped on." She told a reporter that she did not smoke or drink, but she admitted, "if I get mad, I'll cuss a little." Employees portrayed Enid as "a larger-than-life woman who could swear like a sailor on the shop floor and uncannily collect debts from the hardest accounts. Yet she was generous and inspired extreme loyalty from employees." Others described her as having "the biggest heart in the world" and being "a great benefactor to Nocona."[14]

Enid could be a "tough" boss, but she also had a fun-loving side that appealed to employees and charmed interviewers. She loved to tell a good story, and over the years she repeated her favorites time and again.

Enid and Walt Disney at the 1956 grand opening of the Disneyland Hotel. (Courtesy of the Enid Justin - Nocona Boot Company Collection, University of North Texas Special Collections.)

Surprisingly, those stories remained exactly the same through the years, without the embellishment that often comes with time. An invitation in 1956 to the star-studded grand opening of the Disneyland Hotel, built in an orange grove across the street from the new theme park, was an experience she delighted in telling:

> I was at the head table with Walt Disney, his wife, and other folks. Mr. Disney was left-handed and while he was talking, he got my cup of coffee and drank it. When he noticed what he'd done, he apologized and ordered another cup for me . . . and he drank that one too. So, I had two cups of coffee with Walt Disney, but he drank both of them.[15]

Enid's sense of humor seemed to surprise some interviewers. At dinner with a columnist for the Spokane, Washington *Spokesman-Review*, Enid warned, "Be sure and write bootmaker, not bootlegger." When the conversation turned to the oil business, Enid told the reporter, "At our country club in Nocona, we have an oil well that pays all its expenses.

Our cemetery also has an oil well which pays for its upkeep." She only wished that they would bring in a well that would pay the taxes of everyone in town. The reporter described Enid as "so quiet-spoken, with her 'Texas twang,' and so feminine it is hard to place her in the business world," but the lady bootmaker had excelled as a business owner and was deservedly proud of the company she created. "She has a pair of silver boots welded to her radiator, a silver boot on the screen door of her home, her business cards are miniature boots on key rings, and the weathervane atop her home is a spurred boot." The reporter, who seemed enthralled with this true Texas character, concluded her column, "That an attractive and most feminine woman should be the world's greatest maker of cowboy boots is quite an anomaly. But then, can't anything happen in Texas."[16] The statement is more an exclamation than a question.

Another of Enid's favorite stories concerned the making of Nocona's first pair of children's boots. "I was approached by the parents of this tiny little boy," Enid recalled. "They wanted a pair of cowboy boots for him. Well, we weren't set up for such a small size, but I thought the challenge would be fun, so I told the people we'd make him a pair. His folks were just wonderful people, but they cussed like sailors." When the boots were ready, Enid personally presented them. "I put the tiny boots on the boy, and he looked down for a long time before he finally said anything. Finally, he said, 'goddam!' I guess that's the only way he knew to show his approval. I almost died laughing. That little boy is a grown man now and still has those boots. Neither of us will ever forget them, but for different reasons."[17]

There were funny stories, but there were also serious stories that Enid liked to tell:

> One night I was listening to the radio—we did that years ago, before television—and a news reporter was talking about a young man found in Olympia, Washington, suffering from amnesia. The newsman mentioned he was wearing Nocona Boots. Well, I immediately called the sheriff there and told him to look inside the boots for the serial number. I took that number to the factory, traced it down as to who the dealer was who sold the boots, and the young man was identified without further problems.[18]

Another favorite story involved Enid being summoned to testify at a trial in West Texas for a man who had stolen a number of items, including Nocona Boots, from a retail store. He was caught with the stolen property in his possession, and Enid was asked to identify the boots. "His attorney tried to trip me up saying there were so many boots manufactured that I couldn't possibly identify them as ours. I retorted, 'You'd know your own children, wouldn't you? Well, those boots are my children.' I didn't have any more problems with that attorney, and his client was convicted of the theft."[19]

Enid often told the story of her attempt to present a pair of cowboy boots to Pope Pius XII in the 1950s when she was granted an audience with the Holy Father at the Vatican. "The poor fellow was standing there in a pair of thin red slippers," she exclaimed. "I explained to the Pope that I'd wanted to make him a pair of made-to-measure boots with the papal crest on the uppers. Only when I checked with the Vatican's ambassador in Washington to get the foot measurements and a copy of the papal crest, I was informed that the Pope has no use for a pair of cowboy boots. When I told all this to the Pope, he just gave me a sad smile." The reason for the "sad smile" is open to interpretation.[20]

From the 1939 Pony Express Race to papal boots, Enid did not pass up a chance to garner publicity for her company. In the popular column "Tolbert's Texas" in the *Dallas Morning News*, Frank X. Tolbert told of his part in one of those promotions. "Several years ago, Miss Enid made up a size 24 boot which I delivered to the town museum in Bigfoot, Texas, west of San Antonio." The small community was named in honor of its famous resident, Texas Ranger William A. A. "Bigfoot" Wallace, and the Nocona Boot, the largest ever made at the factory, was displayed in his honor. Enid had a number of big-footed customers, the largest being a size 18 worn by a California rancher. Tolbert remarked that he "must look like a right angle."[21]

A photograph displayed in the Nocona museum provides another example of Enid's never missing an opportunity to promote her company. She often took her great-nieces and -nephews, three boys and two girls, on vacations, and she designed matching outfits for the small children to wear on those trips. The photo shows the five children, lined up with their backs to the camera, wearing matching white coveralls with

CHAPTER 8

Enid's great-nieces and -nephews advertise for the company in matching white jumpsuits and red boots. (Courtesy of the Nocona Boot Company Collection, Tales 'N' Trails Museum, Nocona, Texas.)

"Nocona Boot Company, Nocona Tex," appliquéd on the back in large red letters. And, of course, they were wearing matching red boots. When asked about that childhood experience, Enid's eldest great-niece Melanie Chapman Howington recalled that the children were not bothered by the outfits: "We were kids, and we would just go and play and be kids." She added facetiously, "That's how Auntie used us—we were advertising gimmicks."[22]

Over Enid's years in the boot business, she had traveled all over the country, and she was always quick to profess her love for Texas and the United States. "I'm not a bit bashful about being patriotic because I figure that's one way of showing my thanks. I'm proud of the United States and our boots. You know, they kind of go together."[23]

In an article in *Modern People* magazine in 1973, Enid shared the philosophy behind her success: "You've got to keep busy and you've got to be a fighter. I've never let life get me down. Life is a big battle with Father Time and if you ever give in, it's all over." She continued, "Keep your mind active. Live today, not in the past. Channel all your experience and energy into constructive pursuits." And finally, "Get out there and work to help make your life a little happier. It's great therapy. And stay involved. It keeps you young." There is a whole lot of wisdom packed in those short sentences, and Enid was living proof that her philosophy worked—she was 79 at the time of that interview, and she would continue to practice what she preached for the rest of her life.[24]

The year that Enid died, Justin Industries acquired the Tony Lama Company, another boot manufacturer with a proud history. The company began in 1912 when Tony Lama, who had been a cobbler for the US Army stationed at Fort Bliss, opened a shoe-repair and boot-making shop in El Paso. Lama soon gained a reputation for being a quality bootmaker, and by the early 1930s his company was producing forty pairs of boots a day. Much like the Justin family, Lama's six children all became active participants in the business that eventually grew to be the largest producer of western-style boots in the state. The brand was best known for high-end boots crafted from exotic leathers. In 1990, at the time of the merger with Justin Industries, Tony Lama had two plants in El Paso that employed more than 900 workers and produced 2,200 pairs of boots daily.[25]

The acquisition of "Nocona's and Justin's main competitor" was a significant win for Justin Industries. John Jr. proclaimed, "We'd been trying to buy Tony Lama for twenty years." J. T. Dickenson, who had been promoted to vice president of Justin Industries, explained how the merger finally came about. In the mid-'80s Tony Lama was outselling Justin. "While we were shipping around 750,000 pairs a year at Justin Boot Company, they were shipping close to a million pairs," Dickenson explained. "But they started getting sloppy in their quality, and their management wasn't really doing their homework. Family members were running the company, and for whatever reason, their interest started to subside." By 1990, the El Paso company had "some major problems" that allowed Justin Industries to acquire the company by absorbing their debt and purchasing their stock. The Tony Lama Company, like Nocona Boot Company, remained a separate entity within the Justin corporate family structure and continued to operate with local management. The three boot companies remained competitors in the marketplace, but the "big three" of Texas boots were now in Justin hands.[26]

With the big three Texas bootmakers under the umbrella of Justin Industries, one might think that John Jr. was proud of these acquisitions and was interested in growing all three popular brands. But that was not entirely true—his main incentive in acquiring Nocona and Tony Lama was to eliminate competition, and while as an astute businessman he wanted the two companies to remain profitable, he did not want them to eclipse Justin Boot Company. This seemed especially true with Nocona Boot, probably because of the history of rivalry and contention between the two companies. John Tillotson explained what he believed to be John Jr.'s mindset with regard to the Nocona company. "He didn't really want to own it to make it a bigger company, make it more aggressive, more profitable, unless it was less big, less profitable than Justin," Tillotson explained. "In his mind, Nocona was where it was, and it was going to stay there... he did not want Nocona outshining Justin in any way." Steve Pickens gave a more conflicted description of John Jr.'s position on the Nocona company. "He was always proud of Nocona Boot," Pickens maintained, "but Nocona didn't carry his name. He wanted Nocona to do well. He wanted us to make money and so forth, but he never really wanted us to surpass what Justin did."[27]

In the early 1990s, Justin Industries considered consolidating their three boot companies, a move that Pickens opposed because he believed it would homogenize the boot brands that had always had their own unique characteristics. "A Tony Lama boot, a Justin boot, and a Nocona boot may all be full quill ostrich, but they are not the same boot," Pickens asserted. "They do not fit the same, they do not feel the same, they are not manufactured the same, and they have three distinct customers." The boots were constructed differently, on different lasts, and that resulted in differences in fit and customer preference. As an example, in a Nocona boot the upper was sewn into a groove cut in the insole, resulting in a very unforgiving fit. According to Pickens, "It either fit you or it didn't," and that required Nocona to produce a larger range of sizes. In contrast, the Justin boot used a rib, a leather welt sewn to the boot top and then to the sole to hold the two together, and that rib had a certain amount of play that allowed the boot to stretch to fit. Likewise, a customer with a high instep would prefer a Tony Lama boot because their last was designed for a high instep. Each brand—Nocona, Justin, and Tony Lama—was distinctive, and for the short term they would continue to maintain that exclusivity.[28]

For several years after Enid's death, the boot company she founded continued to prosper. From 1989 to 1993, Nocona Boot had a string of record-setting sales and production years. General Manager Dave McGrady noted, "1993 was the second biggest in history after 1992." But those record-breaking numbers began to change in 1994 as boot sales suddenly slumped. "The demand for our product is down, and that's true for the entire industry," McGrady explained. "That's true for Justin Boot Company and Tony Lama Boot Company, and that's true for other companies outside our group."[29]

The downturn in boot sales was not a result of the economy. After a brief recession in 1990–1991, a period of economic expansion began and continued for the remainder of the decade. The 1990s were a time of strong economic growth that peaked in 1994 just as the downturn in boot sales began. The decline in sales was purely fashion driven. Some retail consultants cited a trend for more casual footwear, like loafers and athletic shoes, as the reason for slowing boot sales. Traditionally, two groups of people buy western-style boots: those who have always worn them and those who wear them solely as a fashion statement. When the cowboy boot is no longer high fashion, the second group moves on to whatever footwear is trending at the time. As an example, New Yorkers who clamored for boots during the "urban cowboy" craze had moved on to wearing high-fashion loafers with their suits and jeans. Obviously, the loss of that portion of the market negatively impacted sales volume.[30]

When popular designers like Ralph Lauren and Calvin Klein show western styles in their collections, boot sales climb. But fashion is notoriously fickle, and it had turned away from cowboy style. "The Western and Western-influenced products haven't been in demand," McGrady noted. "Everything is fashion-driven and obviously Western is one fashion that's either in or out." Enid had once made it through hard times without laying off employees by placing a grand piano on the factory floor and telling her employees to play and sing when there was no work to do, but the factory was far too large for that benevolent solution to work in 1994. Nocona Boot Company had more than 450 employees when boot sales began to slump, and downsizing the workforce was a regrettable but necessary measure.[31]

The first job cuts were announced in September. Thirty-two front office employees—some had worked at the boot company for over three decades—were told that their jobs would be phased out over the next few months as Justin Industries announced the decision to consolidate the accounting, payroll, and billing departments of all three boot companies under one roof in Fort Worth. "The boot operation in Nocona will stay like it is as far as manufacturing," Justin Industries president J. T. Dickenson told *The Nocona News* as he "tried to allay fears that the move was the first in the long-rumored, long-feared closing or relocation of the entire Nocona Boot Company operation." Since the 1981 merger, Noconans had worried about the future of their boot company. Dickenson stressed that the cost-cutting measure was designed to eliminate duplicate administrative functions, and the factory would continue to operate in Nocona as it always had.[32]

Less than two months later, twenty-three additional layoffs were announced when sales continued to slump in what was normally the busiest season of the year. The cuts weighed heavily on the company president. "I love all of these people. I don't want to let any of them go, but I can't keep them all." Pickens added, "We tried not to really affect any one department, so we took some from all the departments, and for six months we've been letting attrition take its effect." Nocona Boot started 1994 with 433 employees, and by November that number was down to 355. Pickens did not anticipate further layoffs, but he cautioned that the industry forecast for the coming year was not encouraging.[33]

In spring 1995, Justin Industries announced additional changes in the organizational structure of its boot division. Consolidation continued as sales and marketing operations for the three boot companies joined accounting, payroll, and billing in the Fort Worth office, but proposed changes to top management were quite unexpected. The corporate office announced that a general manager would replace the president as top executive of each boot company. Steve Pickens, who had resisted the consolidation of the three companies, was a casualty of that reorganization. He would be the last president of Nocona Boot Company.[34]

General manager Dave McGrady took over leadership of the company. When asked about the management change, McGrady replied, "I'm proud to have this opportunity, and I'm sad that Steve's not a part of it." He praised Pickens's leadership: "The 12 years that he served as the leader of this company have been the most successful in the history of the company." Pickens had come to Nocona Boot Company in 1983 as a financial analyst, a position he originally believed would be temporary. He stayed on to become general manager and finally president shortly after Joe Justin retired. It was his dream job. Pickens grew up in a small town, and he had always wanted to "run a manufacturing company in rural America" because he believed, as Enid did, that small towns provided the best workforce. "You had third-generation family members—their mom had worked there or their granddaddy worked there . . . and they loved the company." Pickens continued, "They were hardworking, and they loved what they did." Much like Enid, he was proud of Nocona Boot's workforce, and he carried on her legacy in other significant ways. Pickens wanted Nocona Boot Company to be a state-of-the-art factory that produced the best quality boots. "I wanted to be the premier of the line and be known for our quality and our workmanship—that's what I wanted Nocona to be." In many ways, his vision and Enid's were the same. He would later say that the corporate office did him "a huge favor" because downsizing the company was difficult for all concerned. "I'd rather be on the outside than on the inside," Pickens explained. "It hurt me either way, but it would hurt me a lot more if I'm right there having to hand them their final checks."[35]

The pattern of falling boot sales and factory layoffs continued, and by summer 1995, Nocona Boot's workforce was down to 260. Employee numbers had not been that low since the late 1950s. "What's getting us simply is our order rate," McGrady declared. "That old saying that the phone just keeps not ringing." The western apparel industry continued to decline, and in spring 1996 forty-three more employees, all production related, were sent home, leaving Nocona Boot with a total workforce of just over two hundred. McGrady told *The Nocona News* the layoffs "were tough" and cost the company "some quality workers, sometimes spouses or best friends of other workers." The general manager was far from optimistic: "Right now, based on the trends in fashion and the demand we're seeing, we're looking at a long, drawn-out affair." Sales for 1996 were projected to be down 25 percent from the previous year, "which was an historically low year."[36]

Fears that Nocona Boot Company would be relocated or even closed were no longer in the back of people's minds—they were becoming a distinct possibility. Optimism was hard to summon as the market continued to decline over the next two years. In 1997, Justin Industries reported their footwear sales fell 16 percent from the previous year, and the following year those numbers continued to fall. When the Fort Worth conglomerate's entire footwear division failed to make a profit in 1998 (losses, in fact, were reported to be $500,000), company executives decided drastic changes were in order. Under the leadership of John V. Roach, who was named chairman of the board of Justin Industries when John Jr. retired, it was decided that the company would separate its footwear and building material businesses, "arguing that the boot and brick combination is too confusing for investors." The building materials division had remained profitable, but the footwear division needed major reorganization if it were going to regain profitability.[37]

Justin's footwear manufacturers—Nocona Boot, Justin Boot, Tony Lama Company, and Chippewa Shoe Manufacturing Company—would be consolidated under one management with the name Justin Brands. In a Justin Industries press release, Randy Watson, newly named president of the footwear division, announced, "We will immediately put into motion changes that should increase our competitiveness and operating efficiency." With those "changes," Noconans' worst fears became reality.[38]

On Wednesday, August 4, 1999, Justin Industries announced the closing of Nocona Boot Company as well as Fort Worth's Justin Boot Company. According to a Justin senior official, the company could no longer justify operating big plants, like Nocona and Tony Lama, at below capacity. He explained, "The realignment of domestic production will result in the transfer of all manufacturing activities from the Fort Worth and Nocona plants to larger facilities in El Paso and Cassville, Missouri." Going forward, the Nocona brand would be manufactured at the Tony Lama plant in El Paso. According to a New York financial analyst, "Justin's results have suffered because its major boot brands often made competing products that hurt one another's business. That meant smaller production lines and higher costs. It no longer makes sense for Justin and Tony Lama to each do $350 black ostrich boots." The reorganization would reduce duplication in styles and eliminate competing products from the boot lines. The individual boot brands would still be produced, but, as Steve Pickens predicted, they would no longer have the distinctive characteristics each was known for.[39]

In addition to realigning domestic production, Justin management planned to pursue "outsourcing" to Mexico and Asia. Outsource manufacturing became common practice in the consumer electronics industry in the 1970s, and with the success of that industry, other manufacturers moved production overseas or south of the border. The primary advantage was lower labor costs. Investment analysts had criticized Justin Industries for not "moving more decisively" toward outsourcing production. With its reorganization, Justin Brands announced its intention "to sell more lower-cost boots produced at plants in Mexico and China." For several years, Justin's Tony Lama division had produced some products in Mexico but, oddly enough, Nocona Boot Company may have been the first cowboy boot manufacturer to outsource production with its Bootmaker's Collection made in Spain in the 1970s. (Outsourcing, once considered to be the future of United States manufacturing, has proven over time to have a downside. With regard to the boot industry, the negative has always been that many Americans object to their cowboy boots being made in China.)[40]

The economic justification for the closing of the Nocona factory was no consolation for employees, many of whom had spent all their working years producing Nocona Boots; the bottom line for them was that the factory that provided their livelihood was closing down. But for many, it was more than that—the factory was home away from home and fellow employees were like family. One employee explained the feeling of loss: "This has been a lot more than a job to me and to many others." Nocona Boot's remaining 183 employees were informed that their jobs would end as soon as they finished the orders that were in production.[41]

The ramifications of the closing spread far beyond company employees. The town was losing its largest taxpayer, and Mayor Gene Fitzgerald noted, "The county, the schools, and the hospital district are also going to be hurt badly." And Nocona's merchants and businessmen were bracing for hard times with the loss of the boot company's payroll that had pumped around $3.5 million a year into the local economy. The economic impact for the town of 2,800 was staggering, but the psychological impact was equally devastating.[42]

"Nocona, without Nocona Boots, does not seem conceivable," a local newspaper sympathized. "Shutdown of the town's largest employer has sent the community into virtual mourning for an old friend." A longtime Noconan lamented, "The sad thing, apart from the loss of jobs, is that it was kind of our identity." Because of the boot company, the town of Nocona had gained fame that few small towns attain, and the community took great pride in being the home of Nocona Boot Company and its gutsy founder Enid Justin. "Miss Enid would be totally shocked if she learned this boot company was closing," Weldon Parr, a thirty-five-year employee, told a reporter. "I'm just glad she's not around to see it." Ironically, Enid had once voiced her opinion on the subject. "I've seen a lot of plants shut their doors and I've always wondered why their owners allowed it to happen," she told an interviewer. "When you close a plant, the employees are left out in the cold and the town where the plant is located is also hurt. I'm glad I never had to close one." The closing of Nocona Boot Company led many to lament in almost identical words, "Miss Enid is rolling in her grave."[43]

Over the next six weeks, production at Nocona Boot Company slowly and painfully came to an end. As the final boots wound their way along the production line, each individual department shut down when its specific job was completed. *The Nocona News* documented the closing with a group photo of each department's employees on their final day. The cutting department was the first to be terminated on August 11—the newspaper photo showed fourteen men and women grouped around a cutting table on their last day at the factory. The caption listed their names and noted that they "started the process of making the last Nocona-made Nocona Boots." The computer stitching department shut down on August 17 followed by the lasting department on August 19, and the process continued department by department until the final boots reached the end of the production line. On September 2, Nocona Boot's remaining personnel, including supervisors, maintenance workers, and office staff, gathered to watch as the finishing department completed the last boots to be made at the 74-year-old factory. The final pair, made of cognac-colored full quill ostrich, were specially made for the North Montague County Historical Society to be placed in the Nocona museum. General manager Dave McGrady presented the boots to Historical Society president Gary Don King. *The Nocona News* reported, "It was a somber ceremony, made more so by the eerie quiet in the factory building."[44]

Many years earlier, Enid was asked if the noise in the factory bothered her, and she replied, "Only when it stops." Now the noise had stopped, the huge factory was silent, and the story of the lady bootmaker entered the annals of history. It is the story of a woman who dared to enter a profession that belonged to men, and her success in that business earned her the title "First Lady of American Cowboy Boots." The journey was not easy, but that "Texas archetype full of stubborn," as one journalist so vividly described her, never wavered from her original goal: to carry on her father's tradition of making quality western boots in the town they both called home. Against all odds, she built a successful business, a testament to her steadfast commitment, her hard work, and her admitted "love affair with the boot business." That love affair lasted a lifetime and earned Enid Justin her own place in Western history.[45]

EPILOGUE

When Nocona Boot Company closed its doors in fall 1999, there were no longer any Justin family members involved in the business. Enid was gone by 1990. As promised in her will, nephew Joe Justin, who retired from the boot company in 1984, inherited her stock in Justin Industries; he sold it a short time later. John Justin Jr., who led Justin Boot Company (later Justin Industries), for forty-nine years, retired in April 1999 at the age of 82. "For the first time in 120 years," the *Fort Worth Star-Telegram* noted, "there will not be a Justin running the company."[1]

By April 2000, Justin Industries' newly streamlined footwear division, Justin Brands, showed significant increases in sales and earnings. The impressive turnaround helped to finalize the sale of Justin Industries to Berkshire Hathaway, the holding company of billionaire investor Warren Buffett. In July, Buffett's company purchased the Fort Worth–based conglomerate for $600 million. Justin's two divisions, Justin Brands with its four labels of footwear, and Acme Building Brands, makers of bricks and other building products, would operate as a wholly owned subsidiary of Berkshire Hathaway. "It is an absolutely first-class business run by first-class people," Buffett said. "The managers who have produced Justin's outstanding results will continue to run operations from Fort Worth just as they have in the past."[2]

While Justin Brands continued to produce Nocona Boots in El Paso, boot-making resumed in Nocona in spring 2001. The Montague Boot Company (named after the county) began operations in the original Nocona Boot Company factory on Clay Street. The company was started

EPILOGUE

by Jim Williams and his brother Bill Williams Jr., whose Dallas-based Williams Company supplied leather to Nocona and other boot factories across the nation for years. The brothers launched their company in Nocona because of the existing workforce skilled in the art of boot-making. "It wasn't a hard sell," Jim Williams remarked. "Nocona is just full of boot makers. They're teaching us." Wanting to produce private label boots, the owners contracted with retired rodeo cowboy Larry Mahan, whom Jim Williams called "the Michael Jordan of cowboys," to produce boots with the Mahan name. Williams added, "We want to remain a small niche, with an American-made, high-quality product." With around forty employees whose collective experience added up to some 700 years, the company produced high-end boots that were sold exclusively at Cavender's Boot City, a Texas-based western wear retail chain.[3]

In 2014, Montague Boot Company was purchased by the Fenoglio family. Much like the Justins, the Fenoglios are a prominent Nocona family who trace their Montague County roots back to 1886 when their Italian immigrant ancestors first settled the area. The Fenoglio Boot Company continues to manufacture boots for Cavender's, but they also produce high-end boots with the Fenoglio brand. Perhaps the young company will carry on the tradition of other Texas bootmakers of Italian heritage, like Tony Lama and Sam Lucchese. Fenoglio boots are manufactured in a small factory on the west side of Nocona, and the company operates its own retail store in Enid's original factory building on Clay Street.[4]

The historic Nocona Boot factory, with its Art Deco styling and cream-colored brick, for many years was a source of pride for the town, but over time it became an eyesore. Despite changes in ownership and attempts to repurpose the 150,000-square-foot building, the structure continued to deteriorate. The shell of the building was intact, but the interior had been stripped of everything that could be resold or salvaged, and a leaking roof caused further damage to the structure. In fall 2016, with what *The Nocona News* called "the best news in a long time," the decaying building was purchased by Grapevine, Texas, businessman Craig Carter. The new owner planned a multi-use renovation that "preserved the history of the factory and Nocona's leather-goods industry." The transformation over a two-year period was impressive, and by the end of 2018 Carter's vision was realized. The beautifully restored and updated building, complete with the original Nocona Boot Company sign, houses several businesses as well as an event venue. In a fateful turn of events, the building became the new home of Nocona Athletic Goods Company, founded in 1926, only a year after Enid established her boot company. The famous baseball glove manufacturer has its factory and retail store in the east end of the restored boot factory, where it carries on the building's tradition of producing fine leather goods.[5]

When the Nocona Boot Company closed in 1999, the *Washington Post* made a dire prediction about the future of the cowboy boot. "It's the fault of modern times," the newspaper reported. "In places where sales are dependent on fashion whim—in the big cities of the East, for example—cowboy boots, once a rage, are o-u-t. And what's more unsettling for the industry, its core market also is eroding. Slowly but steadily, industry executives said, Texans and others in the West are abandoning cowboy boots, leaving a symbol of their history and culture in the trail dust."[6]

But before that dust cleared, the cowboy boot industry had begun to rebound, proving the *Post*'s prediction to be mistaken. Justin's reorganization of its boot division assured the continuation of iconic brands Justin, Nocona, and Tony Lama. Lucchese Boot Company, founded in San Antonio in 1883, had also undergone changes of ownership and had moved production to El Paso, but that brand also remained strong. In 2002, in addition to big-name brands, Texas had some 100 smaller bootmakers whose clients were often willing to wait a year or more for a pair of custom boots. By 2007, that number had grown to around two hundred custom bootmakers, more than those in the rest of the states combined. To prove the point that cowboy boots continued to be a valued symbol of the state's culture, in January 2007, the 80th Legislature designated "the cowboy boot as the official State Footwear of Texas."[7]

That is not to diminish the popularity of cowboy boots in other states—across the nation there continued to be a market for the iconic footwear. Acme Boot Company, located in Tennessee, became the world's largest manufacturer of cowboy boots in the 1940s and retained that title until the mid-1980s. Like Justin Brands, Acme became a subsidiary of Berkshire Hathaway and continues to produce boots under the Double-H Boots brand label. A number of other states boast famous custom bootmakers, like Blucher Boot Company in Beggs, Oklahoma. (Founder Gus

Blucher worked for Daddy Joe for five years before founding his own company in 1915.) Jennifer June, author of *Cowboy Boots: The Art & Sole*, created a website (dimlights.com) that lists custom bootmakers across the United States, and to date that list includes boot artisans in thirty-three states. Obviously, the art of boot-making continues to thrive, and not just in Texas.[8]

If she were still here, Enid would be pleased by the resurgence in cowboy boot popularity and the proliferation of Texas bootmakers, but she would be especially proud of the women who entered the profession after her. In the early 1980s, two women bootmakers started their own custom boot shops. Melody Dawkins opened Melody's Custom Boots in La Quinta, California, and Deanna McGuffin, who learned the trade from her father, legendary New Mexico bootmaker L. W. McGuffin, began crafting boots at McGuffin Custom Boots in Albuquerque. Others followed in their "bootsteps." Although their numbers remain small, the majority of women bootmakers have small shops that produce custom boots on an individual order basis. Texas bootmaker Stephanie Ferguson, for example, has her own shop in the small town of Millsap, west of Fort Worth.[9]

Although not a bootmaker herself, Wendy Henry, owner of Back at the Ranch Cowboy Boots in Santa Fe, New Mexico, has been designing and manufacturing boots at her factory in El Paso, Texas, since 1990. And the list would not be complete without mention of Beth Cross and Pam Parker, footwear innovators who combined athletic shoe technology with riding boots to create a more comfortable and durable boot for equestrian athletes. Their California-based company, Ariat International, was founded in 1992 and met with immediate success. The multi-million-dollar corporation manufactures cowboy boots, English riding boots, and work boots.[10]

Boot historian Tyler Beard once wrote, "In this male-dominated profession it seems that the survival of a woman bootmaker is a rare and precious thing." Enid Justin started Nocona Boot Company in 1925 with a $5,000 loan and grew it to be one of the top five boot manufacturing companies in the world. Hers is a story of the triumph of one woman's entrepreneurial spirit.[11]

Enid Justin's Creed for Success

I believe what I am doing helps make other people happy.
I believe in earning a promotion every day.
I give twice as much and as a result, receive twice as much.
People like me because I believe people are the most important thing on earth.
I try to make every day better for those I come in contact with.
I believe if I add to prosperity, I will prosper in return.
I believe I control my own "success ceiling."
I will not let my mind think "bad times."
I believe it is easier to win.
I believe it is better to be honest.
I believe in having the best attitude (I believe the magic word is attitude).
I believe opportunities are everywhere.
I have a goal, and I will reach that goal.
I have the seed for achievement—brains.
I am president of my own life.
I will live each day the best I can.
The world pays me the same 1,440 minutes every day that everyone else gets.
I believe you will become what you think about.
I believe to be successful one has to succeed in all areas of life.

NOTES

Introduction

1. President Calvin Coolidge, "The Press Under a Free Government," address to the Society of American Newspaper Editors, January 17, 1925.
2. Donald L. Miller, "Women Entrepreneurs Take the Stage During New York's Jazz Age," September 11, 2014, www.entrepreneur.com/article/237335; Virginia G. Drachman, *Enterprising Women: 250 Years of American Business* (Chapel Hill: University of North Carolina Press, 2002), 4–5. *Enterprising Women* tells the stories of women entrepreneurs throughout the history of the United States who, like Enid Justin, were successful in the business world.
3. Jennifer June, *Cowboy Boots: The Art & Sole* (New York: Universe Publishing, 2007), 22.
4. Donald E. Chipman and Harriet Denise Joseph, *Spanish Texas, 1519–1821*, 2d ed. (Austin: University of Texas Press, 2010), 262–63; D. W. Frommer II, "A History of the Western Boot," *ShoeInfoNet*, http://shoeinfonet.com/shoe-history/history-western-boot, 1–2.
5. Frommer, "A History of the Western Boot," 2.
6. Wayne Gard, *The Chisholm Trail* (Norman: University of Oklahoma Press, 1954), 4; Ramon F. Adams, *Western Words: A Dictionary of the Range, Cow Camp and Trail* (Norman: University of Oklahoma Press, 1945; reprint, London: Forgotten Books, 2017), 15 (page reference is to reprint edition).
7. Tyler Beard, *The Cowboy Boot Book* (Salt Lake City: Peregrine Smith Books, 1992), 8–9; David R. Stoecklein, *The Cowboy Boot: History, Art, Culture, Function* (Ketchum, ID: Stoecklein Publishing, 2004), 16.
8. Stoecklein, *The Cowboy Boot*, 16; *Kansas City Star*, February 11, 1911; *Olathe Mirror*, August 24, 1898.

9. Stoecklein, *The Cowboy Boot*, 14–16.
10. Barbara Brackman, "Legend Posing as History: Hyer, Justin, and the Origin of the Cowboy Boot," *Kansas History* (Spring 1995): 46; Tim McCoy and Ronald McCoy, *Tim McCoy Remembers the West* (Lincoln: University of Nebraska Press, 1977), 30; *El Paso Daily Times*, May 5, 1883.
11. Stoecklein, *The Cowboy Boot*, 19–20; *El Paso Times*, October 21, 1962.
12. Stoecklein, *The Cowboy Boot*, 16–20.
13. Sharon Delano and David Rieff, *Texas Boots* (New York: Viking Press, 1981), 24–27.
14. Enid Justin, *Miss Enid: The Texas Lady Bootmaker*, ed. Dale Terry (Austin: Nortex Press, 1985), vii.

Chapter 1
1. Justin, *Miss Enid*, 90.
2. Ibid., 11.
3. Randolph B. Campbell, *Gone to Texas: A History of the Lone Star State*, 3rd ed., (New York: Oxford University Press, 2017), 332–34.
4. Irvin Farman, *Standard of the West: The Justin Story* (Fort Worth: Texas Christian University Press, 1996), 5–6; Brackman, "Legend Posing as History," 44.
5. Farman, *Standard of the West*, 5–6; Justin, *Miss Enid*, 1–3; Brackman, "Legend Posing as History," 44; Larry Roquemore, "100 Year History of Justin Boot Company," produced by Dally Advertising and Public Relations, 1978 [photocopy], 1–2, Enid Justin Collection, Tales 'N' Trails Museum, Nocona, Texas (hereafter cited as Nocona Museum). There is some question about when Joe Justin left Indiana. It is generally agreed that he came to Texas in 1877, but "H. J. Justin, occupation shoemaker," is listed in the 1878 Lafayette city directory. That same directory lists his brother John as a cigar maker.
6. Campbell, *Gone to Texas*, 290–308.
7. Gard, *The Chisholm Trail*, 89, 96–97; David Minor, "Gainesville, Texas," *Handbook of Texas Online*, accessed April 13, 2018, http://www.tshaonline.org/handbook/online/articles/heg01; Justin, *Miss Enid*, 2; Campbell, *Gone to Texas*, 298, 306.
8. Michael Collins, *Cooke County, Texas: Where the South and the West Meet* (Marceline, MO: Walsworth Publishing Company, 1998), 25; A. Morton Smith, *The First One Hundred Years in Cooke County* (San Antonio: Naylor

Company, 1976), 63.

9. Collins, *Cooke County, Texas*, 25–26; Smith, *The First One Hundred Years in Cooke County*, 63, 71.
10. Witherspoon & Ridings Public Relations Agency, "The Justin Story: A History of H. J. Justin & Sons, Inc." (Fort Worth: Witherspoon & Ridings, c. 1954), Joe Justin Papers, University of North Texas Oral History Collection, Denton, Texas, 2–3; Farman, *Standard of the West*, 8–10; Lee C. Jacobs, *J. R. McChesney: A Lifetime, A Legacy* (Colorado Springs: ColorTek Printing, 1994), 4–5; Roquemore, "100 Year History of Justin Boot Company," 3. Roquemore obtained the story of Justin's journey to Spanish Fort with J. I. Sewell's cargo of liquor from Louise Addington, longtime Nocona librarian and local historian who passed away in 1999 at the age of 92.
11. David Minor, "Montague County," *Handbook of Texas Online*, accessed April 2018, http://www.tshaonline.org/handbook/online/articles/hem16.
12. Lea Anne Morrell, "Spanish Fort, Texas," *Handbook of Texas Online*, accessed April 2018, http://www.tshaonline.org/handbook/online/articles/hns64.
13. Robert S. Weddle, *After the Massacre: The Violent Legacy of the San Sabá Mission* (Lubbock: Texas Tech University Press, 2007), 9, 127.
14. Jeff S. Henderson, ed., *100 Years in Montague County* (Saint Jo, TX: IPTA Printers, 1978), no page numbers.
15. Henderson, *100 Years in Montague County*; Brian Hart, "Red River Station, Texas," *Handbook of Texas Online*, accessed April 2018, http://www.tshaonline.org/handbook/online/articles/hvr24.
16. Farman, *Standard of the West*, 8–10; Justin, *Miss Enid*, 2–3; Witherspoon & Ridings, "The Justin Story," 5.
17. Farman, *Standard of the West*, 10; Witherspoon & Ridings, "The Justin Story," 4–5; *The Monitor*, McAllen, TX, January 22, 1932, reprint of an article originally published in *The Texas Weekly*. Over the years, as the Justin legend grew, many people claimed to have bought the first pair of Justin boots. I have chosen to give credence to Frank See's story because it is the only first-person account.
18. *The Monitor*, January 22, 1932.
19. Farman, *Standard of the West*, 2–10; Roquemore, "100 Year History of Justin Boot company," 5.
20. Farman, *Standard of the West*, 7–13; Justin, *Miss Enid*, 2–4.
21. Roquemore, "100 Year History of Justin Boot Company," 5; Guy Renfro Donnell, "The History of Montague County, Texas" (MA thesis, University of

Texas, 1940), 103; Morrell, "Spanish Fort, Texas," *Handbook of Texas Online*.
22. Farman, *Standard of the West*, 13–14; Morrell, "Spanish Fort, Texas," *Handbook of Texas Online*.
23. Justin, *Miss Enid*, 3–4.
24. Farman, *Standard of the West*, 14–16; Justin, *Miss Enid*, 7; Roquemore, "100 Year History of Justin Boot Company," 4–5.
25. Gard, *The Chisholm Trail*, 258–59; Campbell, *Gone to Texas*, 278–79.
26. David Minor, "Nocona, Texas," *Handbook of Texas Online*, accessed April 13, 2018, http://www.tshaonline.org/handbook/online/articles/hgn03. The Gainesville, Henrietta and Western Railway was later bought by the Missouri–Kansas–Texas line.
27. Melvin Fenoglio, ed., *The Story of Montague County: Its Past and Present* (Dallas: Curtis Media Corporation, 1989), 63; *Handbook Online*, "Nocona, Texas"; Robert H. Williams, "Peta Nocona," *Handbook of Texas Online*, accessed April 17, 2018, http://www.tsha.org/handbook/online/articles/fpefn. In 1836, Cynthia Ann Parker was taken captive by Comanches who attacked her family's settlement in north-central Texas. She lived with the tribe for twenty-four years and had three children with Peta Nocona. Their son Quanah Parker became a well-known chief who led his people into the Reservation Era.
28. Fenoglio, *The Story of Montague County*, 64; *Handbook Online*, "Nocona, Texas."
29. Farman, *Standard of the West*, 18–20.
30. Justin, *Miss Enid*, 7.
31. *Philipsburg Mail*, Philipsburg, Montana, September 30, 1938; H. Allen Anderson, "XIT Ranch," *Handbook of Texas Online*, accessed April 2018, http://www.tsha.org/handbook/online/articles/apx01; Witherspoon & Ridings, "The Justin Story," 6.
32. Farman, *Standard of the West*, 14–15; Justin, *Miss Enid*, 7.
33. Farman, *Standard of the West*, 14–16; Roquemore, "100 Year History of Justin Boot Company," 7.
34. Justin, *Miss Enid*, 7, 11; Witherspoon & Ridings, "The Justin story," 8; Cheryl Coggins Frink, "Breaking Step with Tradition," *Austin American-Statesman*, March 2, 1986. Frink, a staff writer, interviewed Enid Justin in Nocona on April 19, 1985 for the article.
35. J. Dale Terry, "Miss Enid, The Lady Bootmaker," *Texas Highways*, 1977, author's manuscript in University of North Texas Archives, Enid

Justin–Nocona Boot Company Collection, 1929–1982, 01/BA.15 (Box 1, Series 1, Papers), 2.
36. Justin, *Miss Enid*, 11–12; Terry, "Miss Enid, The Lady Bootmaker," 2.
37. Farman, *Standard of the West*, 22; Witherspoon & Ridings, "The Justin Story," 9.
38. *Nocona News*, September 24, 1908.
39. Ibid.; Beth Weese, "The Century Old Boot," *Oklahoma Magazine*, May 21, 2015, accessed April 2020, http://www.okmag.com/blog/the-century-old-boot/. Blucher died in 1932, but his company, now located in Beggs, Oklahoma, still produces custom boots.
40. *Nocona News*, October 1, 1908, May 20, 1909; Witherspoon & Ridings, "The Justin Story," 9.
41. Justin, *Miss Enid*, 13–14.
42. Justin, *Miss Enid*, 18–21, 19–20.
43. Farman, *Standard of the West*, 21–25; *Nocona News*, May 20, 1909.
44. Justin, *Miss Enid*, quote on p. 21.
45. Ralph A. Wooster, *Texas and Texans in the Great War* (Buffalo Gap, TX: State House Press, 2009), 84–95; Roquemore, "100 Year History of Justin Boot Company," 14–15; *Nocona News*, July 5, 1918.
46. Roquemore, "100 Year History of Justin Boot Company," 14; Farman, *Standard of the West*, 29.
47. Roquemore, "100 Year History of Justin Boot Company," 15; Farman, *Standard of the West*, 29–30; Justin, *Miss Enid*, 14; United States Department of the Navy commendation to H. J. Justin, Enid Justin Collection, Nocona Museum.
48. Justin, *Miss Enid*, 20–24; *Nocona News*, January 18, January 25, February 1, 1918.
49. Justin, Miss Enid, 20–24.
50. Ibid., 25; *Nocona News*, July 19, 1918.

Chapter 2

1. *Austin American-Statesman*, March 2, 1986.
2. Justin, *Miss Enid*, 25.
3. Ibid., 24.
4. H. J. Justin, Last Will & Testament, filed August 12, 1918, Cause No. 1994, Probate Minutes of Montague County, Texas, Vol. 14, page 246; Justin, *Miss

Enid, 7; Witherspoon & Ridings, "The Justin Story," 11.

5. Farman, *Standard of the West*, 34; Roquemore, "100 Year History of Justin Boot Company," 16.
6. Lee Darrigrand, "Justin Boot Company: The Standard of the West," *Western & English Fashion*, August 1988, 27; Roquemore, "100 Year History of Justin Boot Company," 16.
7. Farman, *Standard of the West*, 34; Darrigrand, "Justin Boot Company," 27; *Nocona News*, August 21, 1925.
8. Justin, *Miss Enid*, 25: Darrigrand, "Justin Boot Company," 27; Farman, *Standard of the West*, 30–34; Witherspoon & Ridings, "The Justin Story," 11; *Nocona News*, June 20, 1919.
9. Justin Boot Catalog, 1923, Justin Archives, Fort Worth, Texas.
10. Ibid.
11. Farman, *Standard of the West*, 46–49; Witherspoon & Ridings, "The Justin Story," 11.
12. Witherspoon & Ridings, "The Justin Story," 11.
13. Harold Rich, *Fort Worth: Outpost, Cowtown, Boomtown* (Norman: University of Oklahoma Press, 2014), 3–7; Janet Schmelzer, "Fort Worth, TX," *Handbook of Texas Online*, accessed May 2018, http://www.tshaonline.org/handbook/online/articles/hdf01.
14. *Handbook Online*, "Fort Worth, TX"; Rich, *Fort Worth*, 3–7; Farman, *Standard of the West*, 53–55.
15. Farman, *Standard of the West*, 49–50, 53.
16. Ibid., 50–51.
17. *Fort Worth Star-Telegram*, April 24, 1925; *Nocona News*, May 1, 1925.
18. Justin, *Miss Enid*, 26–27.
19. Farman, *Standard of the West*, 50.
20. Justin, *Miss Enid*, 26.
21. Ibid., 27.
22. Enid Justin, interview by Charles Townsend, June 24, 1969, transcript, Southwest Collection, Texas Tech University, Lubbock, Texas, 2; *Nocona News*, May 19, 1911.
23. Enid Justin, interview by Floyd Jenkins, February 26, 1986, transcript, University of North Texas Oral History Collection, Denton, Texas, 12.
24. Justin, *Miss Enid*, 26–27. Farmers and Merchants Bank president Cadmus Steven "Cad" McCall held that position from 1915 until his death in 1953.

Through the years, he would prove to be an enthusiastic supporter of Nocona Boot Company and a trusted adviser to Enid.
25. Judith N. McArthur and Harold Smith, *Texas Through Women's Eyes: The Twentieth Century Experience* (Austin: University of Texas Press, 2010), 1–3, 98; Drachman, *Enterprising Women*, 76–77, 110–13.
26. Patricia Riley Dunlap, *Riding Astride: The Frontier in Women's History* (Denver: Arden Press, 1995), 162–64; "An 80-Year-Old Bootmaker," *New Woman*, July–August 1976, scrapbook clipping in Enid Justin–Nocona Boot Company Collection, Special Collections, BA.15, Box 1825, University of North Texas Archives. In *Red River Women* (Plano, TX: Republic of Texas Press, 1996), Sherrie S. McLeroy tells the stories of eight women, including Enid Justin, who embody the frontier spirit.
27. "An 80-Year-Old Bootmaker"; Justin, *Miss Enid*, 27; *Nocona News*, July 24, 1925.
28. Justin, *Miss Enid*, 28–29; *Nocona News*, August 28, 1925.
29. Justin, *Miss Enid*, 28–29; Enid Justin, interview by Charles Townsend, 2.
30. Enid Justin, interview by Floyd Jenkins, 16; Justin, *Miss Enid*, 28–29.
31. *Nocona News*, July 24, August 7, 28, 1925; March 23, 1934.
32. Justin, *Miss Enid*, 29.
33. Justin, *Miss Enid*, 28–29, quote 30.
34. Enid Justin, interview by Floyd Jenkins, 23–24; Justin, *Miss Enid*, 28–31.
35. "Statement of Nocona Boot Company," December 31, 1925, included in Joe Justin, interview by Carol Lipscomb, transcript, University of North Texas Oral History Collection, Denton, Texas; Justin, *Miss Enid*, 31–32; "An 80-Year-Old Bootmaker"; *Nocona News*, October 9, 1925.
36. Henderson, "Search for Crude in Montague County," in *100 Years in Montague County*, n.p.; *Nocona News*, March 16, 1917; June 5, 1925; July 24, 1925.
37. Justin, *Miss Enid*, 32–33.
38. *Austin American-Statesman*, March 2, 1986; Justin, *Miss Enid*, 30; United States Patent Office; Boot Tongue, patent 1,726,269, application filed February 19, 1924.
39. Justin, *Miss Enid*, 29; Enid Justin, interview by Charles Townsend, 3; Nocona Boot Company Credit Report, produced by R. G. Dun & Co., July 24, 1931, Justin Archives, Fort Worth, Texas.
40. Justin, *Miss Enid*, 33.

NOTES

41. Justin, *Miss Enid*, 33–34; Enid Justin, interview by Charles Townsend, 2–3.
42. Justin, *Miss Enid*, 33–34.
43. Justin, *Miss Enid*, 33–35; Enid Justin, interview by Floyd Jenkins, 18–21.
44. Justin, Miss Enid, 35–36; Richard L. Himmel, "Nocona Boot Company," *Handbook of Texas Online*, accessed January 2010, http://www.tshaonline.org/handbook/online/articles/hdf01.
45. Enid Justin, interview by Charles Townsend, 3; Justin, *Miss Enid*, 29, 58.
46. Justin, *Miss Enid*, 37–39, 38.
47. Ibid., 36–38.
48. Enid Justin, interview by Charles Townsend, 3; Justin, *Miss Enid*, 37–39.
49. Justin, *Miss Enid*, 39.
50. Ibid.
51. Justin, *Miss Enid*, 44–46, quote 44. On June 25, 1910, Congress passed the Mann Act, also known as the White-Slave Traffic Act, which made it illegal to "transport any woman or girl" across state lines "for any immoral purpose." The law was ostensibly aimed at keeping innocent girls from being lured into prostitution, but it also offered a way to make a crime out of many kinds of consensual sexual activity.
52. Justin, *Miss Enid*, 44–45.
53. Ibid., 40–45, quote 45; Enid Justin, interview by Floyd Jenkins, 15–16, quote 16.
54. Delano and Rieff, *Texas Boots*, 114; Enid Justin, interview by Charles Townsend, 2.
55. Justin, *Miss Enid*, quote 63.

Chapter 3

1. "Boots in a Woman's World," April 1969, clipping in Enid Justin, interview by Charles Townsend, Southwest Collection, Oral History Program, Texas Tech University, Lubbock, Texas.
2. *Nocona News*, March 23, 1934; Justin, *Miss Enid*, 28–29, 37; Enid Justin, interview by Charles Townsend, 7–8; W. E. Justin to Enid Justin, February 4, 1926, scrapbook, Brad Taylor Papers, Enid Justin Collection, Nocona Museum.
3. Enid Justin, interview by Charles Townsend, 5.
4. Campbell, *Gone to Texas*, 332–34; David M. Kennedy, *Freedom from Fear: The American People in Depression and War, 1929–1945* (New York: Oxford University Press, 1999), 10–13.

NOTES

5. Jacobs, *J. R. McChesney*, 85.
6. Jane Pattie, *Cowboy Spurs and Their Makers* (College Station: Texas A&M University Press, 1991), 42; Jacobs, *J. R. McChesney*, 5; Collins, *Cooke County, Texas*, 45.
7. Jacobs, *J. R. McChesney*, 73.
8. Jacobs, *J. R. McChesney*, 73–74; Pattie, *Cowboy Spurs*, 42.
9. Pattie, *Cowboy Spurs*, 42–43; Jacobs, *J. R. McChesney*, 74–75. In much that is written about McChesney, the town of Broken Arrow is incorrectly identified as Broken Bow, a town located in McCurtain County, 150 miles from Tulsa in the southeast corner of Oklahoma. In telling the McChesney story, Lee Jacobs related a slightly different account of the blacksmith shop purchase. According to Jacobs, McChesney went to Tulsa with a twenty-dollar gold piece. He paid $18.50 for the blacksmith shop and used the remaining $1.50 to buy groceries.
10. Pattie, *Cowboy Spurs*, 42–43; Jacobs, *J. R. McChesney*, 74–75.
11. Pattie, *Cowboy Spurs*, 43.
12. Collins, *Cooke County, Texas*, 29, 45.
13. Collins, *Cooke County, Texas*, 45; Jacobs, *J. R. McChesney*, 75–76; Lee C. Jacobs, *A McChesney Manual: Scrutinizing Bits and Spurs of an Innovative Creator* (Colorado Springs: self-published, n.d.), 18.
14. Pattie, *Cowboy Spurs*, 45; Jacobs, *J. R. McChesney*, 80.
15. Jack Thomas, "History of the Texas Spur," *The Western Horseman* (August 1973): 86–87; Jacobs, *A McChesney Manual*, 39.
16. Thomas, "History of the Texas Spur," 87; Jacobs, *A McChesney Manual*, 39.
17. Jacobs, *J. R. McChesney*, 5; Jacobs, *A McChesney Manual*, 39; Pattie, *Cowboy Spurs*, 45–47; Joe Justin, interview by Carol Lipscomb, 38.
18. Collins, *Cooke County, Texas*, 45; Jacobs, *J. R. McChesney*, 76.
19. Michael Tower, "Pauls Valley," Encyclopedia of Oklahoma History and Culture, Oklahoma Historical Society, accessed October 2019, https://www.okhistory.org/publications/enc/entry.php?entry=PA019.
20. Jacobs, *J. R. McChesney*, 13, 77, 83; Pattie, *Cowboy Spurs*, 45–47. August Buermann Manufacturing Company of Newark, New Jersey, maker of Star Brand spurs, was the largest manufacturer in the country.
21. *Pauls Valley Democrat*, January 10, 1928; Pattie, *Cowboy Spurs*, 47–48; Jacobs, *J. R. McChesney*, 77–78.
22. Enid Justin, interview by Floyd Jenkins, 63; *Pauls Valley Democrat*, January 15, 1928; Jacobs, *J. R. McChesney*, 78; Pattie, *Cowboy Spurs*, 48; *Nocona News*, July

25, 1930; R. G. Dun & Co., Nocona Boot Company Credit Report, July 24, 1931, Justin Archives.
23. Jacobs, *J. R. McChesney*, 85.
24. Contract between Nocona Boot Company and R. J. Kerruish, September 4, 1930, Enid Justin Collection, Nocona Museum.
25. Jacobs, *J. R. McChesney*, 86–89; Luciel Leonard, interview by Carol Lipscomb, August 3, 1995, transcript, University of North Texas Oral History Collection, Denton, Texas, 5–6.
26. Luciel Leonard, interview by Carol Lipscomb, 5–6.
27. Jacobs, *J. R. McChesney*, 86, 89; Pattie, Cowboy Spurs, 17–25.
28. Jacobs, *J. R. McChesney*, 85–86.
29. Ibid., 135; Pattie, *Cowboy Spurs*, 48.
30. Jacobs, *J. R. McChesney*, 87, 95, 105.
31. Ibid., 105. When Nocona Boot Company ceased production of McChesney bits and spurs in 1948, some of the equipment was acquired by spur-maker Adolph Bayers of Gilliland, Texas, and eventually found a home in the Panhandle-Plains Historical Museum in Canyon, Texas.
32. Enid Justin, interview by Charles Townsend, 3; Enid Justin, interview by Floyd Jenkins, 73–74; Justin, *Miss Enid*, 52; Kennedy, *Freedom from Fear*, 58–59, 163; R. G. Dun & Co., Nocona Boot Company Credit Report, March 3, 1933, Justin Archives.
33. *Nocona News*, March 23, 1934; construction contract between Nocona Boot Company and C. E. McCarley, Builder, March 21, 1934, Enid Justin Collection, Nocona Museum.
34. *Nocona News*, May 27, 1932; Farman, *Standard of the West*, 74.
35. Enid Justin, interview by Charles Townsend, 4; Justin, *Miss Enid*, 52; "Unusual Occupations," accessed October 2019, www.shieldspictures.com/unusualoccupations.html.
36. Enid Justin, interview by Charles Townsend, 4. For a detailed account of the shift in Texas's public image from southern to western, see Light Cummins, "History, Memory, and Rebranding Texas as Western for the 1936 Centennial," in *This Corner of Canaan: Essays in Honor of Randolph B. Campbell*, eds. Richard B. McCaslin, Donald E. Chipman, and Andrew J. Torget (Denton: University of North Texas Press, 2013).
37. Farman, *Standard of the West*, 73–74.
38. *Nocona News*, August 20, 1937.

39. Justin, *Miss Enid*, 28.
40. *Wichita Daily Times*, April 25, 1938.
41. Leslie Humphrey to H. J. Justin & Sons, April 29, 1938; Enid Justin to Earl Justin, April 29, 1938, Justin Archives.
42. Earl Justin to Enid Justin, copy to Leslie Humphrey, May 3, 1938, Justin Archives.
43. Earl Justin to Enid Justin, May 3, 1938; Leslie Humphrey to Earl Justin, May 6, May 17, 1938; Earl Justin to Leslie Humphrey, May 14, 1938, Justin Archives.
44. Earl Justin to Enid Justin, May 3, 1938, Justin Archives.
45. Enid Justin to Earl Justin, May 11, 1938, Justin Archives.
46. Justin, *Miss Enid*, 63.
47. Ibid., 62–63.
48. Scrapbook clipping dated May 7, 1937, in Enid Justin-Nocona Boot Company Collection, BA.15, Box 1826, University of North Texas Archives. The Wagner Act, also known as the National Labor Relations Act of 1935, made the federal government the arbiter of employer-employee relations through the creation of the National Labor Relations Board. The law recognized for the first time the right of workers to organize and bargain collectively with their employers.
49. Ibid.
50. Congressman Ed Gossett, 13th District, to Enid Justin, April 11, 1939, Enid Justin-Nocona Boot Company Collection, BA.15, Box 1819, University of North Texas Archives.
51. Enid Justin, interview by Charles Townsend, 5; *Nocona News*, February 10, 1939.
52. *Nocona News*, February 3, 1939; Justin, *Miss Enid*, 75–76; Pony Express Race Scrapbook, Enid Justin Collection, Nocona Museum.
53. *Nocona News*, February 10, 1939.
54. Ibid.; Justin, *Miss Enid*, 76–77.
55. Pony Express Race Scrapbook.
56. Western Union Telegram, March 6, 1939, Pony Express Race Scrapbook.
57. Justin, *Miss Enid*, 77–79; Pony Express Race Scrapbook.
58. *Nocona News*, May 12, 1939; Justin, *Miss Enid*, 74–79; Pony Express Race Scrapbook. Shannon Davidson was killed a few years later in a tragic farm accident.
59. Pony Express Race Scrapbook; Justin, *Miss Enid*, 79.
60. Enid Justin, interview by Floyd Jenkins, 95; Justin, *Miss Enid*, 78.

61. Enid Justin, interview by Charles Townsend, 5; Justin, *Miss Enid*, 79.
62. *Austin American-Statesman*, March 2, 1986.

Chapter 4
1. Justin, *Miss Enid*, 81.
2. Ibid., 46–47.
3. Ibid.
4. Ibid., 48
5. Ibid., 48–49; Enid Justin, interview by Floyd Jenkins, 65.
6. Justin, *Miss Enid*, 49; Joe Justin, interview by Carol Lipscomb, March 23, 1995, transcript, University of North Texas Oral History Collection, Denton, Texas, 20.
7. Justin, *Miss Enid*, 49–50.
8. Ibid., 50.
9. *Nocona News*, April 12, 26, 1940.
10. *Nocona News*, August 28, 1975.
11. *Nocona News*, July 18, 1941.
12. Ibid.; Enid Justin, interview by Charles Townsend, 5.
13. Arthur Herman, *Freedom's Forge: How American Business Produced Victory in World War II* (New York: Random House, 2012), 164–65, 193–99.
14. Luciel Leonard, interview by Carol Lipscomb, August 3, 1995, transcript, University of North Texas Oral History Collection, Denton, Texas, 12; Enid Justin, interview by Charles Townsend, 3.
15. Justin, *Miss Enid*, 52–53; Enid Justin, interview by Charles Townsend, 3–5; Luciel Leonard, interview by Carol Lipscomb, 11–12.
16. Ibid.
17. Enid Justin, interview by Charles Townsend, 4; Justin, *Miss Enid*, 52–53.
18. Justin, *Miss Enid*, 53; Enid Justin, interview by Charles Townsend, 5.
19. Herman, *Freedom's Forge*, 262–66; Luciel Leonard, interview by Carol Lipscomb, 9,11; War Labor Board File, Steve Pickens Papers, Enid Justin Collection, Nocona Museum.
20. WLB File, Steve Pickens Papers, Enid Justin Collection, Nocona Museum.
21. Ibid.; Kennedy, *Freedom from Fear*, 620, 640–41.
22. , Enid Justin to Earl Justin, July 7, 1944, WLB File, Steve Pickens Papers, Enid Justin Collection, Nocona Museum.
23. Ibid.

24. "Request for Review," c. May 25, 1944, WLB File, Steve Pickens Papers, Enid Justin Collection, Nocona Museum.
25. Enid Justin to Ed Gossett, July 31, 1944, Gossett to Justin, August 2, 1944, WLB File, Steve Pickens Papers, Enid Justin Collection, Nocona Museum.
26. Enid Justin, interview by Charles Townsend, 7; "General Practice as to Salary Raises Relative to Straight Time Workers," WLB File, Steve Pickens Papers, Enid Justin Collection, Nocona Museum.
27. Enid Justin to A. H. Hertwig, November 27, 1943, WLB File, Steve Pickens Papers, Enid Justin Collection, Nocona Museum; Luciel Leonard, interview by Carol Lipscomb, 11–12.
28. Luciel Leonard, interview by Carol Lipscomb, 15–16; Justin, *Miss Enid*, 54.
29. Justin, *Miss Enid*, 54, 83.
30. Ibid., 54.
31. Campbell, *Gone to Texas*, 378–79.
32. Enid Justin to E. J. Gilbert, January 13, 1947, Steve Pickens Papers, Enid Justin Collection, Nocona Museum; *Nocona News*, March 14, 1947; *Wichita Daily Times*, July 30, 1947; "Female Bootmaker Added to Texas Gallery of Notables," *Boot and Shoe Recorder*, March 15, 1948, scrapbook clipping, Brad Taylor Papers, Enid Justin Collection, Nocona Museum.
33. Enid Justin, interview by Charles Townsend, 5–6; Justin, *Miss Enid*, 55–56.
34. Justin, *Miss Enid*, 55; Enid Justin, interview by Charles Townsend, 6.
35. Justin, *Miss Enid*, 55–56; Enid Justin, interview by Charles Townsend, 5–6. In *Up the Chisholm Trail: The Cattle Trails of Montague County* (Gale Cochran-Smith, ed., Montague County Historical Commission, 2017, 46–47), maps illustrate the many branches of the Chisholm Trail in the county, including the one just east of the site of Nocona Boot Company.
36. *Nocona News*, March 14, 1947.
37. Ibid.; Justin, *Miss Enid*, 56–57.
38. Justin, Miss Enid, 56; *Nocona News*, August 1, 1947, August 28, 1975.
39. *Nocona News*, August 1, 1947; Justin, *Miss Enid*, 56.
40. *Nocona News*, July 25, 1947, June 4, 1948; Justin, *Miss Enid*, 56.
41. *Fort Worth Press*, June 10, 1948; Justin, *Miss Enid*, 56–57.
42. *Wichita Falls Record News*, June 10, 1948.
43. Luciel Leonard, interview by Carol Lipscomb, 17–18; Justin, *Miss Enid*, 55–56; *Wichita Falls Record News*, June 10, 1948. Alfred Randolph Bill Tandy was a veteran pilot who often flew to Nocona to do business with Enid. During

NOTES

WWII, Tandy flew a B-26 Marauder, a twin-engine medium bomber, over Europe on fifty successful missions. The Tandy Leather Company in Tulsa was not connected to the Hinckley-Tandy Leather Company (later to become Tandy Leather Factory and Radio Shack) begun in Fort Worth in 1919 by Bill's grandfather Dave Tandy and partner Norton Hinckley. https://tulsahistory.org/hall-of-fame/alfred-randolph-bill-tandy.

44. Luciel Leonard, interview by Carol Lipscomb, 14; *Nocona News*, June 4, 1948; August 28, 1975.
45. *Nocona News*, June 4, 1948; *Wichita Falls Record News*, June 10, 1948; Justin, *Miss Enid*, 57.
46. Justin, *Miss Enid*, 57–58, 85.
47. Ibid., 85; Luciel Leonard, interview by Carol Lipscomb, 43.
48. Justin, *Miss Enid*, 84–85.
49. Ibid., 84.
50. Marcia Taylor, interview by Carol Lipscomb, May 31, 1995, transcript, Oral History Collection, University of North Texas, Denton, Texas, 6–7; Delano and Rieff, *Texas Boots*, 96–99; "She Shoes Cowboys," February 1949, scrapbook clipping, Enid Justin Collection, Nocona Museum.

Chapter 5
1. Justin, *Miss Enid*, 57.
2. Ibid., 51; *Nocona News*, August 28, 1975.
3. Farman, *Standard of the West*, 67–68; Bob Hyatt, "How to Make Boots," *Preview of Texas*, c. 1952, copy of article in Brad Taylor Papers, Enid Justin Collection, Nocona Museum.
4. Beard, *The Cowboy Boot Book*, 14–15; "List of Westerns on Television," accessed October 2018, https://en.wikipedia.org/wiki/list_of_westerns_on_television.
5. *Dallas Morning News*, June 29, 1958; *Nocona News*, August 1, 1952.
6. *Fort Worth Star-Telegram*, March 24, 1950; *Nocona News*, August 1, 1952; W. N. Furey, "Nocona Boots the U.S., Makes 'War' Helmets." *Fort Worth Press*, October 12, 1953, scrapbook clipping, Brad Taylor Papers, Enid Justin Collection, Nocona Museum.
7. *Nocona News*, June 23, 1950; Justin, *Miss Enid*, 64–65.
8. Justin, *Miss Enid*, 64–65; Enid Justin, interview by Charles Townsend, 9.
9. *Nocona News*, June 23, 1950, December 15, 1951, December 12, 1952.
10. Rachael Barber to Willard Haselbush, August 12, 1948, Justin Archives.

NOTES

11. W. E. Justin to Bob Travis, July 11, 1946; Rachel Barber to Willard Haselbush, August 12, 1948, Justin Archives. The documents relating to the three newspaper articles were found paper-clipped together in the Justin Archives, possibly as evidence for the lawsuit.
12. Adams, *Western Words*, 86 (page reference is to reprint edition).
13. Farman, *Standard of the West*, 51.
14. Ibid.; Enid Justin, interview by Charles Townsend, 3.
15. Farman, *Standard of the West*, 95–103.
16. Ibid., 103.
17. *Nocona News*, May 30, 1952, August 1, 1952; "Dear Mae Manners," November 14, 1950, scrapbook clipping, Brad Taylor Papers, Enid Justin Collection, Nocona Museum.
18. "La Semaine du Texas en France," Executive Report 1655, July 3, 1952, *New York Herald Tribune*, European Edition, Paris, August 5, 1952, BA.15, Box 1815, Special Collections, University of North Texas Archives.
19. "Texas Week on the Riviera," Executive Report 1741, July 18, 1952, Box 1815, Special Collections, University of North Texas Archives; *Nocona News*, July 24, 1958.
20. *Nocona News*, June 13, 1952; Justin, *Miss Enid*, 70; "Gavel From Here to Open Governors Meeting Today," June 29, 1952, scrapbook clipping, Enid Justin Collection, Nocona Museum.
21. Justin, *Miss Enid*, 70.
22. *Nocona News*, August 28, 1953, April 9, August 20, 1954; Farman, *Standard of the West*, 127–28; Delano and Rieff, *Texas Boots*, 95; "Texas Women of Distinction" award certificate, March 10, 1953, scrapbook, Brad Taylor Papers, Enid Justin Collection, Nocona Museum.
23. *Nocona News*, August 1, 1952; "Female Bootmaker Added to Texas Gallery of Notables," *Boot and Shoe Recorder*, March 15, 1948, scrapbook clipping, Enid Justin Collection, Nocona Museum. Lake Success on New York's Long Island was the temporary home of the UN from 1946 to 1951.
24. Enid Justin, interview by Charles Townsend, 9; *Nocona News*, July 24, 1958, August 28, 1975.
25. Joe Justin, interview by Carol Lipscomb, March 23, 1995, transcript, University of North Texas Oral History Collection, Denton, Texas, 44–45, 52; Farman, *Standard of the West*, 128.
26. Joe Justin, interview by Carol Lipscomb, 46–53; *Nocona News*, September 10,

1954; Enid Justin, interview by Charles Townsend, 7–8.

27. Joe Justin, interview by Carol Lipscomb, 51–52; Luciel Leonard, interview by Carol Lipscomb, August 3, 1995, transcript, University of North Texas Oral History Collection, 13.
28. Joe Justin, interview by Carol Lipscomb, 47–48; Luciel Leonard, interview by Carol Lipscomb, 23.
29. *Nocona News*, July 19, 1957; Farman, *Standard of the West*, 148–49.
30. *Nocona News*, August 21, 1958, August 6, 1959, August 28, 1975.
31. Justin, *Miss Enid*, 63–64.
32. Ibid.; Luciel Leonard, interview by Carol Lipscomb, 24–25; Enid Justin, interview by Charles Townsend, 6–7.
33. Justin, *Miss Enid*, 84.
34. "Only Woman Cowboy Boot-Maker Has Shop on Chisholm Trail," *Quarter Horse Journal*, April 1954, scrapbook clipping, BA.15, Box 1823, Special Collections, University of North Texas Archives.
35. *Nocona News*, January 30, 1953, January 20, 1956; Farman, *Standard of the West*, 224.
36. *Nocona News*, June 13, 1952, September 2, 1955.
37. *Nocona News*, May 28, 1954; "Texas in Review," Texas Archive of the Moving Image, accessed July 2019, https://www.texasarchive.org/library/index.php/Category:Texas_in_Review.
38. Blanche to Enid Justin, June 2, 1954, scrapbook, Brad Taylor Papers, Enid Justin Collection, Nocona Museum. The letter from Blanche (no last name) to Enid was written on Dickson-Jenkins Manufacturing Company stationery. The Fort Worth apparel manufacturer most probably sold western clothing to the Nocona Boot Company retail store. Blanche and Enid were likely business acquaintances.
39. *Wichita Falls Record News*, June 10, 1948; "Nocona Literally Lifts Itself by Bootstraps," c. 1948, scrapbook clipping, Brad Taylor Papers, Enid Justin Collection, Nocona Museum.
40. *Nocona News*, September 5, 1952.
41. *Nocona News*, February 14, 1941, September 5, 1952.
42. Ibid.
43. *Nocona News*, September 5, 1952, "Nocona Literally Lifts Itself by Bootstraps," c. 1948, clipping, Brad Taylor Papers, Enid Justin Collection, Nocona Museum; "Nocona Athletic Goods Story," accessed June 2019, www.nokona.

com/our-story/. In 2006, the 80-year-old Nocona Athletic Goods factory burned. The cause was an overheated box fan, the loss estimated at $5 million. The factory moved to Enid's old downtown location, where the company resumed production ten days after the fire, and none of the employees lost any wages. In 2017, the company, still partially owned by the Storey family, relocated to the renovated 1948 Nocona Boot Company building on US Hwy. 82. It remains one of a handful of companies that manufacture baseball gloves in the United States.

44. *Nocona News*, June 4, 1948, June 13, 1952.
45. Ibid.
46. *Nocona News*, June 4, 1948, June 13, 1952; F & E Leather exhibit, Nocona Museum.
47. *Nocona News*, September 5, 1930, June 4, 1948.
48. *Nocona News*, July 23, 1937; Application for Registration of Trade-Mark, June 23, 1937; Department of Commerce, U.S. Patent Office to Nocona Boot Company, September 28, 1937; Enid Justin to C. A. Snow, September 11, 1937. Papers relating to Nocona Baby Shoe Company are attached to Joe Justin, interview by Carol Lipscomb, Oral History Collection, University of North Texas, Denton, Texas.
49. *Nocona News*, July 23, 1937, April 8, 1938; A. Billings to C. A. Snow, October 4, 1937; C. A. Snow to Enid Justin, October 7, 1937; Enid Justin to C. A. Snow, September 11, 1937; Edward Clark, Secretary of State, to C. A. Snow, October 4, 1937. Papers attached to Joe Justin, interview by Carol Lipscomb.
50. *Nocona News*, June 13, 1952; *Fort Worth Press*, October 12, 1953; *Dallas Morning News*, May 9, 1941.
51. *Wichita Daily Times*, April 10, 1948; "Leather Industry," *Handbook of Texas Online*, accessed February 28, 2019, https://www.tshaonline.org/handbook/online/articles/dr101.
52. "Tex Tan Western Leather has long history in Yoakum," *Victoria Advocate*, Victoria, Texas, February 5, 2006; Mary M. Orozco-Vallejo, "Yoakum, TX," *Handbook of Texas Online*, accessed August 2018, http://www.tshaonline.org/handbook/online/articles/hfy01.
53. Orozco-Vallejo, "Yoakum, TX," *Handbook of Texas Online*; Enid Justin, interview by Floyd Jenkins, November 13, 1981, transcript, Oral History Collection, University of North Texas, Denton, Texas, 42–44.
54. Justin, *Miss Enid*, 38–39, 67; Enid Justin, interview by Charles Townsend, 9.

55. Justin, *Miss Enid*, 67; Delano and Rieff, *Texas Boots*, 164.

Chapter 6

1. "Rusty Steps in to Aid Company," c. 1976, scrapbook clipping, Enid Justin Collection, Nocona Museum.
2. Rob Patterson, "Her Boots Were Like Her Children," *Western & English Today*, March/April, 2007, 40; Enid Justin, interview by Charles Townsend, 6; Donna Bearden and Jamie Frucht, *The Texas Sampler: A Stitch in Time* (Austin: Governor's Committee on Aging, a Bicentennial Publication, 1976), 160.
3. Cheryl Runquist, "Boots in a Woman's World," April 1969, newspaper clipping included in Enid Justin, interview by Charles Townsend, Southwest Collection, Texas Tech University; William T. Rives, "She Shoes Cowboys," February 1949, article in Enid Justin Collection, Nocona Museum.
4. "Miss Enid Justin: The Nocona Boot Lady," *Western & English Today*, October 1987, 13; McLeroy, *Red River Women*, 235.
5. *Fort Worth Star-Telegram*, July 18, 1968; *San Francisco Examiner*, November 9, 1972; *Colorado Springs Gazette Telegraph*, August 11, 1972; *East Oregonian*, Pendleton, Oregon, September 22, 1973.
6. McLeroy, *Red River Women*, 237; Justin, *Miss Enid*, 58; *Las Vegas Sun*, January 22, 1973; *San Francisco Examiner*, November 9, 1972.
7. Purchase Agreement, March 23, 1965, included in Joe Justin, interview by Carol Lipscomb, March 23, 1995, transcript, Oral History Collection, University of North Texas, Denton, Texas.
8. Dorothy D. DeMoss, "Clothing Manufacture," *Handbook of Texas Online*, accessed November 2018, http://www.tshaonline.org/handbook/online/articles/dlc02.
9. *Nocona News*, April 8, July 29, 1965; Purchase Agreement, included in Joe Justin, interview by Carol Lipscomb.
10. *Nocona News*, June 3, July 29, August 5, 1965; Purchase Agreement, Joe Justin, interview by Carol Lipscomb.
11. *Nocona News*, April 4, 1969, January 8, 1970; Luciel Leonard, interview by Carol Lipscomb, August 3, 1995, Oral History Collection, University of North Texas, Denton, Texas, 32; Runquist, "Boots in a Woman's World." Action-Line's purchase of Texas Togs assets and lease of its former location were not negotiated with Enid but with Mel Chapman, owner of Nocona Belt Company. Chapman, who also held the position of vice president and general

manager of Nocona Boot Company, purchased the old downtown boot factory building from Enid around the time that Texas Togs closed, so it appears that he acquired the assets of that defunct firm when he purchased the building. Chapman's belt manufacturing company, begun in 1968, was a successful addition to Nocona's leather industry. He would eventually leave Nocona Boot Company to concentrate on his belt business.

12. Luciel Leonard, interview by Carol Lipscomb, 30–31; Joe Justin, interview by Carol Lipscomb, 77–78; Justin, *Miss Enid*, 64; *Nocona News*, August 28, 1975. The profit-sharing plan remained in place until 1981, when Nocona Boot Company merged with Justin Industries and the program was discontinued.
13. Farman, *Standard of the West*, 143–44. Farman gives the incorrect date of 1954 for the lawsuit, as court records show the suit took place in 1964.
14. Ibid., 144–47.
15. Ibid., 146–47.
16. District Court of Montague County, Texas, 97th Judicial District, *John Justin Jr. v. Nocona Boot Company, Inc., et al.*, Cause No. 14633, September 25, 1964, Plaintiff's Original Petition, 3.
17. Ibid.; *John Justin Jr. v. Nocona Boot Company, Inc.*, Defendant's Answer to Original Petition, 1–4.
18. *John Justin Jr. v. Nocona Boot Company, Inc.*, Judgment.
19. Farman, *Standard of the West*, 148; Justin, *Miss Enid*, 59; *Capital Horseman*, May 1969, scrapbook clipping, Brad Taylor Papers, Enid Justin Collection, Nocona Museum.
20. Enid Justin, interview by Charles Townsend, 4, 7; Justin, *Miss Enid*, 65–66; *Fort Worth Star-Telegram*, July 18, 1968.
21. *Nocona News*, October 14, 1971; Enid Justin, interview by Charles Townsend, 7; Justin, *Miss Enid*, 65.
22. *Nocona News*, August 28, 1975; Otis Nelson to R. S. Lemon, December 5, 1963, Enid Justin Collection, Nocona Museum.
23. Enid Justin, interview by Charles Townsend, 4, 8; *Fort Worth Star-Telegram*, July 18, 1968; *Standard Times*, New Bedford, MA, February 17, 1967.
24. Enid Justin, interview by Charles Townsend, 10.
25. Enid Justin, interview by Charles Townsend, 7–8.
26. *Nocona News*, October 14, 1971; *Wichita Falls Record News*, September 17, 1971.
27. Delano and Rieff, *Texas Boots*, 11; Beard, *The Cowboy Boot Book*, 17.

28. *Shiner Gazette*, Shiner, Texas, July 4, 1974.
29. "Nocona News" (Nocona Boot Company newsletter), August 1972, Enid Justin Collection, Nocona Museum.
30. Ibid.; *Nocona News*, April 20, 1972; "Nocona Hits Profit Trail in Eastern Boot Trend," *American Shoemaking*, May 3, 1972, clipping in Enid Justin Collection, Nocona Museum. Mel Chapman became vice president in 1971 after the death of R. S. "Ruff" Lemon.
31. *Nocona News*, April 20, 1972; *The Sunday Oklahoman*, Oklahoma City, December 10, 1972.
32. "Nocona News" (NBC newsletter), March 1973, Enid Justin Collection, Nocona Museum.
33. *Fort Worth Star-Telegram*, May 31, 1973; *Wichita Falls Times*, May 27, 1973; Justin, *Miss Enid*, 59; "Nocona News" (NBC newsletter), June 1974, Nocona Museum.
34. *Nocona News*, May 10, 1973, August 28, 1975; "Nocona News" (NBC newsletter), June 1973, Nocona Museum.
35. "She Gets a Boot out of Work," *Wichita Falls Times*, c. 1973, scrapbook clipping, Enid Justin Collection, Nocona Museum; "Miss Enid, Bootmaker," *Single Magazine*, September 1973, scrapbook clipping, Enid Justin Collection, Nocona Museum; *Nocona News*, February 8, 1973; *Industry News* 4, No. 5, May 1973, scrapbook clipping, Enid Justin Collection, Nocona Museum.
36. *Nocona News*, September 20, 1973.
37. "Miss Enid Justin—Honorary Life Member of the Texas Hereford Association," *The Texas Hereford*, January 1973, scrapbook clipping, Enid Justin Collection, Nocona Museum; *Nocona News*, February 1, 8, 1973; Justin, *Miss Enid*, 26, 88.
38. *Nocona News*, May 4, 1972.
39. *Nocona News*, December 20, 1973; *Daily Oklahoman*, Oklahoma City, October 29, 1973, Justin, *Miss Enid*, 87.
40. "She Gets a Boot out of Work," *Wichita Falls Times*, c. 1973, scrapbook clipping, Enid Justin Collection, Nocona Museum; *Salt Lake Tribune*, July 24, 1974; "They Died with Their Boots On . . . and the Boots Were Justin's," *Master Shoe Rebuilder*, March 1974, scrapbook clipping, Enid Justin Collection, Nocona Museum.
41. *Deseret News*, Salt Lake City, Utah, July 25, 1974; *Las Vegas Sun*, June 16, 1974; Justin, *Miss Enid*, 59–60. H. J. Justin & Sons was renamed Justin Industries, Inc., on October 16, 1972, after acquiring Acme Brick Company.

NOTES

42. Joe Justin, interview by Carol Lipscomb, March 23, 1995, transcript, Oral History Collection, University of North Texas, Denton, Texas, 80–81.
43. Joe Justin, interview by Carol Lipscomb, 57–64.
44. Ibid.
45. "Nocona News" (NBC newsletter), June 1974, Enid Justin Collection, Nocona Museum.
46. "Nocona News" (NBC newsletter), June, December 1974, Enid Justin Collection, Nocona Museum; *Nocona News*, August 28, 1975.
47. Justin, *Miss Enid*, 68; George Dolan column, "Shabby Boots Result in gift," *Fort Worth Star-Telegram*, scrapbook clipping, c. 1964, Enid Justin-Nocona Boot Company Collection, BA.15, Box 1826, University of North Texas Archives.
48. *Nocona News*, January 6, 1972, August 28, 1975; *Oklahoma City Times*, December 8, 1972; *Gazette Telegraph*, Colorado Springs, August 11, 1972; Justin, *Miss Enid*, 72–73.
49. Justin, *Miss Enid*, 72–73; *Nocona News*, August 28, September 18, 25, 1975.
50. *Nocona News*, August 28, 1975.
51. Ibid.; Justin, *Miss Enid*, 61; "Nocona News" (NBC newsletter), July 1975.
52. *Nocona News*, August 28, 1975.
53. Ibid.; Justin, *Miss Enid*, 60; *Deseret News*, Salt Lake City, Utah, July 25, 1974; 1974 Nocona Boot Company Catalog, Enid Justin Collection, Nocona Museum.
54. Voices of Oklahoma Oral History Project, interview with Ray Ackerman, September 30, 2009, accessed February 2019, https://www.voicesofoklahoma.com/wp-content/uploads/2013/09/19.mp3.
55. "Case Histories," *Texas Monthly*, 1979, scrapbook clipping, "Even Smallest Detail Painstakingly Realistic," *Lifestyle*, c. 1979, scrapbook clipping, Enid Justin-Nocona Boot Company Collection, BA.15, Box 1826, University of North Texas Archives.
56. "Even Smallest Detail Painstakingly Realistic," *Lifestyle*, c. 1979, scrapbook clipping, Enid Justin-Nocona Boot Company Collection, BA.15, Box 1826, University of North Texas Archives.
57. Voices of Oklahoma Oral History Project, interview with Ray Ackerman.
58. "Case Histories," *Texas Monthly*, c. 1979, scrapbook clipping, Enid Justin-Nocona Boot Company Collection, BA.15, Box 1826, University of North Texas, Denton, Texas.

NOTES

59. Ibid.; Enid Justin, interview by Floyd Jenkins, November 13, 1981, transcript, Oral History Collection, University of North Texas, Denton, Texas, 41; Voices of Oklahoma Oral History Project, interview with Ray Ackerman.
60. *Nocona News*, March 2, 1978; *Denton Record Chronicle*, Denton, Texas, November 11, 1976; "Nocona News" (NBC newsletter), September 1975, Enid Justin Collection, Nocona Museum. Nocona Boot Company's Bicentennial boot is on display in the Nocona Museum.
61. Justin, *Miss Enid*, 60; *Nocona News*, October 14, 1979; *Denton Record Chronicle*, October 11, 1976.
62. "United States Bicentennial," accessed July 2019, https://en.wikipedia.org/wiki/United-States-Bicentennial.

Chapter 7

1. "Boot Hill News" (NBC newsletter), Enid Justin Collection, Nocona Museum.
2. "Nocona News" (NBC newsletter), December 1976, Enid Justin Collection, Nocona Museum.
3. Joe Justin, interview by Carol Lipscomb, March 23, 1995, transcript, Oral History Collection, University of North Texas, Denton, Texas, 68–69; *Nocona News*, October 14, 1976.
4. *Wichita Falls Times*, April 14, 1977; "Nocona News" (NBC newsletter), Spring 1977, Enid Justin Collection, Nocona Museum.
5. *Wichita Falls Times*, October 14, 1976; "Nocona News" (NBC newsletter), Fall 1977, Enid Justin Collection, Nocona Museum; *Nocona News*, October 14, 1976.
6. *Nocona News*, September 15, 22, 1977; "Nocona News" (NBC newsletter), Fall, Winter 1977, Enid Justin Collection, Nocona Museum.
7. *Moulton Eagle*, Moulton, Texas, October 14, 1977, February 17, 1978; "Nocona News" (NBC newsletter), Spring 1977, Enid Justin Collection, Nocona Museum. According to the *Moulton Eagle*, the Moulton Boot Company was "fully operational" in February 1978, producing boots under the trade name "Shenandoah." The boots were distributed "to various firms throughout the United States."
8. *Moulton Eagle*, March 11, 1977; "Nocona News" (NBC newsletter), Spring 1977, Enid Justin Collection, Nocona Museum.
9. *Nocona News*, March 2, 1978; "Nocona News" (NBC newsletter), Spring, Fall 1977, Enid Justin Collection, Nocona Museum; "Nocona introduces

Bootmakers Collection," *Western Outfitter*, June 1977, scrapbook clipping, Enid Justin-Nocona Boot Company Collection, BA.15, Box 1826, University of North Texas Archives.

10. Enid Justin, interview by Floyd Jenkins, November 13, 1981, transcript, Oral History Collection, University of North Texas, Denton, Texas, 71–73; District Court of Montague County, Texas, 97th Judicial District, *Joe Justin v. Enid Justin, et al.*, Cause No. 18,706, July 17, 1980; Oral Deposition of Chester B. Taylor, October 7, 1980, 63–64.
11. *Nocona News*, March 2, 1978.
12. "Nocona News" (NBC newsletter), Spring 1978, Enid Justin Collection, Nocona Museum.
13. Enid Justin, interview by Floyd Jenkins, 81; Joe Justin, interview by Carol Lipscomb, March 23, 1995, transcript, Oral History Collection, University of North Texas, Denton, Texas, 72–73.
14. *Nocona News*, March 2, 1978; "Nocona News" (NBC newsletter), Spring 1978, Enid Justin Collection, Nocona Museum.
15. *Washington Post*, February 13, 1979. Yankee manager Billy Martin may have gained his boot knowledge while managing the Texas Rangers in 1974—it was a winning season.
16. Justin, *Miss Enid*, 61; Delano and Rieff, *Texas Boots*, 36–40.
17. "Nocona News" (NBC newsletter), Summer 1979, Enid Justin Collection, Nocona Museum.
18. Ibid.; *GQ*, August 1979.
19. "Nocona News" (NBC newsletter), Spring 1976, Enid Justin Collection, Nocona Museum.
20. Ibid.; "Rusty Steps in to Aid Company," c. 1979, newspaper clipping, Enid Justin Collection, Nocona Museum.
21. Alice Kessler-Harris, *In Pursuit of Equity: Women, Men, and the Quest for Economic Citizenship in 20th Century America* (New York: Oxford University Press, 2001), 7–8, 213–25, 258–59; Ryan Bergeron, "The Seventies': Feminism Makes Waves," August 17, 2015, CNN, accessed July 2019, https://www.cnn.com/2015/07/22/living/the-seventies-feminism-womens-lib/index.html, 2–5.
22. Ibid.
23. Elizabeth Hayes Turner, Stephanie Cole, and Rebecca Sharpless, eds., *Texas Women: Their Histories, Their Lives* (Athens: University of Georgia Press, 2015), 277–79; Campbell, *Gone to Texas*, 409–11; Sherilyn Brandenstein, "Texas

ERA," *Handbook of Texas Online*, accessed November 2019, http://www.tsha-online.org/handbook/online/articles/mlt02.

24. Ibid.; "Women of the Year: Great Changes, New Chances, Tough Choices," *Time* magazine, January 5, 1976.

25. Fane Downs and Nancy Baker Jones, eds., *Women and Texas History* (Austin: Texas State Historical Association, 1993), 141–42; Campbell, *Gone to Texas*, 409–11; Justin, *Miss Enid*, 82.

26. *Chickasha Daily Express*, Chickasha, Oklahoma, March 16, 1977; *Corsicana Daily Sun*, Corsicana, Texas, April 26, 1977; *Denton Record Chronicle*, Denton, Texas, November 11, 1976.

27. *The Hereford Brand*, Hereford, Texas, May 25, 1978; "Nocona News" (NBC newsletter), Winter 1978, Enid Justin Collection, Nocona Museum. In 1994, the Cowgirl Hall of Fame moved to Fort Worth, and in 2002 the museum moved into its permanent location, a 33,000-square-foot building designed by architect David M. Schwarz in the Cultural District.

28. *Austin American-Statesman*, March 2, 1986; "Nocona News" (NBC newsletter), Summer 1979, Enid Justin Collection, Nocona Museum.

29. "Nocona News" (NBC newsletter), Summer 1980, Enid Justin Collection, Nocona Museum.

30. "Nocona News" (NBC newsletter), Fall 1977, Summer 1978, Enid Justin Collection, Nocona Museum.

31. Ibid.; *Santa Fe New Mexican*, December 4, 1980.

32. "Nocona News" (NBC newsletter), Winter 1976, Fall 1977, Summer 1978, Enid Justin Collection, Nocona Museum.

33. *Wichita Falls Record News*, November 9, 1976; "Nocona News" (NBC newsletter), Summer, Winter, 1976, Enid Justin Collection, Nocona Museum.

34. Ibid.; "Nocona Horsehide: A New Breed," c. 1976, scrapbook clipping, Enid Justin-Nocona Boot Company Collection, BA.15, Box 1383, University of North Texas Archives.

35. "Nocona News" (NBC newsletter), Summer 1976, Enid Justin Collection, Nocona Museum.

36. *Santa Fe New Mexican*, December 4, 1980; *Odessa American*, Odessa, Texas, September 22, 1980; "Nocona Roundup" (NBC newsletter), Winter 1980, Tales 'N' Trails Museum, Nocona, Texas.

37. "Nocona News" (NBC newsletter), Summer 1980, Enid Justin Collection, Nocona Museum.

38. Max Marshall, "*Dallas* at 40: The Inside Story Behind the Show That Changed Texas Forever," *Texas Monthly*, October 2018. As an example of *Dallas*'s influence on the popularity of western attire, J. R. Ewing's cowboy hat is in the collection of the Smithsonian National Museum of American History.
39. Joe Justin, interview by Carol Lipscomb, 70–71; Justin, *Miss Enid*, 61; Enid Justin, interview by Floyd Jenkins, 38, 53; "Nocona Roundup" (NBC newsletter), Winter 1980, Summer 1981, Enid Justin Collection, Nocona Museum.
40. Justin, *Miss Enid*, 61; Luciel Leonard, interview by Carol Lipscomb, August 3, 1995, transcript, Oral History Collection, University of North Texas, Denton, Texas, 44; *Nocona News*, October 18, 1990; "Nocona Roundup" (NBC newsletter), Winter 1980, "Nocona News" (NBC newsletter), Summer 1976, Enid Justin Collection, Nocona Museum.
41. *Nocona News*, August 28, 1975; "Nocona News" (NBC newsletter), September 1974, Enid Justin Collection, Nocona Museum.
42. District Court of Montague County, Texas, 97th Judicial District, *Joe Justin v. Enid Justin, et al.*, Cause No. 18,706, July 17, 1980, Oral Deposition of Enid Justin, October 9, 1980, 12, 29,36; Deposition of Chester Taylor, 10–11.
43. Deposition of Enid Justin, 12, 36; Deposition of Chester Taylor, 10–12.
44. District Court of Montague County, Texas, 97th Judicial District, *Joe Justin v. Enid Justin, et al.*, Cause No. 18,706, July 17, 1980, Oral Deposition of John Justin Jr., October 9, 1980, 6, 10; Joe Justin, interview by Carol Lipscomb, 63.
45. Deposition of Enid Justin, 16, 33; Deposition of John Justin Jr., 6, 10, 13–14.
46. *Fort Worth Star-Telegram*, August 28, 1980; District Court of Montague County, Texas, 97th Judicial District, *Joe Justin v. Enid Justin, et al.*, Cause No. 18,706, July 17, 1980, Agreement of Employment (May 16, 1974), 1. District Court of Tarrant County, Texas, 141st Judicial District, *Justin Industries, Inc. v. Enid Justin, et al.*, Cause No. 141-62433-80, September 8, 1980, Plaintiff's Original Petition, 3.
47. Farman, *Standard of the West*, 150; Deposition of John Justin Jr., 44–45.
48. Deposition of Enid Justin, 42; Deposition of Chester Taylor, 52–53.
49. Farman, *Standard of the West*, 151–52; Deposition of Enid Justin, 33, 90.
50. District Court of Montague County, 97th Judicial District, *Joe Justin v. Enid Justin, et al.*, Cause No. 18,706, July 17, 1980, Plaintiff's Second Amended Petition, 3.
51. Deposition of Enid Justin, 18, 42–43, 54.
52. Deposition of Chester Taylor, 53.

53. Ibid., 46, 54–55, 78.
54. Ibid., 2; Farman, *Standard of the West*, 151–52; *Fort Worth Star-Telegram*, August 28, 1980; District Court of Montague County, Texas, 97th Judicial District, *Joe Justin v. Enid Justin, et al.*, Cause No. 18,706, September 8, 1980, Plea in Abatement of Defendant Justin Industries, Inc., 3.
55. *Waco Citizen*, Waco, Texas, August 28, 1981; *Fort Worth Star-Telegram*, August 28, 1980; Joe Justin, interview by Carol Lipscomb, 64; Farman, *Standard of the West*, 152; Enid Justin, interview by Floyd Jenkins, 35.
56. Enid Justin, interview by Floyd Jenkins, 60–61.
57. *Waco Citizen*, August 28, 1981; *Paris News*, Paris, Texas, March 4, 1981; "Tony Lama Acquires Hyer Assets," scrapbook clipping, Enid Justin Collection, Nocona Museum.
58. "Nocona Roundup" (NBC newsletter), Summer 1981, Enid Justin Collection, Nocona Museum; *Nocona News*, March 5, 1981; Justin, *Miss Enid*, 61–62.
59. Enid Justin, interview by Floyd Jenkins, 55–56.
60. Ibid., 89.
61. Justin, *Miss Enid*, 61, 85; "Nocona Roundup" (NBC newsletter), Spring 1983, Enid Justin Collection, Nocona Museum; *Nocona News*, January 27, 1983, October 18, 1990; Steve Pickens, interview by Carol Lipscomb, January 30, 2020, transcript, Nocona Museum, 6.
62. *Nocona News*, February 10, 1983. Dr. Todd A. Fore pursued a career in civil service and in 2019 was named Deputy Assistant Secretary of the Army for Civilian Personnel.
63. Joe Justin, interview by Carol Lipscomb, 65–67.
64. Ibid.; Steve Pickens, interview by Carol Lipscomb, 9–11; John Tillotson, interview by Carol Lipscomb, November 25, 2019, transcript, Nocona Museum, 1–2.
65. Justin, *Miss Enid*, 86–89.

Chapter 8

1. Lori Grossman, "The Way to a Cowboy's Sole," *Texas Co-op Power*, November 2012, 29.
2. Steve Pickens, interview by Carol Lipscomb, January 30, 2020, transcript, Enid Justin Collection, Nocona Museum, 21–22, 25.
3. Ibid., 13–14. In Farman's *Standard of the West: The Justin Story*, J. T. Dickenson, president of Justin Industries boot division, took credit for the decision to close

Nocona's satellite plants—a contradiction to Pickens's statement.
4. Nocona Boot Company Catalogs, 1986, 1987, 1988, Enid Justin Collection, Nocona Museum; John Tillotson, interview by Carol Lipscomb, November 25, 2019, transcript, Enid Justin Collection, Nocona Museum, 5–6; Steve Pickens, interview by Carol Lipscomb, 16.
5. Beard, *The Cowboy Boot Book*, 49–50; *Wichita Falls Times Record News*, September 26, 1988; *Nocona News*, September 1, 1988.
6. Steve Pickens, interview by Carol Lipscomb, 5.
7. Ibid., 20–21; Beard, *The Cowboy Boot Book*, 50.
8. *Nocona News*, July 7, September 1, 1988; Steve Pickens, interview by Carol Lipscomb, 13.
9. *Wichita Falls Times Record News*, September 26, 1988; *Nocona News*, September 29, 1988.
10. *Nocona News*, July 7, 1988, December 21, 1989, July 27, 1990.
11. Steve Pickens, interview by Carol Lipscomb, 14–15; *Wichita Falls Times*, December 17, 1978; *Nocona News*, October 18, 1990.
12. State of Texas House of Representatives, H.R. No. 1023, May 27, 1991.
13. *Nocona News*, October 18, 1990; Justin, *Miss Enid*, 81; *Fort Worth Star-Telegram*, August 6, 1999.
14. *Fort Worth Star-Telegram*, August 6, 1999; Joe Justin, interview by Carol Lipscomb, 80; Justin, *Miss Enid*, 81; *Oklahoma City Times*, December 8, 1972; Rob Patterson, "Her Boots Were Like Her Children," *Western & English Today*, March/April 2007, 40–42.
15. Justin, *Miss Enid*, 69–70.
16. *Spokesman-Review*, Spokane, Washington, September 24, 1965.
17. Justin, *Miss Enid*, 68.
18. Ibid., 69.
19. Ibid.
20. *Dallas Morning News*, January 22, 1977.
21. Ibid.
22. Melanie Chapman Howington, interview by Carol Lipscomb, January 24, 2020, transcript, Nocona Museum, 2.
23. "America's First Lady of Cowboy Boots," *Modern People*, c. 1973, scrapbook clipping, Enid Justin-Nocona Boot Company Collection, BA.15, Box 1826, University of North Texas Archives.
24. Ibid.

25. Myrna Zanetell, "Tony Lama Company," *Handbook of Texas Online*, accessed November 19, 2019, http://www.tshaonline.org/handbook/online/articles/dlt01.
26. Farman, *Standard of the West*, 232–34; *Port Arthur News*, Port Arthur, Texas, April 1, 1994. Throughout its history, the Tony Lama Company had been managed by Lama family members, and in 1994, John Justin Jr. continued that tradition by appointing Rudolph E. Lama, grandson of the founder, as the new president and chief executive officer of the El Paso company.
27. John Tillotson, interview by Carol Lipscomb, 2, 6; Steve Pickens, interview by Carol Lipscomb, 7, 17.
28. Steve Pickens, interview by Carol Lipscomb, 7–9, 26, 30.
29. *Nocona News*, July 27, 1995.
30. *Herald Palladium*, Southwest Michigan, August 15, 1999: Joseph Stiglitz, "The Roaring Nineties," *Atlantic Magazine*, October 2002, 18–20.
31. *Nocona News*, March 7, 1996; *Herald Palladium*, August 15, 1999.
32. *Nocona News*, September 15, 1994.
33. Steve Pickens, interview by Carol Lipscomb, 28; *Nocona News*, November 10, 1994.
34. Steve Pickens, interview by Carol Lipscomb, 29; *Nocona News*, April 20, 1995.
35. Steve Pickens, interview by Carol Lipscomb, 1–2, 8, 32.
36. *Nocona News*, July 27, 1995, March 7, 1996.
37. *Bowie News*, Bowie, Texas, August 8, 1999; *Fort Worth Star-Telegram*, August 6, 1999; *Herald Palladium*, August 15, 1999; *Nocona News*, July 15, 1999; *Washington Post*, August 20, 1999.
38. *Washington Post*, August 20, 1999; *Nocona News*, July 15, 1999.
39. *Fort Worth Star-Telegram*, October 1, 1999; *Nocona News*, Special Edition, August 5, 1999.
40. *Fort Worth Star-Telegram*, October 1, 1999; *Nocona News*, July 15, August 5, 1999.
41. *Fort Worth Star-Telegram*, August 6, 1999; *Nocona News*, August 12, 1999.
42. Ibid.
43. *Fort Worth Star-Telegram*, August 6, 1999; *Bowie News*, August 8, 1999; Justin, *Miss Enid*, 60.
44. *Nocona News*, August 19, 29, September 2, 9, 1999.
45. Cheryl Runquist, "Boots in a Woman's World," April 1969, clipping in Enid Justin, interview by Charles Townsend, Southwest Collection, Texas

Tech University, Lubbock, Texas; *Washington Post*, August 20, 1999; *Austin American-Statesman*, March 2, 1986.

Epilogue

1. *Fort Worth Star-Telegram*, March 21, 1999.
2. *Fort Worth Star-Telegram*, June 20, 2000.
3. *Lubbock Avalanche-Journal*, Lubbock, Texas, February 24, 2002.
4. Robert Fenoglio, phone interview by Carol Lipscomb, March 6, 2020.
5. *Nocona News*, October 6, 2016.
6. *Washington Post*, August 20, 1999.
7. June, *Cowboy Boots*, 220; 80th Legislature of the State of Texas, 80(R) HCR 151, January 9, 2007.
8. G. Daniel DeWeese, "The Boot Seen Round the World," *True West Magazine*, September 12, 2009; Jennifer June, "Custom Made Cowboy Boots," accessed December 2019, http://www.dimlights.com; Blucher Custom Boot Company Records, 1915–1999, National Cowboy and Western Heritage Museum, Oklahoma City, Oklahoma.
9. June, www.dimlights.com; Tyler Beard, *Art of the Boot* (Salt Lake City: Gibbs Smith, 1999), 84, 136; Tyler Beard, *Cowboy Boots* (Salt Lake City: Gibbs Smith, 2004), 94–97.
10. Wendy Henry, "Back at the Ranch Cowboy Boots," accessed January 2020, www.backattheranch.com; Ariat Boots, accessed January 2020, www.ariat.com.
11. Beard, *Cowboy Boots*, 25.

BIBLIOGRAPHY

Primary Sources

ARCHIVAL MATERIAL

Archival material used in this book is preserved in the collections listed below. Individual documents, articles, interviews, letters, scrapbook contents, and the like are cited in the notes.

Blucher Custom Boot Company Records, 1915–1999. National Cowboy and Western Heritage Museum, Oklahoma City, Oklahoma.
Enid Justin Collection, Tales 'N' Trails Museum, North Texas Society of History and Culture, Nocona, Texas (cited as Nocona Museum).
Enid Justin-Nocona Boot Company Collection, 1929–1982, 01/BA.15, University of North Texas Archives, Denton, Texas.
Justin Archives, Fort Worth, Texas.
Southwest Collection, Oral History Program, Texas Tech University, Lubbock, Texas.
University of North Texas Oral History Collection, Denton, Texas.
Voices of Oklahoma Oral History Project, www.voicesofoklahoma.com.

COURT DOCUMENTS

H. J. Justin, Last Will & Testament, filed August 12, 1918, Cause No. 1994, Probate Minutes of Montague County, Texas, Vol. 14.
Joe Justin v. Enid Justin, et al., District Court of Montague County, Texas, 97th Judicial District, Cause No. 18,706, July 17, 1980.

BIBLIOGRAPHY

John Justin Jr. v. Nocona Boot Company, Inc., et al. District Court of Montague County, Texas, 97th Judicial District, Cause No. 14633, September 25, 1964.

Justin Industries, Inc. v. Enid Justin, et al., District Court of Tarrant County, Texas, 141st Judicial District, Cause No. 141-62433-80, September 8, 1980.

NEWSPAPERS

Austin American-Statesman, Austin, Texas, March 2, 1986.
Bowie News, Bowie, Texas, August 8, 1999.
Chickasha Daily Express, Chickasha, Oklahoma, March 16, 1977.
Corsicana Daily Sun, Corsicana, Texas, April 26, 1977.
Daily Oklahoman, Oklahoma City, Oklahoma, October 29, 1973.
Dallas Morning News, Dallas, Texas, May 9, 1941; June 29, 1958; January 22, 1977.
Denton Record Chronicle, Denton, Texas, November 11, 1976.
Deseret News, Salt Lake City, Utah, July 25, 1974.
East Oregonian, Pendleton, Oregon, September 22, 1973.
El Paso Daily Times, El Paso, Texas, May 5, 1883.
El Paso Times, El Paso, Texas, October 21, 1962.
Fort Worth Press, Fort Worth, Texas, June 10, 1948, October 12, 1953.
Fort Worth Star-Telegram, Fort Worth, Texas, April 24, 1925; March 24, 1950; July 18, 1968; July 18, 1968; May 31, 1973; August 28, 1980; March 21, August 6, October 1, 1999; June 20, 2000.
Gazette Telegraph, Colorado Springs, Colorado, August 11, 1972.
Herald Paladium, Southwest Michigan, August 15, 1999.
The Hereford Brand, Hereford, Texas, May 25, 1978.
Kansas City Star, Kansas City, Missouri, February 11, 1911.
Las Vegas Sun, Las Vegas, Nevada, January 22, 1973; June 16, 1974.
Lubbock Avalanche-Journal, Lubbock, Texas, February 24, 2002.
The Monitor, McAllen, Texas, January 22, 1932.
Moulton Eagle, Moulton, Texas, March 11, 1977; October 14, 1977.
New York Herald Tribune, European edition, Paris, August 5, 1952.
The Nocona News, Nocona, Texas, 1908–2018.
Odessa American, Odessa, Texas, September 22, 1980.

Oklahoma City Times, Oklahoma City, Oklahoma, December 8, 1972.
Olathe Mirror, Olathe, Kansas, August 24, 1898.
Paris News, Paris, Texas, March 4, 1981.
Pauls Valley Democrat, Pauls Valley, Oklahoma, January 10, 15, 1928.
Philipsburg Mail, Philipsburg, Montana, September 30, 1938.
Port Arthur News, Port Arthur, Texas, April 1, 1994.
The Salt Lake Tribune, Salt Lake City, Utah, July 24, 1974.
San Francisco Examiner, San Francisco, California, November 9, 1972.
Santa Fe New Mexican, Santa Fe, New Mexico, December 4, 1980.
Shiner Gazette, Shiner, Texas, July 4, 1974.
Spokesman Review, Spokane, Washington, September 24, 1965.
Standard Times, New Bedford, Massachusetts, February 17, 1967.
The Sunday Oklahoman, Oklahoma City, Oklahoma, December 12, 1972.
Victoria Advocate, Victoria Texas, February 10, 2006.
Waco Citizen, Waco, Texas, August 29, 1981.
Washington Post, Washington, DC, February 13, 1979; August 20, 1999.
Wichita Daily Times, Wichita Falls, Texas, April 25, 1938; July 30, 1947; April 10, 1948.
Wichita Falls Record News, Wichita Falls, Texas, June 10, 1948; September 17, 1971; November 9, 1976.
Wichita Falls Times, Wichita Falls, Texas, May 27, 1973; October 14, 1976; April 14, 1977; December 17, 1978.
Wichita Falls Times Record News, Wichita Falls, Texas, September 26, 1988.

Secondary Sources
BOOKS

Adams, Ramon F. *Western Words: A Dictionary of the Range, Cow Camp and Trail*. Norman: University of Oklahoma Press, 1946; reprint, London, England: Forgotten Books, 2017.
Beard, Tyler. *Art of the Boot*. Salt Lake City: Gibbs Smith, 1999.
———.*The Cowboy Boot Book*. Salt Lake City: Peregrine Smith Books, 1992.
———.*Cowboy Boots*. Salt Lake City: Gibbs Smith, 2004.

BIBLIOGRAPHY

Bearden, Donna, and Jamie Frucht. *The Texas Sampler: A Stitch in Time.* Austin: Governor's Committee on Aging, a Bicentennial Publication, 1976.

Campbell, Randolph B. *Gone to Texas: A History of the Lone Star State*, 3rd ed. New York: Oxford University Press, 2017.

Chipman, Donald E., and Harriet Denise Joseph. *Spanish Texas, 1519–1821*, 2d ed. Austin: University of Texas Press, 2010.

Cochran-Smith, Gale, ed. *Up the Chisholm Trail: The Cattle Trails of Montague County.* Montague County Historical Commission, 2017.

Collins, Michael. *Cooke County, Texas: Where the South and the West Meet.* Marceline, MO: Walsworth Publishing Company, 1998.

Cummins, Light. "History, Memory, and Rebranding Texas as Western for the 1936 Centennial." In *This Corner of Canaan: Essays in Honor of Randolph B. Campbell*, edited by Richard B. McCaslin, Donald E. Chipman, and Andrew J. Torget. Denton: University of North Texas Press, 2013.

Delano, Sharon, and David Rieff. *Texas Boots.* New York: Viking Press, 1981.

DeWeese, G. Daniel. "The Boot Seen Round the World." *True West Magazine*, September 2009.

Drachman, Virginia G. *Enterprising Women: 250 Years of American Business.* Chapel Hill: University of North Carolina Press, 2002.

Downs, Fane, and Nancy Baker Jones, eds. *Women and Texas History.* Austin: Texas State Historical Association, 1993.

Dunlap, Patricia Riley. *Riding Astride: The Frontier in Women's History.* Denver: Arden Press, 1995.

Encyclopedia of Oklahoma History & Culture Online. Oklahoma Historical Society, Oklahoma City, Oklahoma.

Farman, Irvin. *Standard of the West: The Justin Story.* Fort Worth: Texas Christian University Press, 1996.

Fenoglio, Melvin, ed. *The Story of Montague County: Its Past and Present.* Dallas: Curtis Media Corporation, 1989.

Gard, Wayne. *The Chisholm Trail.* Norman: University of Oklahoma Press, 1954 (paperback edition, 1979).

Handbook of Texas Online. Texas State Historical Association & General Libraries, University of Texas at Austin, 1999.

Henderson, Jeff S, ed. *100 Years in Montague County*. Saint Jo, TX: IPTA Printers, 1978.

Herman, Arthur. *Freedom's Forge: How American Business Produced Victory in World War II*. New York: Random House, 2012.

Jacobs, Lee C. *J. R. McChesney: A Lifetime, A Legacy*. Colorado Springs: ColorTek Printing, 1994.

———. *A McChesney Manual: Scrutinizing Bits and Spurs of an Innovative Creator*. Colorado Springs: self-published, n.d.

June, Jennifer. *Cowboy Boots: The Art & Sole*. New York: Universe Publishing, 2007.

Justin, Enid. *Miss Enid: The Texas Lady Bootmaker*. Edited by Dale Terry. Austin: Nortex Press, 1985.

Kennedy, David M. *Freedom from Fear: The American People in Depression and War, 1929–1945*. New York: Oxford University Press, 1999.

Kessler-Harris, Alice. *In Pursuit of Equity: Women, Men, and the Quest for Economic Citizenship in 20th Century America*. New York: Oxford University Press, 2001.

McArthur, Judith N., and Harold Smith. *Texas Through Women's Eyes: The Twentieth Century Experience*. Austin: University of Texas Press, 2010.

McCoy, Tim, and Ronald McCoy. *Tim McCoy Remembers the West*. Lincoln: University of Nebraska Press, 1977.

McLeroy, Sherrie S. *Red River Women*. Plano: Republic of Texas Press, 1996.

Pattie, Jane. *Cowboy Spurs and Their Makers*. College Station: Texas A&M University Press, 1991.

Rich, Harold. *Fort Worth: Outpost, Cowtown, Boomtown*. Norman: University of Oklahoma Press, 2014.

Smith, A. Morton. *The First One Hundred Years in Cooke County*. San Antonio, TX: Naylor Company, 1976.

Stoecklein, David R. *The Cowboy Boot: History, Art, Culture, Function*. Ketchum, ID: Stoecklein Publishing, 2004.

Turner, Elizabeth Hayes, Stephanie Cole, and Rebecca Sharpless, eds. *Texas Women: Their Histories, Their Lives*. Athens: University of Georgia Press, 2015.

Weddle, Robert S. *After the Massacre: The Violent Legacy of the San Sabá Mission*. Lubbock: Texas Tech University Press, 2007.

Wooster, Ralph A. *Texas and Texans in the Great War*. Buffalo Gap, TX: State House Press, 2009.

ARTICLES

"Nocona Hits Profit Trail in Eastern Boot Trend." *American Shoemaking*, May 3, 1972.

Brackman, Barbara. "Legend Posing as History: Hyer, Justin, and the Origin of the Cowboy Boot." *Kansas History* (Spring 1995): 34–47.

Darrigrand, Lee. "Justin Boot Company: The Standard of the West." *Western & English Fashion*, August 1988.

Frommer, D. W., II. "A History of the Western Boot." ShoeInfoNet, accessed February 2015, http://shoeinfonet.com/shoe-history/history-western-boot.

Frink, Cheryl Coggins. "Breaking Step with Tradition." *Austin American-Statesman*, March 2, 1986.

Grossman, Lori. "The Way to a Cowboy's Sole." *Texas Co-op Power*, November 2012.

Marshall, Max. "*Dallas* at 40: The Inside Story Behind the Show That Changed Texas Forever." *Texas Monthly*, October 2018.

Miller, Donald. "Women Entrepreneurs Take the Stage During New York's Jazz Age." *Entrepreneur*. September 11, 2014, www.entrepreneur.com/article/237335.

"Miss Enid Justin: The Nocona Boot Lady." *Western & English Today*, October 1987.

Patterson, Rob. "Her Boots Were Like Her Children." *Western & English Today*, March/April 2007.

Stiglitz, Joseph. "The Roaring Nineties." *Atlantic Magazine*, October 2002.

Thomas, Jack. "History of the Texas Spur." *The Western Horseman*, August 1973.

Weese, Beth. "The Century Old Boot." *Oklahoma Magazine*, May 21, 2015.

"Women of the Year: Great Changes, New Changes, Tough Choices."

Time magazine, January 5, 1976.

UNPUBLISHED SOURCES

Donnell, Guy Renfro. "The History of Montague County, Texas." MA thesis, University of Texas, 1940.

INDEX

Entries in italics refer to images.

(Note: Justin Boot refers to the company making Justin Boots, regardless of the company name at the time.)

Ackerman, Ray, 142
Ackerman McQueen Advertising, 141–43
Acme Boot Company, 201
Acme Brick Company/Acme Building Brands, 195, 199, 224n41
acquisitions/mergers; by Justin Boot, John, Jr. on, 190–91; of Justin Boot by Berkshire Hathaway, 199; of Justin Leather Goods Company by Justin Boot, 26; of McChesney Bits & Spurs, by Nocona Boot Company, 55, 119; of Nocona Boot Company and Justin Boot, 169–73; of Nocona Boot Company by Weyenberg Shoe Manufacturing Company, 168–70; of Tex Tan Boot Company, by Nocona Boot Company, 130; of Tex Tan Western Leather Company by the Tandy Corporation, 114; of Texas Togs, by Action-Line Inc., 121, 222n11; of Texas Togs, by Nocona Boot Company, 119–21; of Tony Lama Company, by Justin Boot, 190
Action-Line Inc, 121, 222n11
Adams, Ramon F., xviii, 96
advertising campaigns: football stars in, 160–62, *161*, *162*; Guess jeans and, 180–81; Let's Rodeo, 141–43, *142*, 156–57, 183. *See also* publicity/promotions
affair, of Julius, 44–45, 212n51
air-conditioning/heating, 85–86, 125
airport improvements, Nocona, 128
Alexander, R. R., 39
Allen, S. A., 10

American Federation of Labor, 105
American Shoe Designer Award, 131
American West. *See* Western culture
amnesia, man with, 187
Amsco Steel Products Company, 104, 135–36, 170
apparel. *See* Western wear
Ariat International, 202
Arizona Highways, 134
Asia, manufacturing in, 196
Atkins Building, *41–42*; expansions of, 58, 74; Fenoglio retail in, 200; Justin Boot at, early, 13; Montague Boot Company in, 199–200; Nocona Athletic Goods in, 201, 221n43; Nocona Boot Company, move into, 35–36; Texas Togs and, 120–21
Autry, Gene, 92, 111

Back at the Ranch Cowboy Boots, 202
Barnett, W. D. "Slim," 55
Battle of Pease River, 12
Beard, Tyler, 92, 128, 202
beef, demand for, 5
belts, 111–12, 135, 176, 183
benefits, of employees, 94, 121, 223n12
Berkshire Hathaway, 199, 201
Bicentennial, 143–45, *145*
bits and spurs, 52–54, *53*, 55–57, *56*, 56–57, 214n31. *See also* McChesney, J. R.
blacksmiths, 49, 51
Blucher, G. C. "Gus"/Blucher Custom Boot Company, xix, 19, 201–2, 209n39
blue jeans, 128, 154
bonds, war, 79–80
Boot and Shoe Workers' Union, 105
boot box, 182
boot components: heels, xvii–xviii, 9, 42, 102;

243

INDEX

leather (*see* leather); shanks, 104–5, 115, 126; stitching (*see* stitching); toes, xviii, 42–43, 75, 102, 105, 129
boot industry: decline in, 192, 194–95, 201; history of, xvi–xviii; innovations in (*see* innovations); longevity of, 32, 91, 128, 202; movies, influence on, xx, 92, 165–66; in 1980s, 174, 179; in New York, 155; quality in, 156 (*see also* quality, of Nocona Boot Company); television, influence on, 92, 99, 108, 166; women in, xx, 202; during World War I, 21–22; during World War II, 74–75. *See also* boot makers
boot makers: Acme Booth Company, 201; Blucher Custom Boot Company, xviii–xix, 19, 126, 201–2, 209n39; C. H. Hyer & Sons, xviii–xix, 126, 174; Coffeyville Pattern Boots, xviii; Dehner Boot Company, 82; Fenoglio Boot Company, 200; Kirkendall Boot Company, 78, 82; Lucchese Boot and Shoe Factory, xix, 180, 201; Moulton Boot Company, 150, 226n7; in 1920s, xvii–xx; Olsen-Stelzer Boot and Saddlery, 45, 110; Tandy Leather Company, 111, 130; Tex Tan Western Leather Company, 114, 130; Tony Lama Company, xix, 101, 173–74, 190–91, 195, 232n26; Whitbern Boots, 72–73
boot styles. *See* styles, of boots
Bootmaker's Collection, *151*, 151–52
boots, children's, 187
bridle bits. *See* bits and spurs
Bright, William, xviii
Broadus, William, 12
Broken Arrow, Oklahoma, 49, 213n9
Brown, Reagan, 150
Brown, William, 170, 172
Buchwald, Art, 99
Buckeridge, B. B., 30
Buffett, Warren, 199
Buie, Judi, 155
Bull Hide, 164–65
Burford, Wallace, 83

C. A. Snow & Co., 112
C. H. Hyer & Sons, xviii–xix, 126, 174
Calvin Klein, 192
Campbell, Earl, 160–61, *161*
Campbell, Sam, 129, 140, 152–54
Carpenter, Ken, 59
Carpenter, Liz, 159
Carter, Amon, *66*, 66–67
Cash, Johnny, 145
catalogs: Justin Boot, 22, 28–29, *29*, 152;
McChesney and, 51–52; Nocona Boot Company, *93*, 93–94, *127*, 137, 165; self-measurements and, 15
Cato, O. C., 14–15
cattle industry: and drives, end of, 10, 12; early, 5–6; in Fort Worth, 30; importance of, 132; in Montana, 14–15
Cavender's Boot City, 200
celebrities: Autry, Gene, 92, 111; Campbell, Earl, 160–61, *161*; Cash, Johnny, 145; Disney, Walt, 186, *186*; Franklin, Tony, 162; Kelly, Grace, 120; Mahan, Larry, 200; Martin, Billy, 154, 227n15; Maynard, Ken, *89*; McCoy, Tim, xix; McCrea, Joel, 134; Moore, Clayton, 92; Murphey, Michael Martin, 166; Rainier III (Prince of Monaco), 120; Reagan, Ronald, 176; Rogers, Roy, 111; Thompson, Hank, 166; Walker, Jerry Jeff, 156–57, *157*; and Western wear, effect on, 92; Wier, Rusty, 157. *See also* politicians
Centennial Celebration (Texas), 59
Chapman, Mel, 129, 131, 135, 222n11, 224n30
Chapman, Zana (niece of Enid), 135
Chapman Howington, Melanie (great-niece of Enid), 189
character, of Enid: as businesswoman, 47–48, 124, 185–87; deception and, 172–73; generosity of, 80, 132–33, 138, 187 (*see also under* employees: treatment of, by Enid); humor of, 186; as strong-willed, 17; toughness of, 72, 124, 185; work ethic of, 18, 34, 37–38, 118, 135
Chickasaw Nation, 54
children's boots, 187
Chippewa Shoe Manufacturing Company, 195
Chisholm Trail, 5, 7, 30, 82, 217n35
Chisholm Trail Roundup, 106–7, *107*
Christmas traditions, 95
circle letter, 63
Clifton, Jack, 67
clothing. *See* Western wear
clubhouse, Justin family, 13, *15*, 20, 22, 26
Cobine, John, xviii
Cockrell, Lila, 159
Coffeyville Pattern Boots, xviii
collective bargaining, 63
Comanche Indians, 6, 208n27
computers, 125, 134–35
Cooper, W. O, 115, 168
cork, 76
Cow Palace Rodeo, 176
Cowboy Boot Book, The (Beard), 128
cowboy boots. *See* boot headings

INDEX

Cowboy Boots: The Art & Sole (June), 202
Cowboy Saloon, 9
cowboys: in advertising campaign, 141–43; boot needs of, xvi–xviii, 8–9, 42–43; Cowboy Hall of Fame, 134; culture of, 34; in history, xvii–xviii, 5, 7; in Spanish Fort, 9; spurs and, 51; and woman as boot maker, hesitancy to, 38. *See also* cattle industry; rodeos
Cowgirl Hall of Fame, 160, 228n27
craft kits, 111
Crain, Jack, 110
Crain, Kathleen, 120
Crain, Sam, 120
Creed for Success, 157–58, 203
creeping paralysis, 21
Cross, Beth, 202
Cushion Shanks, 104–5, 115, 126
custom boots, xix–xx, 19, 94, 128, 137, 140, 201–2

Daddy Joe. *See* Justin, Herman Joseph "Daddy Joe"
Dallas (TV show), 166, 229n38m
Dallas Fashion Arts, 101
Davidson, Shannon, 67–68, *69*, 70, 215n58
Dawkins, Melody, 202
dealers, 28, 102, 118, 127, 130, 174
deaths: Anna Jo (daughter), 25; Daddy Joe, 23, 25–26; Enid, 184
debt, of Nocona Boot Company, 37–38
Dehner Boot Company, 82
Denver Post, The, 95–96
deposition, of Enid and Justin Boot merger, 172–73
Depression, Great, 57–58
diamonds, 118
Dickenson, J. T., 178, 190, 193, 230n3
discrimination, 153–54
Disney, Walt, 186, *186*
divorces, of Enid, 44–45, 72
Dodson, Calvin, 82
domestic production, 195–96
Double H Boots, 201
Drake, John, 112
drought, 12, 22
dude ranches, 59–60

economy: in 1920s, xv, 48; in 1940s, 80; in 1950s, 103–4; in 1970s, 165; in 1980s, 184; of communities, local, 128; during Great Depression, 57–58; of Nocona, post-factory, 196; from oil industry, 73; postwar boom, 80; during World War I, 21–22
education, of Enid, 17–18
employees: benefits of, 94, 121, 223n12; diversity of, 153–54; during Great Depression, 58; of Justin Boot, early, 16–17, 19, 28; labor unrest and, 62–64; layoffs of, 63, 104, 192–94; long-term, 167–68; merger of Nocona Boot Company and Justin Boot and, 173–74; post-factory close, 196–97; treatment of, by Enid, 86–87, 94–95, 118–19, 135, 171; Whitman as, 72; during World War II, 76, 78–79. *See also* labor issues
Enid Drive, 148, *149*
Equal Employment Opportunity Commission, 153–54
Equal Pay Act, 159
Equal Rights Amendment, 158–59
equestrian boots, 202
Erdman, Henry, xix
exotic leather, 22, 28, 102, 115, 163–64, 183
Eyes for the Navy, 22

F & E Leather Company, 108, 110–11, 113
F. E. Schmitz Co., 139
factories. *See* locations, of Nocona Boot Company
Fair Labor Standards Act, 64
Fairbanks, Jerry, 59
family, conflict among: identities of companies, separation of, 62; Justin name, Enid's use of, 95–97; newspaper errors, on, 60–62, 95–96; on Nocona Boot Company start, 32–33; patents and, 39; on stock ownership, 122–24; Texas in Review and, 107–8
family dynamics: business conflict among (*see* family, conflict among); business dichotomy of, 75–78; as children, 16–17, 20; great-nieces and nephews of Enid, 188–89, *189*
Farenthold, Frances "Sissy," 159
Farman, Irvin, 97, 122, 124
Farrah, 119
fashion, boots as, xx. *See also* styles, of boots
Feminine Mystique, The (Friedan), 158
feminism. *See* women
Fenoglio Boot Company, 200
Ferguson, Stephanie, 202
50th anniversary celebration, 138–39
fire, at Justin home, 44
Fisher, Henrietta, 119
Fisher, Nathan, 119
Flex-Line Sole, 105
Florsheim, Thomas, 168

INDEX

football, 161–62
footwear industry, 74–75, 80, 129, 192, 195, 199, 201–2. *See also* boot makers
Fore, Todd, 176, 230n62
Formby, Margaret, 160
Fort Worth, Texas, 29–32, 35
Franklin, Tony, 162
Friedan, Betty, 158
Fuller, Carroll, 154
funding, for Nocona Boot Company, xv, 33–34, 39
funeral, of Enid, 184
Future Farmers of America (FFA), 132–34

Gainesville, Texas, 5–6, 51, 167
gambling, 176
Garner, Ethel, 110
Garner, Floyd, 110
gender inequality. *See* women
Gold Nugget, 129
Golden Gate Exposition, 64
good faith agreement, with Joe Justin, 135–36, 169–72
Gordon, Dale, 142–44, 153
Gossett, Ed, 64, 78
governors' conference, *100*, 100–101
Grace, Bill, 9
grained leathers, 164
Grand Ole Opry, 156
Great Depression, 57–58
Greenwood, Vennie, 67
growth, fear of, 47, 103, 117
growth, periods of: 1927, 39; 1929–1930, 41; 1930s, early, 58; 1940s, 73–74, 79; 1960s, early, 117; 1970s, 127, 129; 1975, 139; 1976, 145; 1978, 152–53; 1980s, 166–67, 184; 1989–1993, 192
Guess jeans advertisement, 180–81

Hall, Earl P., 83
Harris, A., 98
Hayes, Melanie, 133
Haynes, S. B., 82
heating/air-conditioning, 85–86, 125
heels, xvii–xviii, 9, 42, 102
Hellinger, David, 148
Henry, Wendy, 202
Hero Boot Box, 182
Hickman, Tom R., 28
hides/tanneries, 114. *See also* tanneries
Hinckley, Norton/Hinckley-Tandy Leather Company, 111, 217n43
Hispanics, in workforce, 153–54

H. J. Justin & Sons. *See* Justin Boot
Holcomb, Marguerite, 137
Hollister, Oklahoma, 23
home, Justin, 13, *14*, 44. *See also* clubhouse, Justin family
Honky Tonk Queen Contest, 166
horses, Enid's avoidance of, 53, 64, 67–68, 70, 87–88, 106
Horton, Sandy, 8
Howard Paine Saddlery, 112
Hubbard, Richard B., 6
Hudson, Shorty, 67
Humble Oil and Refining Company, 107–8
Humphreys, G. W., 26
Hyer, Charles, xviii–xix
Hyer Boot Company, xviii–xix, 126, 174

Indians (Native Americans): Battle of Pease River, 12: Chickasaw Nation, 54; Comanche Indians, 6, 208n27; Taovaya Indians, 7; Wichita Indians, 6–7
innovations: bits and spurs, 52–53, *53*, 55, 57; decorative stitching, 16; Flex-Line Sole, 105; lasts, xviii; Needle Toe Cushion, 105; revolving shoe tree, 124–25, *125*; riding boot technology, 202; Seamless Saddle Side, 105; self-measuring kits, xviii–xix, 14–16; Thin-Line Cushion Shank, 104–5, 126; tongue of oil field boot, 39; watchbands, 111
insurance, 94

Jacksboro, Texas, 40, 147
jeans, 128, 154
Jester, Beauford, 84
Jettons, 94–95
Jim Thorpe–All American (Warner Brothers), 110
Johnson, Lyndon, 159
Johnson, Virginia, 82
Jordan, Barbara, 159
Jordan, D. C., 12
Jordan Estate, 81–82
June, Jennifer, xvi, 202
Justin, Anis (sister), 21
Justin, Annie (née Allen, mother), 10, 16
Justin, Dorris "Myrl" (sister), 40
Justin, Enid, *35*, *88*, *177*; appearance of, 20, 87, 117–18; boot industry involvement, break in, 25, 31; character of (*see* character, of Enid); civic involvement of, 132–33, 138; daughter of, 21, 23, 25; death of, 184; on death of Daddy Joe, 23, 25; diamonds and, 118; education of, 17–18; 80th birthday of, 134; and

246

INDEX

father, relationship with, 4, 18, 20, 23; final years of, 178; health of, 167, 174–75; home of, adult, 88–89, 187; home of, childhood, 13, *14*, 15, 20, 44; honors of, 134, 138–39; horses and, 87–88, 106; at Justin Boot, early years, 4, 17–18; marriages of, 20, 44–45, 71–73 (*see also* Stelzer, Julius L. (husband)); park development by, 138; perjury and, 172–73; Pickens, Steve and, 182–83; retirement of, 131, 135, 175–76; salary of, 37, 47, 76–78; as sales force, 39–41; siblings of, 13 (*see also* individual siblings); as speaker, 157, 160; as storyteller, 186–88; on success, 189–90, 203; as woman pioneer, xvi, 47, 101, 107, 159–60, 185

Justin, Herman Joseph "Daddy Joe" (father), 11; career of, early, xviii–xix, 5–6, 8–10; death of, 23, 25–26; family of, 4, 13 (*see also* individual names); health of, 21; innovations by, xix, 14–16; marriage of, 10; Nocona, move to, 12; personality of, 17; recognition of, 22; younger years of, 4–5, 206n5

Justin, Joe (nephew): career, early, 103; and Enid, relationship with, 103–4, 169–71; good faith agreement and, 135–36, 169–72; layoff and rehiring of, 169–72; Nocona Boot Company, return to, 135–36; at Nocona Boot Company, 1950s, 103–4; Nocona Boot Company sale and, 168–69; on profit-sharing plan, 121; retirement of, 176–77, 199; Spanish boots and, 152; on Vernon location, 147

Justin, John (brother), *16*, 17–18, 21, 32, 39, 72, 103

Justin, John, Jr. (nephew): and Justin, Joe, 103, 178; on Justin Leather Goods Company, 26, 169–70; on Justin name, Enid's use of, 96–97; management of Justin Boot by, 97–98, 103; on Nocona Boot Company, post-Enid, 191; retirement of, 199; on stock ownership conflict, 122–24; on Tony Lama Company acquisition, 190. *See also* family, conflict among; succession plan

Justin, Nicholas (grandfather), 4

Justin, Samuel "Avis" (also "Sam," brother), *16*, 17, 21, 97

Justin, William (uncle), 10

Justin, William "Earl" (brother), 17–18, 21, 26, 32, 61–62, 77, 95, 103

Justin Boot: beginnings of, 9–10, 13, 16–17, 207n17; brick business of, 195, 199, 224n41; catalogs for, 27; closing of, 195; conflicts with Nocona Boot Company (*see* family, conflict among); consolidations and, 193, 195; dealers of, 28; employees of, early, 16–17, 19, 28; factory, early, *16*; fit, of boot, 191; Fort Worth, Texas, move to, 3–4, 29–30, 35; growth of, 18–20; management of, xix, 18, 97–98, 103, 193, 195, 199; mechanized factories for, 18; Nocona Boot Company merger with (*see* succession plan) and Nocona Boot Company rivalry (*see* family, conflict among); praise for, 96; publicity for, 19–20, 27–28, 157; World War I, during, 21–22

Justin Industries. *See* Justin Boot

Justin Leather Goods Company, 26–27, 108–9, 113

Justin name, Enid's use of, 60–62, 95–97

Keck, Pat, 118

Keller, E. D. "Gene," 33, 36–37, 39, 102, 168

Kelly, Dee, 172–73

Kelly, Grace, 120

Kennedy, John F., 158

Kerruish, R. J., 55

Kirkendall Boot Company, 78, 82

labor issues: shortages, 76, 147, 153; unionization, 105, 215n48; unrest, 62–64. *See also* employees

lace-up boots, 38–39

Lama, Rudolph E., 232n26

Lama, Tony, xix, 190. *See also* Tony Lama Company

lasts, xviii, 73, 76

layoffs, 63, 104, 192–94

leather: Bull Hide, 164–65; buying, 114–15; embossed, 126; exotic, 22, 28, 102, 115, 163–64, 183; grained, 164; and Justin Leather Goods Company, 26–27, 108–9, 113; manufacturing of in Nocona (*see* leather, in Nocona); purchase of, 162–65; quality, 42; shortage, 22, 76; sole, for military footwear, 74–75; Troutbrook, 28, 137; varieties of, 102, 126 (*see also under this heading*: exotic); work, Spain, 151–52

leather, in Nocona: about, 109; community of, 113; F & E Leather, 110–11; Hinckley-Tandy Leather Company, 111; Howard Paine Saddlery, 112; Justin Leather Goods, 109, 113; Nocona Athletic Goods, 110, 220n43; Nocona Baby Shoe Company, 112–13; Nocona Belt & Novelty Company, 112, 222n11; Nocona Leather Goods Company, 109–10; Nocona Sandal Company, 112;

INDEX

praise of, 107–8
Ledbetter, T. J., 28
Leddy, M. L., xix–xx
legal issues: Justin, Joe, position at Nocona Boot Company and, 135–36, 169–72; Justin name, on use of, 61–62, 96–97; Nocona Baby Shoe Company, 112; on oil field boot tongue, 39; and option contract with Justin Boot, 171–73 (*see also* succession plan); Salary Stabilization and, 77–78; Spanish boots and, 152; on stock ownership of Nocona Boot Company and Justin Boot, 123–24 (*see also* succession plan); theft, of Nocona Boots, 188; on tongue, 39; with Weyenberg Shoe Manufacturing Company, 170; on *Wichita Daily Times*, 61–62; women's rights and, 159
Lemon, R. S. "Ruff," 104–5, 115, 124, 126, 224n30
Leonard, Luciel, 55, 79, 86, 104, 121
Library of Congress exhibit, 143
Life, 99
Linn, Darla, 119
liquor sales, 53
"Little Texan," 112
livestock industry. *See* cattle industry
livestock shows, 106
locations, of Nocona Boot Company: Atkins Building (*see* Atkins Building); of belt production, 183; US Hwy 82 (*see* Nocona Boot Company factory, US Hwy 82 location); Gainesville plant, 167, 179–80; Moulton plant, 114, 150–51; Vernon plant, 147–50, *149*, 153, 179–80
Lucchese, Salvatore "Sam," xix
Lucchese Boot and Shoe Factory, xix, 180, 201
Lunn, J. W., 86

machinery: accumulation of, 32, 36, 47; in Nocona Boot Company factory, US Hwy 82, 86; expansion of, 1940, 73–74; innovative, 124–25, *125*, 140; at Justin Boot, 1908, 18–19
Maddox, J. W., 38
magazines: *Arizona Highways*, 134; *GQ*, 155; Guess advertisement in, 180; *Life*, 99; *Modern People*, 189; *Newsweek*, 99; *Playboy*, 158; *Sidesaddle*, 160; *Texas Monthly*, 143, 162; *Time*, 99, 159; *Western & English Today*, 117; *Western Outfitter*, 134
Mahan, Larry, 200
mail: Enid's opening of, 86, 118, 135; Pony Express Race and, 64–70, *65–66, 68–69*

mail-order, xviii–xix, 14–16. *See also* catalogs
Man of the Year, 159
Marcus, Stanley, 128
markets, of Nocona Boot Company: cowboys, 38; oil field workers, 38, 48; rodeos, 106; "urban cowboy," 143, 165–66, 192; women, 58–59, *127*, 128–29, 180, *181*; young adults, 156–57
marriages, of Enid, 20, 44–45, 71–73. *See also* Stelzer, Julius L. (husband of Enid)
Martin, Billy, 154, 227n15
Maynard, Ken, *89*
McCall, Cadmus Steven "Caddy" (or "Cad"), 33, 81–92, 84, 109, 210–11n24
McChesney, J. R./McChesney Bits and Spurs, *50*; as businessman, 48–49, 51, 213n9; Daddy Joe and, 6, 52; death of, 54; early years of, 49, 213n9; Gainesville, Texas, move to, 6, 51–52; Pauls Valley, Oklahoma, move, 53–54; sale of business to Nocona Boot Company, 55; spur designs, 52–53, *53*
McChesney, Rosetta (née Madison), 49, 51–52
McChesney, Thomas Carwin, 49, 51–52
McCoy, Tim, xix
McCrea, Joel, 134
McDonald, Atwood, 123
McGrady, Dave, 192
McGuffin, Deanna, 202
McInerney, T. C., xviii
McQueen, Angus, 141
media: magazines (*see* magazines); movies (*see* movies); newspapers (*see* newspapers); radio, 84, 106, 131, 156; television (*see* television); Western Wear, influence on, xx, 92, 99, 108, 165–66; women, portrayal of by, 158. *See also* publicity/promotions
Melody's Custom Boots, 202
mergers. *See* acquisitions/mergers
Mexico, manufacturing in, 196
military footwear, 74–75, 80
Miller, Donald L., xvi
minority employees, 153–54. *See also under* women: in workforce
Model T Fords, for bits and spurs, 56–57
Modern People, 189
Moiser, Paul, 150
Montague, Daniel, 6
Montague County, Texas, 6
Montana, 14
Moore, Clayton, 92
Moore, Reevely A., 26
Morris, Meel, 8–9
Mosier, Paul, 131

248

INDEX

Moulton Boot Company, 150, 226n7
Moulton, Texas, factory, 114, 150–51
movies: Enid in, 59; leather goods in, 110; Western wear, influence on, xx, 92, 165–66
Moyer, Bob, 67
Muenster, Texas, 20
Murphey, Michael Martin, 166
museums, 130, 160, 188, 197

National Cowboy Hall of Fame, 134
National Organization for Women, 158
National War Labor Board (WLB), 77
Native Americans. *See* Indians (Native Americans)
Needle Toe Cushion, 105
Neiman-Marcus, 119–20, 128
Nelson, Otis, 121, 123
newspapers: *Denver Post, The*, 95–96; *Nocona News, The*, 22–23, 31, 36, 121, 197; *Washington Post*, 201; *Wichita Times*, 60–62
Newsweek, 99
Nix, Mary Lee, 184
Nocona, Texas: about, 12–13; airport in, 128; as Boot Capital of the World, 98; city parks in, 138; Daddy Joe's desire to keep company in, 33; factory in, post–Justin Boot merger, 170; leather manufacturing in (*see* leather, in Nocona); Montague Boot Company in, 199–200; post-factory, 196–97, 199–200; rodeos in, 106–7
Nocona, Peta, 12, 110, 208n27
Nocona Athletic Goods, 110, 201, 220n43
Nocona Baby Shoe Company, 112–13
Nocona Belt & Novelty Company, 112, 135, 222n11
Nocona Boot Company: 25th anniversary of, 94; 50th anniversary, 138–39; beginnings of, 3–4, 31–35; challenges of (*see* family, conflict among; legal issues); closing of, 195–97, 199; debt of, 37–38; events and (*see* publicity/promotions); fit of boot, 191; funding of, 33–34, 39, 47; honors of, 98–101, 128, 131, 142; and Justin Boot rivalry (*see* family, conflict among); Justin family members working at, 102–3; post-merger, 173–76; quality of (*see* quality, of Nocona Boot Company); sale of, 168–69; sales area of, 139–40; succession plan of (*see* succession plan); training program, 148. *See also* Nocona Boot Company, post-Enid
Nocona Boot Company, post-Enid; advertising and, 180–81; belts, 183; boot styles and, 180–82; consolidations with Justin Boot, 193, 195; cost cutting at, 179–80; Justin, John, Jr. on, 191; layoffs in, 192–94; made to order product, 179; shutdown of, 193, 195–97, 199. *See also* Nocona Boot Company
Nocona Boot Company factory, US Hwy 82 location, *83*; assets of, 85–86; expansions of, 117, 129–30; grand opening for, 84–85, *85*; groundbreaking for, 82–83; location of, 81–82; Nocona Athletic Goods in, 2017, 220n43; research trips for, 82
Nocona Boot Company Riding Club, 184
Nocona Leather Goods Company, 108–10
Nocona News, The: building, 121; on Justin Boot move to Fort Worth, 31; "Mortuary," 22–23; on Nocona Boot Company close, 197; on ownership, Nocona Boot Company, 36
Nocona Rodeo Association, 106
Nocona Sandal Company, 112
North Field (oil drilling), 31, 38, 48
Norton Shoe Shop/Norton Shoe Company, xvi, 5, 18–19

oil industry, 30–31, 38, 48, 73
Old West. *See* western culture
Olsen, Carl, 45
Olsen-Stelzer Boot and Saddlery, 45, 110
100 Clay Street building, 26–27, *27*, 35–36
order delivery backups, 40, 73–74, 81, 127, 129–30, 150, 165–66
outsource manufacturing, 196

Parker, Cynthia Ann, 12, 208n27
Parker, Pam, 202
parks, city, 138, 183–84
Parr, Weldon, 197
Parton, L. A., 64
patents: on Nocona name for shoe manufacturing, 112; oil field boot tongue and, 39; self-measuring kit, 16; of Thin-Line Cushion Shank, 126
Pauls Valley, Oklahoma, 53–54
pegs, 115
perfume, 162
perjury, 172–73
Peta Nocona, 12, 110, 208n27
Petrie, Dick, 130, 137
Pickens, Steve, 176, 178–79, 182–85, 191, 193–95
piecework, 79, 104, 125
Pius XII (pope), 188
Playboy, 143

249

playground, 138, 183–84
politicians: Cato, O. C., 15; Jester, Beauford, 84; Reagan, Ronald, 176; Shivers, Allan, 100; Smith, Preston, 128; Stevenson, Adlai, 101; Talmadge, Herman, *100*; women, 159. *See also* celebrities
Pony Express Race, 64–70, *65–66*, *68–69*, 149
Pribble, Bill, 101
prices of boots: 1909, xix; 1915, 20; 1942, 79; 1950s, 102; 1975, 140; 1977, from Spain, 151; early 1920s, 27; early Justin Boots, 9
production, wartime, 74
profit-sharing program, 121, 223n12
Progressive Era, xvi
publicity/promotions: in 1973, 131–32; boot, oversize, 188; boot boxes, 182; Campbell, Earl and, 160–61, *161*; Daddy Joe and, 19–20; dude ranches, 59–60; governors' conference, *100*, 100–101; *GQ* cover, 155; Great American Honky Tonk Queen Contest, 166; Justin, John, Jr. on, 124; Justin Boot, 19–20, 22, 27–28; ladies' boots, 58–59; livestock shows, 106; movies, Enid in, 59; Pony Express Race, 64–70, *65–66*, *68–69*; radio, 84, 106, 131, 156; rodeos and, 106, *107*, 141, 200; Texas Centennial Celebration, 59; Texas in Review, 107–8; Texas Week on the Riviera, *98*, 98–99. *See also* advertising campaigns

quality, of Nocona Boot Company: commitment to, 102, 156; Justin Boot and, 16; of materials, 41–42, 114–15; at Moulton factory, 131; and Spanish boots, 152
Quigley, Lloyd, 163, 165

race, Pony Express, 64–70, *65–66*, *68–69*, 149
Radford, Jimmy, 99
radio, 84, 106, 131, 156
railroads/railway, 12, 30, 114
Rainier III (Prince of Monaco), 120
Ralph Lauren, 192
Reagan, Ronald, 176
recession, 184
Red River Station, 7
regulations, wartime, 74–77
repair, boot, 8, 37, 111, 183, 190
retail sales, 18, 39–41, 93–94, 128–29, 182–83, 200
retirement, of Enid, 131, 135, 175–76
Ritchie, Berry, 162–64
rivalry, Nocona Boot Company and Justin Boot. *See* family, conflict among

Roach, John V., 195
Roberts, Tommy, 153
rodeos: advertising campaign and, 141–43, *142*, 156–57, 183; all-girl, 160; boot market as, 106; boots for, 129; in Nocona, 106–7; publicity and, 106, *107*, 141, 200
Roe v. Wade (1973), 159
Rogers, Roy, 111
Roosevelt, Eleanor, 158
Roosevelt, Franklin D., 22, 74
roper boot, 180, *181*
Russell, Charles M., 28

saddles, 105, 114
salary, of Enid, 37, 47, 76–78
Salary Stabilization, 77–78
sales force: Enid as, 39–41; for Justin Boot, 28–29; for Nocona Boot Company, 41. *See also* dealers
Samuels, Sidney, 96
schooling, Enid, 17–18
Schrock, J. W., 9
See, Frank P., 8–9
Seamless Saddle Side, 105
self-measuring system, xviii–xix, 14–16
Semaine du Texas, *98*, 98–99
Seneca Falls Convention, 158
Sewell, J. I., 6
Shabay Brothers Store, 40
shanks, 104–5, 115, 126
sheepskin, 76
shifts, of work, 153, 180
Shive, S. C., xvii
Shivers, Allan, 100
shoe boots, 180–82, *182*
shoe production, 91, 98, 112–13, 168
shortages: labor, 76, 147, 153; material, 22, 76
Sidesaddle, 160
Singer sewing machines, 17–18, 36
Smallwood, W. R., 112
Smith, Preston, 128
soldiers, cowboy boots and, 80
soles, 140
Spain, manufacturing in, *151*, 151–52
Spanish, language, 153
Spanish Fort, Texas, xix, 6–10, 12, 207n10
Speers, L. E., 67
Speights, Clara Beth, 185
sporting goods, 109–10
spurs, 52–54, *53*, *56*. *See also* bits and spurs
stamps, souvenir, 65–66
Standard of the West: The Justin Story (Farman), 122

250

INDEX

Steinem, Gloria, 158
Stelzer, Anna Jo (daughter), 21, 23, 25
Stelzer, Julius L. (husband): daughter, death of, 23; infidelity of, 44–45, 212n51; at Justin Boot, 20–21, 25, 33; at Nocona Boot Company, 33, 36–37, 39, 44; post-marriage to Enid, 45; relationship with Enid, 20
Stevenson, Adlai, 101
stitching: decorative, 16, 43; by machines, 18, 36, 140; soles, 140; during World War II, 75
stock shows, 106
stock/stockholders: in 1970s, Nocona Boot Company, 127–28; annual meetings for, 122; of Daddy Joe, distribution of, 25–26; Enid's of Justin Boot, 31, 33, 199; issuance of, Nocona Boot Company, 39; Justin Boot move to Fort Worth and, 30–31; merger with Justin Boot and, 170, 173, 175; old rock building purchase with, 47; ownership conflict, between Nocona Boot Company and Justin Boot, 122–24; transfer from Sam to John Jr., 97
Storey, Robert E., 109–10
strokes, Enid and, 167
styles, of boots; in 1950s, 102; in 1975, 137; Bicentennial, 143–45, *144*; cowboys' needs and, xvi–xviii, 8–9, 42–43; custom, xix–xx, 19, 94, 128, 137, 140, 201–2; as decorative, 43–44; dress, 1930, *43*; fancy, 91–92, *92–93*, 102, 155; in history, xvii–xviii; ladies', 58–59; leather types of (*see* leather); Neck, The, 43–44; rodeos and, 129; roper, 180, *181*; shoe boots, 180–82, *182*; during World War II, 74–75
succession plan: interest in Nocona Boot Company, 131; Justin, Joe and good faith agreement, 135–36, 169–72; Justin Boot merger, 169–70; merger with Justin Boot, 169–73; sale of, to Weyenberg Shoe Manufacturing Company, 168–70
Sykes, T. J., 67

Tandy, Bill, 84, *85*, 217n43
Tandy, Charles, 111, 114
Tandy Leather Company, 111, 130
tanneries, 42, 76, 114–15, 162, 164
Taovaya Indians, 7
Taylor, Chester, 152, 168, 172–73, 184
Taylor, Marsha (niece), 89, 184
television: *Dallas*, 166, 229n38m; sponsorships on, 106–8; *Today*, 99; Western wear, influence on, 92, 99, 108, 166
Terry, Dale, xx, 80

Tex Tan Boot Company/Tex Tan Western Leather Company, 114, 130
Texas Angus Association, 132
Texas fever, 10, 12
Texas First job creation program, 148
Texas Hereford Association, 132, *133*
Texas Hide and Leather Company, 114
"Texas in Review," 107–8
Texas Monthly, 143, 162
Texas Togs, 119–21, 222n11
Texas Week on the Riviera, *98*, 98–99
Texas Women of Distinction, 101
Thin-Line Cushion Shank, 104–5, 115, 126
"This is Your Life," of Enid, 138–39
Thompson, Hank, 166
Thompson, Jess, 39
Thrasher, Mack, 83–84
Tillotson, John, 180, 191
Time, 99, 159
toes of boots, 42–73, 75, 102, 105, 129
Tolbert, Frank X., 188
Tony Lama Company, xix, 101, 173–74, 190–91, 195, 232n26
training program, 148, 153
travel, of Enid: for Nocona Boot Company factory, US Hwy 82 build, 82; during later years, 131, 145; for machinery, 124; for publicity (*see* publicity/promotions); retirement, in, 176; sales, 40–41, 118
Travolta, John, 165
Trim-Foot Company, 82
Troutbrook leather, 28, 137
Tuck, Taylor, 67
Turner, Leona M., 160
25th anniversary celebration, 138–39
Tyler Rose, 160–61, *161*

unionization, 105, 215n48
United Shoe Machinery Company, 36
"Unusual Occupations," 59
Urban Cowboy, 165–66
Uselton, Chris, 67–68

Valadez, Ramon, 131
Vatican, 188
Vernon plant, 147–50, *149*, 153
Vernon Regional Junior College, 148
veteran, boots for, 80

wages, 77–79, 104, 125. *See also* salary, of Enid
Wagner Act, 63, 215n48
Walker, Jerry Jeff, 156–57, *157*
Wallace, William A. A. "Bigfoot," 188

war. *See* World War I; World War II
war bonds, 79–80
War Labor Board (WLB), 77–78
War Production Board (WPB), 74–75
warehouses, 139, 154, 179, 183
Watson, Randy, 195
Welhausen, Carl, 114
Wellington boots, xvii
Western culture: apparel of (*see* Western wear); ethos of, 34; in Fort Worth, 30; women in, 34
Western & English Today, 117
Western Heritage Center, 134
Western Outfitter, 134
Western wear: in 1970s, late, 154; beginnings of, 59–60; Bicentennial and, 143–44, *144*; decline in, 192; industry, 92–94, 119; longevity of, 128; media, influence on, xx, 92, 99, 108, 165–66; Texas on the Riviera and, *98*, 98–99; Texas Togs, Nocona Boot Company purchase of, 119–21; Texas Week on the Riviera and, *98*, 98–99; women and, 58–59, *127*, 128–29, 160, 180, *181*
Western Words: A Dictionary of the Range, Cow Camp and Trail (Adams), 96
Weyenberg Shoe Manufacturing Company, 168–70
Whitbern Boots, 72–73
Whitman, Harry, 71–73
whooping cough, 22–23
Wichita Daily Times, 60–62
Wichita Falls, Texas, 72–73
Wichita Indians, 6–7
Wier, Rusty, 157
Wilkes, T. B., 109
Williams, Bill, Jr., 200
Williams, Jim, 200
Williamson-Dickie, 119
women: boot makers, 202; boots for, 58–59, *127*, 128–29, 180, *181*; in business, xv, xvi, xx, 33–34, 36; in Future Farmers of America (FFA), 132–34; politicians, 159; rights movement, xvi, 158–59; in the West, 34; in workforce, xvi, 33–34, 76, 153, 180
workforce. *See* employees; labor issues
World War I, 21–23, 34
World War II: contributions by Nocona Boot Company during, 79–80; growth of Nocona Boot Company during, 74, 79; labor during, 76, 78–79; material shortages during, 76; regulations during, 74–75; Salary Stabilization and, 77–78; sporting goods production and, 109

XIT Ranch, 14–15

Yoakum, Texas, 113–14

www.ingramcontent.com/pod-product-compliance
Lightning Source LLC
Chambersburg PA
CBHW020049170426
43199CB00009B/226